The Good Divorce

The Good Divorce

KEEPING YOUR
FAMILY TOGETHER
WHEN YOUR
MARRIAGE
COMES APART

Constance Ahrons, Ph.D.

HarperCollins*Publishers*

HarperCollins books may be purchased for educational, business, or sales promotional use. For information please write: Special Markets Department, HarperCollins Publishers, Inc., 10 East 53rd Street, New York, NY 10022.

Designed by Alma Hochhauser Orenstein

Library of Congress Cataloging-in-Publication Data

Ahrons, Constance R.
   The good divorce / by Constance R. Ahrons.
        p.   cm.
   Includes bibliographical references and index.
   ISBN 0-06-016973-7
   1. Divorce—United States—Longitudinal studies.
HQ834.A67 1994
306.89'0973—dc20   94-15798

94 95 96 97 98 ❖/HC 10 9 8 7 6 5 4

To the many families who gave so generously of themselves
and who shared their intimate lives with me.
Without them this book would not exist.

Contents

Introduction

The Good Divorce?

The Good Divorce? My eighty-five-year-old mother, looking puzzled, shook her head in disbelief. We were sitting in the living room of the retirement home in which she lived, and when a friend of hers walked in, she announced proudly: "My daughter is writing a book. It's called *Divorce Is Good.* Thinking she had not heard me, I politely corrected her, only to hear her repeating her version of the title to another friend. Again, I felt the need to correct her. Again, to no avail. Now, two years later, my mother still refers to the title of this book *her* way. Same words, reverse order, vastly different meanings.

Every thirteen seconds, someone gets divorced. Each year, in the United States alone, over one million families experience divorce. Each year, for every two couples that get married, one couple gets divorced. Not one of these couples likes getting divorced. They agonize over it, usually for years, and say it has been the most difficult time of their lives. It ranks right at the top of the personal stress index, second only to death of a loved one. It is an extraordinarily painful experience that invades one's whole life space.

Is divorce good? The answer is a resounding "no." Divorce is what it is: a fact of our society; a social institution. Its purpose is to act as a safety valve for bad marriages. In fact, most people say that this function is the only thing that is good about divorce. For most, it is better to go through that temporary, excruciating pain than to continue to live with the permanent, excruciating pain of a bad marriage.

But if divorce isn't good, is there such a thing as a good divorce? The answer is a resounding "yes." Not only do such divorces exist, but about half of divorced couples today actually manage to end up with one. In these good divorces, couples part without destroying the lives of those they love. Their children continue to have two parents. The divorced parents continue to have good relationships with their children. The families of these good divorces continue to be just that— families.

This is a book about such good divorces. I show divorces that run counter to our stereotypes—divorces that many people find suspect. These good divorces don't make headlines. What they do is model, for individuals and society, the beginnings of a quiet social revolution. I show how, as good divorces catch on, they will catalyze acceptance of an already existing but generally unaccepted cultural phenomenon— multiparent families that span two or more households.

The Binuclear Family Study

This book is based on my landmark longitudinal study of family relationships after divorce. Funded by the National Institutes of Mental Health (NIMH) and the University of Wisconsin, this groundbreaking research is the first of its kind to study *normal* divorced families.

During the initial stages of the study I developed the concept of *binuclear family*. A binuclear family is any family that spans two households. Nuclear families have one nucleus, one shared household; binuclear families split into two nuclei, two households, each headed by one parent. The family continues to be a unit even though it shifts from a nuclear structure to a binuclear one.

Ninety-Eight Normal Binuclear Families

Interestingly, most of the research funds in this field are apportioned to those who study mental illness rather than mental health. The result is that the vast bulk of the studies and clinical literature about divorce has been based on families with some psychiatric history, families with some identified problem or dysfunction. In contrast, my study was based on ninety-eight normal families from the midwestern United States. The study is unique because I selected the participants randomly from the public divorce records, from the pool of all divorces in 1978 in one Wisconsin county. (The appendix contains a further description of the methodology and sample characteristics.)

The idea was that by using a random sample, I would find families of divorce that were *actually* the norm in a certain geographical area, not families whom I supposed represented all families of divorce.

When I first proposed to do this study, the NIMH review committee expressed grave doubts that, through this random selection process, I could find sufficient subjects—families in which both exspouses would agree to participate. Although two prior longitudinal studies—Judith Wallerstein and Joan Kelly's much publicized Marin County study of sixty families and Mavis Hetherington's Virginia study comparing forty-eight divorced families with forty-eight married families—also interviewed both spouses, their subjects were not randomly selected. Wallerstein and Kelly advertised for their sample and offered them a clinical intervention program as part of the study, and the Hetherington sample of four-year-olds and their parents was referred by lawyers and schools. After a year of testing out the viability of my approach—in Wisconsin, Illinois, and California—I proved not only that it was possible, but also that it was crucial to use a random sample if we wanted to accurately document the divorce process and its aftermath.

Why Study Both Exspouses?

The inclusion of both exspouses was an important aspect of this study. As much attention as divorce has received in recent years, it is surprising that the relationship between exspouses has remained such an anomaly. In fact, my study was the first to have the relationship between exspouses as its major focus.

Most of the prior research—and even most of the current research, including large-scale survey studies—relies on the responses of only one partner. Although women are usually the spokespersons for the family, they still provide only one side of the story. As a clinician, I knew from years of experience that couples (whether married or divorced) usually hold very different views of their relationship. To form a complete picture of the divorce process requires the perspectives of both exspouses.

Two Pictures of the Same Divorce . . . Two Different Divorces

As I expected, differences in the two halves of an excouple's story emerged; in fact, once their names were deleted, we often couldn't tell who had been married to whom. Partners differed on such essential details as when they first separated, who had decided to divorce, what were the reasons, how involved fathers were with their children, the amount and regularity in payment of child support, and the actual time each parent spent with the children. One father said he spent every Saturday with his children and his former wife said he rarely saw them. A mother said she had sole custody of the children and her exspouse said they had joint custody.

As you will see, some of these discrepancies were truly individual differences, some were gender differences, and some were adversarial or positional differences sparked by a legal battle over custody.

Mapping the Families Over Time

Over the course of six years, my graduate assistants and I interviewed these 196 parents three times, at one, three, and five years after their divorce. We began each set of interviews by constructing a diagram—a map of that family's kinship network—and expanded the map as the families changed configuration through such factors as remarriages and new births.

Ninety-six of the ninety-eight families remained in the study for the entire period. The fact that all but two of the families (one dropped out due to the death of a child) participated for five years is remarkable—most longitudinal studies lose half their participants over the years. Many of the interview subjects told us they continued to participate because this was a pioneering project, that they wanted other divorced couples to learn from them, that they learned a lot just from our interviews, and that no one had ever before asked them about what was good, perhaps even better, in their lives after their divorce.

An unintended—but even more interesting—reason was that this study helped its participants to feel more normal. When we asked certain questions, they realized that others were explicitly communicating about the divorce process in the same way that they were implicitly thinking about it. In one section of the interview, we used statements printed on cards instead of verbal questions—statements such as, "Sometimes I wish my ex was dead," and "I want to punish her (or him) for all the wrongs done to me." The subject sorted the cards into five piles, labeled "always," "often," "sometimes," "rarely," and "never." Just recognizing the unsayable (there was a lot of laughing and crying during this part of the interview) helped people to see that their feelings were not outrageous, crazy, or, it turns out, unthinkable.

These in-depth interviews allowed me to learn how divorce changed these families, to find a range of normalcy, and to compare and understand how, five years later, some spouses had managed to uncouple without causing psychological harm to their family whereas others had not. To better understand the complexities of how divorced families function, and the reasons for these complexities, we also interviewed ninety-one new partners who joined these families as stepparents. In total, my graduate students and I interviewed 287 people several times over five years. They each told us from their very personal perspective what living in a divorced family was really like.

Cross-National Study

In 1981, I presented a paper reporting preliminary findings from the first interviews of the Binuclear Family Study at an international sociological conference. There, in Leuven, Belgium, I met, for the first time, a group of European social scientists who were collaborating on a research project organized by the Vienna Centre. Much to our surprise, we found that our studies had very similar designs. In all the countries—Finland, Sweden, Hungary, Denmark, The Netherlands, Poland, and Norway—both exspouses were participants in the research; as in the Binuclear Family Study, all had dependent children.

Several months later, I was asked to join the Vienna Centre research project. Meeting twice a year, over the next three years we analyzed our data from a cross-national perspective.

We expected to find vast differences between families from different countries. Our actual findings came as quite a surprise. Allowing for the differences in the legal processes, cross-culturally, the emotional adjustment processes were remarkably similar.

Supplementary Studies

In addition to the major longitudinal study of binuclear families and the cross-national study, my examples, case stories, and conclusions are drawn from many other sources. Over the past fifteen years I have conducted several smaller studies about divorce from different generational and sample perspectives: a study of forty-one joint-custody parents from San Diego County who were interviewed at two different intervals postdivorce; a study of seventy-eight grandmothers who experienced the divorce of a son or a daughter; and a study of thirty young adult children between the ages of nineteen and twenty-five who had recently experienced their parents' divorce.

In dozens of additional interviews for this book, I have met scores of other parents and children. Because the participants in the Binuclear Family Study were mainly white, middle-class midwesterners, I wanted to broaden my understanding by interviewing people from different ethnic and geographic backgrounds, in different stages of the life cycle.

My twenty-five years as a therapist also add richness and depth. A unique intimacy and trust is generated over several years of hard work on a relationship. At times I will draw upon client stories as well.

The ideas for this book have been with me for a long time, as far back as 1976 when I first started studying divorce. I was teaching at the University of Wisconsin then and beginning my research about divorce and its aftermath. In my private practice as a family therapist at the time, I was also seeing more and more people who were dealing with the terrifying disorganization that divorce brings. In both spheres of my work life, now, as I did then, I see people who have good divorces, people who have bad ones, and those whose divorces have elements of both. In my personal life I have also experienced divorce, both its good and bad dimensions. I have lived the family and role permutations that are the aftermath of divorce: I have been a single parent, a second wife, and a stepmother; I've been an adversarial exspouse and a friendly one; I've done the research at the personal as well as the academic level.

This book is meant to be the companion piece to *Divorced Families,* the academic and professional training book I co-authored in 1987 with Roy H. Rodgers. It comes in response to the many divorced people—students, clients, colleagues—who encouraged me to write a book that speaks more directly to them. A book that, for a change, looks at the good news and not just the bad news about divorce.

My greatest hope is that *The Good Divorce* will be a powerful antidote for millions of divorced parents: an antidote to the negativity of society about divorce. If you are tired of hearing only doomsday reports, if you're tired of having your home labeled as a "broken home," if you're tired of being the scapegoat for many of society's major problems—this book is written for you.

In this book I challenge society's traditional view—that divorce is one of life's greatest failures. Binuclear families make up a major part of our society today. These families want to know—and deserve to know—how to function in the best possible ways available to them, how to minimize the stress, and most of all, how to feel normal.

The Good
Divorce

1

What's Good in Divorce
VALUING FAMILY

M Y OLDER DAUGHTER got married twenty-five years after her father and I divorced. A large family group took part in the ceremony, including my exhusband, his wife, their two children, and my younger daughter. Looking at the video, I see two proud and happy parents walking their daughter down the aisle. From these images of smiling, laughing people, a stranger could never tell that this couple had not been husband and wife for the past twenty-five years, unless, fast forwarding to the altar scene, they noticed the three beaming parents to the right of the bride. In this scene we three parents stand together tightly holding hands, laughing and crying, deeply moved. This family constellation is like many others around the world—families in which one or both sets of parents are divorced.

Those who witnessed our stormy, acrimonious parting in 1965 would never have predicted that my exhusband and I could share the wedding of our child politely, let alone joyously. No-fault divorces didn't exist back then. To be released from an incompatible union, one of us had to prove the other undeniably at fault. We needed to produce a clearly demonstrable reason to end it, such as adultery or abuse. Already engaged in a furious, pitched battle, we were forced by the no-fault issue to raise the stakes still higher. We knew that the one proved to be at fault would be socially shamed, and probably economically penalized as well. Worst, he or she would be considered responsible for destroying our family's chance to live the American dream. I was the one who left, and for two miserable years my husband and I battled constantly over custody, visitation, and child support. There were private detectives, a kidnapping, several lawyers, and two years of legal fees that took me the next ten years to pay off. That painful time of my life was almost thirty years ago, and even today it is hard to write about.

Some things have changed dramatically since I joined the ranks of the formerly married. Between 1966 and 1976 the divorce rate in the United States doubled. While demographers disagree about their projections of divorce rates in the twenty-first century, they agree that we will never return to pre-1970 rates. In the next century, between four and six out of every ten marriages in the United States are projected to end in divorce.

The cold fact of divorce has not dampened our ideal of marriage. About half the marriages that took place in 1993 in the United States were remarriages in which one or both partners had been divorced. Dramatic legal reforms, such as no-fault and joint custody, have replaced the punitive and moral stance of earlier years. Today, divorce is on the verge of becoming acceptable; serial monogamy has become a popular lifestyle. But the social shame somehow lingers.

The Good Divorce Is Not an Oxymoron

When I tell people the title of this book I usually get one of two distinct reactions. Either I hear a knee-jerk response, an incredulous: "Isn't saying 'good divorce' a contradiction in terms, like saying 'sweet sorrow' or 'cruel kindness'?" The other set of people—increasing in numbers lately—say, "It's about time. Finally. We're tired of hearing only about the horrors of divorce. We need models to help us do what we want—and need—to be able to do." These listeners invariably have a story about someone they know (it might even be themselves) who fits the definition of the binuclear family. They'd just never put a name to it. They go on to describe some family with this *strange* relationship where they and their new spouses and all their respective kin spend Thanksgiving or some such holiday together—and everyone seems content.

The good divorce is not an oxymoron. A good divorce is one in which both the adults and children emerge at least as emotionally well as they were before the divorce. Because we have been so inundated with negative stories, divorce immediately carries with it a negative association. Even though we have difficulty conjuring up positive images of divorce, the reality is that most people feel their lives improved after their divorces.

In a good divorce, a family with children remains a family. The family undergoes dramatic and unsettling changes in structure and size, but its functions remain the same. The parents—as they did when they were married—continue to be responsible for the emotional, economic, and physical needs of their children. The basic foundation is that exspouses develop a parenting partnership, one that is sufficiently cooperative to permit the bonds of kinship—with and through their children—to continue.

If people are going to divorce and remarry (and even redivorce) in droves, as by all predictions they are, then structuring a good divorce process, family by family, has become absolutely essential. Our *sanctioning* the process must be incorporated into our dreams of the good life, not treated as the root cause of all of our social nightmares.

Healthy Language, Normal Families

Sanctioning divorce means, first of all, developing a healthy language in which we can speak about it—words such as *binuclear* that can reflect images of a healthy, divorced family, rather than words such as *broken home*. I chose the term *binuclear family* because I wanted it to parallel nuclear family. Quite simply, I wanted to normalize families of divorce by putting them on the same par as nuclear families.

Because our language for families of divorce is so clouded by negative perceptions, I have chosen not to hyphenate words such as binuclear, exspouse, exhusband, exwife, stepparent, stepkin, stepfamily. The hyphens imply that these words are additions or modifications of other words. In this book these terms are accepted as complete within themselves. Perhaps we'll feel a bit itchy at first with such a language modification, but—as with any other change in the norm—in time we'll grow comfortable with it.

The terms *exspouse, expartner,* and *stepparent* aren't perfect, as they pejoratively describe people who lack a relationship and are substitutes for parents, but since they are the terms in common usage, I'll use them too—with hopes that soon we shall come up with better words.

Eskimos have many words for snow, but we have pitifully few words to describe the relationships that exist between people previously bonded by marriage, now bonded through children. The terms *ex, former wife,* and *former husband* are in wide use, but all of these rely on past relationships to define the present. Margaret Mead, in 1971, wrote, "The vulgar 'my ex' is all that we have to deal with the relationship which may involve twenty years and five children. We should be able to do better—and soon." It is over two decades later and we still haven't even begun to name these significant relationships. When we do, we will be well on our way to reintegrating a huge, partially disenfranchised portion of society.

To recognize families of divorce as legitimate, we first have to shatter a deeply ingrained myth—the myth that only in a nuclear family can we raise healthy children. Society still sends us the message: "To raise children effectively means they have two heterosexual parents, and *only* two. Single-parent families, gay and lesbian families, binuclear families, and stepfamilies are all bad and abnormal. The only normal family is the nuclear family."

This nuclearcentric definition, and all language that is nuclearcentric, causes immeasurable harm to children of divorce and can break kinship ties. It causes them to feel deviant, to feel stigmatized, to feel shamed.

As Noam Chomsky said in *Language and the Problem of Knowledge,* "Language can enlighten or imprison." The negative language so common to divorce imprisons millions of families by making them feel that they are somehow bad and unacceptable. By changing our language to more neutral language we will help raise the self-esteem of children and adults in these families. So that binuclear families can be fully accepted as the normal, common family forms they now are, we must also coin names for each of the significant relationships throughout the spectrum of postdivorce kinship.

Is a Normal Binuclear Family Abnormal? Is an Abnormal Binuclear Family Normal?

When I started the Binuclear Family Study, I didn't know what I would find. The existing divorce literature identified only the *adjustment problems* of children and adults. But I knew from my therapy practice and my personal observations that some postdivorce families seemed well adjusted. I didn't know, however, whether or not these histories were highly unusual.

One very important question I wanted to explore was: Why do some fathers stay involved with their children after divorce, while others slowly disappear?

Although the answer to this question is complex and depends on the subtle intricate weaving of individual personalities and family dynamics, one important factor consistently emerged. The fathers who stayed involved with their children after divorce had better relationships with their exwives than the fathers who had minimal or no involvement.

The stereotypes of warring exspouses and deadbeat dads are accurate for some divorced families. But this study clearly revealed that equally as many divorced families cannot be categorized in this way. These exspouses were not at war—some were even friendly. Surprisingly, more people than anyone imagined were constructing new daily realities that didn't fit the typical profiles or stereotypes of the single-parent family.

When I first heard from the James family, who managed to keep the kids in one house while they took turns moving in and out every month, I was amazed at their flexibility, their ability to provide a stable life for their adolescent children. I was impressed with another family, Jean and Tom Turner, who, in spite of continuing conflict, managed a very good shared child-rearing arrangement. Jean Turner and Tom's second wife, Marilyn, were amicable and talked on the phone weekly, communally making the necessary plans for meeting the children's needs. They weren't great friends, but they weren't enemies either. Both of these families, and many others like them, were able to keep the children's interests primary. The goal of providing a healthy family for their children was a hallmark for many parents in the study. These parents established a surprising variety of innovative ways to create their binuclear families.

Exspouses: Friends and Foes

Astonishingly—given society's prejudices—in the Binuclear Family Study almost 50 percent of the couples had amicable relationships. They'd worked their way through difficult crises, but one year after the legal divorce (usually two to three years after the initial separation) these forty-eight couples had civil relationships. Most wouldn't call each other friends exactly, but they were usually cooperative and they respected one another's relationship with the children. Some, however, were really friends and shared many aspects of their lives besides their children.

The divorced couples we interviewed ranged from one extreme of caring and supportive friends all the way to the other extreme of hostile and bitter foes. Although the ninety-eight couples could be placed along a continuum, they can also be typed according to their style of communication and interaction. (In Chapter 3 I will discuss these types more fully and describe how the typologies were formed.)

At first I specified four types of couples, and gave them scientific names. On my way to New York to present these typologies for the first time at a professional conference, I made a stopover to visit my daughters. At lunch on our way to the airport I was telling them about the findings. My daughters listened attentively as I described the groups. First, there was the most dysfunctional group, "Low-Quality Communication with Little or No Direct Interaction." Then, a little bit better, but still problematic, was "Moderate Interaction with Low-Quality Communication." Moving along the continuum, I explained, were the "Moderate Interactors with High-Quality Communication," followed by the last group of couples, who had "High-Quality Communication as Well as High Interaction."

As I gave my daughters more details and described some couples who fit into each category, they said they were getting too confused to follow me. They took their pencils in hand and grabbed a stack of paper napkins. Pretty soon the napkins were filled with hand-scrawled names that were more colorful, more descriptive, and more likely to be remembered.

The amicable group separated into two distinct smaller groups. The majority of them (about one-third of the total sample) were named *Cooperative Colleagues*. These were couples who coped with their anger in productive ways. They managed their conflicts well and the children didn't get caught up in them. One of the major characteristics of this group was their ability to separate their parental responsibilities from their spousal discontents.

A second group of amicable couples, whom I called *Perfect Pals,* were a small but significant minority who remained best friends after divorce. They continued to enjoy an intimate, although nonsexual, relationship. Although their relationships had some conflicts, and anger flared at times, they remained close and caring.

The remaining 50 percent of couples fit the prevailing stereotypes. These couples were arch-enemies. They divided almost equally into two groups: *Angry Associates* and *Fiery Foes*. Interestingly, what differentiated Angry Associates from Cooperative Colleagues was not so much the amount of their anger, but rather *how* they expressed it. Angry Associates were not able to confine their anger to their marital differences; it infused all the relationships in the family.

The Fiery Foes were the real prototypical examples of bad divorces. These couples' rage tainted their families' lives, leaving continued pain and distress for years afterward. Fiery Foes were the ones who made headlines, having custody battle after custody battle, resorting sometimes to violence in their pursuit for revenge.

A fifth type—*Dissolved Duos*—were not present in the study, as I interviewed only couples who'd preserved some contact. *Dissolved Duos* are those exspouses who totally discontinue contact with each other and one parent disappears completely from the children's lives. This is rare. Even the worst parent usually tries to maintain some contact, and usually—unless there's a history of criminality, abuse, or insanity—the primary parent allows some minimal contact.

These descriptive, alliterative, and easy-sounding names replaced the more scientific terminology. I used them in my talk in New York that day, and they caught on immediately.

Why are the typologies important? Because the style of interaction and communication a couple develops postdivorce affects all their future intimate relationships.

Interestingly, not only does the type of postdivorce relationship a couple develops affect the entire functioning of their family, but it also carries over into their remarriages. One of the most significant findings was that amicable exspouses, when they found new partners, were happier in their remarriages than were hostile or unfriendly exspouses.

Another surprise came in the form of the wishes and desires of the divorced spouses, whatever the quality of the relationship. Almost everyone interviewed wished that he or she was on better terms with his or her ex—even the ones who had bad relationships. They expressed sentiments such as these: "I really miss hearing about his old friends and the people he works with"; "I wish she would tell me more about her life"; and "I wish there was less bitterness between us." When we asked them to describe *an ideal divorced parenting relationship,* even the fieriest of foes mentioned the importance of open and frequent communication.

Household, Family, Kinship

Who or what is family? Author Letty Cottin Pogrebin likens it to a hydra: "It has remained 'family' regardless of which of its functions or people are lopped off; and because, without the permission of Western culture, it has changed and thus managed to stay alive in new and diverse forms, it has ultimately proven itself more useful, more responsive, and more human than its critics may have dreamed possible."

Household, family, and kinship are not identical terms. Just look at the many debates about surrogate parents, adoptive parents, and biological parents. The problem of kinship definition goes way beyond the issues of divorce. Even the experts don't agree.

Take, for example, the well-publicized case of Marissa, a child born to a surrogate mother. When Robert and Cynthia Moschetta contracted with Elvira Jordan to have "their" baby through artificial insemination, they did not realize that six months after Marissa's birth, they were going to divorce. All three parents now claimed Marissa was theirs; all three had experts to back them up. Who were the rightful parents? What were Baby Marissa's best interests? The presiding judge finally awarded joint custody to Robert, the genetic father, and to Elvira, the genetic surrogate mother. The adoptive mother, Cynthia, Marissa's primary caregiver for sixteen months, was not even awarded visitation rights.

Another case—the celebrated case of Baby M—however, was decided in exactly the opposite way. When the surrogate mother reneged on her contract and filed for custody, the ensuing litigation centered on whether a parent is defined by relationship or by genes. The adoptive parents, who were perceived as the emotional parents, won custody; the genetic surrogate mother was awarded visitation only.

These decisions are of great significance for binuclear families. First, they introduce a joint custody issue: Can two parents in a conflictual relationship share custody? The judge decided they could. Second, can a child have more than two parents (i.e., stepparents and biological parents) and still have a normal family? The judge again decided yes. So, although there is thorough disagreement about the particulars, the generalities are beginning to fall into place. Family is not strictly genetic, nor is it strictly emotional, and it is not defined by household. It is all three things, and how each family defines itself must be decided family by family.

Anthropologist Paul Bohannan explains the difference between household and family. Family is a matter of kinship, and kinship is a matter of genes. Household, on the other hand, is a matter of geography. Once a child is born, husband and wife become a kind of kin. Although they are not blood relatives, their child is the common descendant. Not even adoption, even though it negates legal rights associated with kinship, can break kinship ties. The binuclear family is kinship in action.

Two Households, One Kinship Structure

The simple truth is that while there are bad divorces, there are also good ones. While some divorces result in serious problems for their families, many do not. Millions now live with the reality of divorce as a normal passage in their lives, and, as my research shows, one-half of these families manage to forge a constructive relationship. When they do so, the children of these families are not irreparably damaged.

Although good divorces are as varied as good marriages, they have an important common denominator. Most basic is the absence of malice and a mutual concern for the well-being of the children. The partners have similar goals: to maintain their family relationships while moving ahead with their separate lives.

In this book we will see exspouses who are very friendly, and others who choose not to be. There are many routes by which people reach their end—a civil, well-functioning, two-parent family—even if the exspouses start as badly as did my first husband and I.

One tightly held secret is that out of many bad marriages come good divorces. In this book we will see unlikely candidates who had horrible times in the early stages, but who over time healed some of the wounds. We will see more likely candidates too—those who from the beginning managed a cooperative relationship. In between are many variations, and many partners who continue to struggle.

Whole Homes, Not Broken Homes

Our negative image of divorce is so powerful—not only for families but for society as a whole—that to even try to imagine it as good means we have to shake up some deeply entrenched beliefs. Despite the fact that in American society, and in most European countries as well, divorce is now as much of a social institution as marriage, we still view divorce as deviant, as abnormal or pathological. We glorify the so-called intact family and stigmatize divorced families as broken and incomplete. Is divorce as bad as society makes it out to be? What portion of the negative consequences of divorce is inherent in the dissolving of a spousal relationship—and what portion is inherent in custom, in social habit?

Suppose exspouses were encouraged—even expected—to maintain civility when they split up. Would we still have such destructive acrimony around divorce? Now suppose that exspouses had some socially approved rituals to help them cope with the losses of an ended relationship, like we do when a loved one dies. Would these couples (who adequately grieved for their ended marriage) have to defend themselves with so much anger?

Why, when one out of two American marriages ends in divorce, do we persist in negativity? Perhaps we need to perpetuate the myth that divorce is unmitigated disaster because we feel in doing so we may preserve marriage. Perhaps we feel that if there's such a thing as a good divorce, then too many people will flee their marriages. If unhappy couples knew some excouples with good divorces, if they knew their bad marriage was harming their children, if the long-term effects of a good divorce on a family turned out to be positive . . . where would this all lead? Perhaps we fear that nobody normal would be left behind, nobody who believed in duty, home, and family.

Divorce Is Now Normal

Drawing by Koren; © 1992 *The New Yorker* Magazine, Inc.

Are Nuclear Families Faring Any Better?

Today, we must question the basic assumption of the nuclear family, no matter how much we revere it. In a society in which serial marriages are becoming the norm, we cannot keep degrading the option of divorce. We cannot scapegoat divorce for more than its proper share of society's ills. We cannot equate recognizing the better implications of divorce with being antimarriage, antireligious, or antifamily.

I do not sanction the irresponsible splitting of marriages; nor do I wish my readers to run right out and get a divorce. I do not think that single-parent families, stepfamilies, gay and lesbian families are better than the traditional nuclear family, merely that they exist and that happiness can come out of these situations as well as the other. Upholding the myth of the nuclear family in preference to the reality is antiwomen, antimen, and antifamily. Upholding the myth that the children of divorce are necessarily miserable and abnormal denies the reality that many divorced families can and will continue to be two-parent, normal, and healthy—albeit binuclear.

A recent cartoon, now made into postcards and T-shirts, shows a large empty auditorium with only *two* people in the audience. The banner reads: "Annual Conference of Adult Children of Normal Families." Perhaps the doomsayer must look at who's out there.

Not Abnormal . . . Not Alone

Over and over again, in my research, my therapy office, and at my lectures, I have heard divorced couples express feelings of shame and isolation, confusion and anguish. To the terrible pain of the breakup of their spousal relationship has been added the pain of ostracization, the pain of anchorlessness and of having no social models that can help them to organize the barrage of new, often unwelcome, physical and emotional details.

I remember the terror I felt in 1965 when I decided, after years of soul-searching, to separate from my first husband. I had never before lived alone. Married at nineteen, I had gotten pregnant at twenty. I was now twenty-eight. As much as I tried to picture how I would live as a divorced mother of two young children, I could not construct anything but a disastrous image. I didn't know anyone who was divorced. The social image of the divorcee at that time—a woman of harsh bitterness and easy virtue—did not help. The only fact I knew for sure was that I was far too miserable to continue living in a love-less, empty relationship. But I couldn't explain that to my family, because my husband happened to be nice. He wasn't a wife-beater, a gambler, an alcoholic, or a drug addict. We had a pleasant home and from the outside, at least, we looked fairly happy. Therefore, the only conclusion to be drawn by society was that I was crazy. My discontent was seen as pathological.

After the decision, I felt that some people saw me as a pariah. I was beginning graduate studies in social work at a large midwestern university. During the previous year—when my husband and I were together—we'd lived in university housing. When we separated, I was told I had to move. University housing was for married graduate students with families. Outraged, I managed eventually to convince the housing director that even after divorce, two children and their mother still constituted a family. My daughters and I also had to contend with their teachers' automatic assumption that now that they came from a broken home, they would of course be expected to have problems in school.

This prejudice, which still exists and which I label *divorcism,* is damaging to divorced families. In the years to follow, my own experiences, as well as those of my research participants, clients, and friends, revealed many general injustices. The first was that we exspouses felt like second-class citizens, ashamed and alone.

The Pointing Finger of Divorcism

Divorcism is like any other prejudice—an unreal expectation caused by lack of knowledge. Being the recipient of divorcism is like being judged by any other prejudice. It makes people angry; it makes people fundamentally doubt themselves.

People begin life, postdivorce, in confusion and anguish. Will their family still be a family? Are fifteen years of intimacy with their extended family, say with their exspouse's nephews and nieces, now suddenly over? In divorcing, have they undergone an amputation in which any ghostly feeling of love is now to be discounted or ignored? Many people in my studies asked, Where did they now fit into a larger social picture? Were they doing this right? How did other people manage their life after divorce? Why were their mutual friends, upon hearing of the divorce, saying such things as, "It's hard to believe," or worse, "We stuck it out!"? The implication being, "You two are failures, and your kids don't have a chance of surviving this."

Divorce is not something you do and it's over. You live divorce for the rest of your life, unless you were married for a short period and had no children. Divorce is a label you wear, and in this society, a handicap until we prove it otherwise.

Many personal information forms, such as patient information requested at the doctor's office or an application for a credit card, have a "divorced" box to check. Why do they want this information? Interestingly, if you then remarry, you check "married." Why are you any less divorced after a remarriage? And why aren't you then "single" after you divorce?

I imagine an account executive saying, "Hmm, divorced. Who's responsible for paying the bills?" Or a doctor attributing an ailment to the stress of divorce, without even asking the patient whether the divorce (which may have occurred many years prior) is creating serious stress.

People who haven't experienced divorce think I'm a little paranoid about this subject. But never have I felt that response from a divorced person. They always nod in relief. They always add a story.

Once an external label (such as "divorced") is applied, internal feelings may subsequently be shaped by society's reaction to the connotations of that label. John F. Kennedy once said that the greatest enemy of truth is not the lie, which is deliberate, contrived, and dishonest, but the myth, which is persistent, pervasive, and unrealistic. Divorcist statements point to such myths—myths that label divorce as shameful and pathological—which are all the more dangerous to the soul because they are implied rather than explicit.

Divorce Has Gotten a Bad Rap

Castigated by divorcists, negatively sanctioned by society, spoken about in worst-case language, divorce—the potentially neutral split of a nonworking marriage—has certainly gotten a bad rap in the professional literature. But what about in the popular literature?

Turning to newspapers and books, we see the same phenomenon. We read almost exclusively about negative outcomes, that is, divorces in which children and adults are irreparably damaged. In film and television, also, we see the most sensational divorces—the ugly, dysfunctional, lethal ones that end up in litigation. The much publicized Woody Allen–Mia Farrow case is an example. The media links divorce to virtually every social ill: drug abuse, family violence, even the Los Angeles riots.

When politicians don't know where to place culpability for society's ills, they blame the family, that once-hallowed bastion now crumbling at the roots, mainly (they continue) because of one thing and one thing only—divorce.

True, the public display of rage leading to violence and even sometimes to death is dramatic. And divorce is an easy scapegoat. But these worst cases that make so many media headlines, and that tax our court system with prolonged and public bitterness, are in fact the tiny minority—they constitute less than 10 percent of the total number of divorces.

Who's to Blame?

The loss of the traditional nuclear family is almost always blamed on women. It is women who have left the home and entered the workplace in large numbers; it is women who demand more equality in the world and at home; it is women who initiate most divorces. Susan Faludi, in her best-selling book, *Backlash: The Undeclared War Against American Women,* argues convincingly that blaming women for the increased divorce rate is really just another way to blame feminism for the breakdown in America's values.

Yes, it's true that more divorces are initiated by women, in Europe as well as the United States. Yes, all of it is true, even that the increase in divorce coincided with the resurgence of the women's movement. But all this does not necessarily add up to the statement, "Divorce is bad and it destroys the family." Rather it adds up to the statement that women, rather than having to stay in unfulfilling, destructive, or abusive marriages, are now more able to leave because of increased economic, psychological, and social independence.

Is the Cup Half Empty . . . Or Half Full?

Two of the most popular recent books on this subject imply that divorce is destructive for women, children, and families. Interestingly, neither documents divorce as destructive for men.

Worrying about whether the cup of divorce is half empty or half full might seem a fairly useless argument to some. It is not, because the argument, once supported by books and studies, is used by policymakers. Society's attention to the issue, including publicity, programmatic funding, educational and judicial policy, and even legislation, can hinge on a debate of this kind. Lenore Weitzman's *The Divorce Revolution* shows the economic decline of women, and hence children, postdivorce.

Although her research has been criticized as containing serious inaccuracies—the *degree* of economic decline she's reported has been disputed—it's true that divorce does leave women poorer.

My research corroborates the drop in women's income after divorce demonstrated by most other studies, although not to the severe degree that Weitzman shows. Much to my surprise, though, many of these women said they felt more satisfied with their financial situation after the divorce than during the marriage. The reasons: they had more control over the money they did have; also they felt relieved not to have to account to their husband for their expenditures.

One woman in my study told a story similar to many others. "Sure, our so-called 'family' income was higher than what I have now, but I didn't even get to see most of it, let alone spend it. I got an allowance and had to fight for anything over that I needed." Another woman whose income had dropped almost in half explained why even that reduced sum was better than the money she had access to in the marriage. "He always put his needs first. There were his toys—his car, his boat, his fishing weekends with the boys. The kids and I got what was left over, which wasn't even as much as we have now."

The Weitzman study has been used by politicians to support the negative consequences of divorce and to support more punitive, regressive divorce laws—an outcome not intended by the author. In other words, the book has been used as a vehicle for blaming the victims, rather than as the start of an inquiry into how to better balance the disparate economics of divorce.

The other study that has received national attention is Judith Wallerstein's research on sixty families from Marin County, California. Presented in a popular book by Wallerstein and Sandra Blakeslee, *Second Chances,* the focus is on the negative consequences for children after their parents divorce. The press and politicians have been quick to publicize these findings, lending support to the conclusion that divorce inevitably leaves pathology in its wake. What gets overlooked, however, is that at the ten-year follow-up almost half (45 percent) of the children did *not* experience any long-term psychological damage. In fact, Wallerstein states: "They emerged as competent, compassionate and courageous people." Although Wallerstein accurately reports that two-fifths (41 percent) of the children were doing poorly, she nevertheless focuses almost exclusively on this minority of children, telling sad tales of children's distress some ten years later. The remaining 14 percent, Wallerstein notes, were "strikingly uneven in how they adjusted to the world."

Why don't we hear about the majority group, the almost half of her sample who came through without psychological scars?

The fact that Wallerstein found less than half the children damaged should be encouraging news. It is even more encouraging given that the sixty families she studied were volunteers solicited for a counseling program whose aim was to help troubled couples through divorce. What about the people who didn't feel they needed counseling?

And because Wallerstein didn't have a comparison group of married families, we are also left wondering: *Are children from nuclear families faring any better?*

In spite of all the bad press, there is encouraging news about postdivorce families. Most of my interview subjects, the subjects in the cross-national study, and those in many other recent studies, said fervently that they were much happier several years postdivorce than they had been during marriage. Even though most women's incomes had dropped sharply, they enjoyed their new control over their lives, their finances not being dependent on their partner's behavior or goodwill. Both the men and the women spoke poignantly about their wish that they'd separated sooner. Though they'd stayed together for the children, in retrospect they said that this had been a mistake, and that their children were better off in an honest and well-functioning household, even if it was a household that had experienced divorce.

It all depends on whether you see the cup as half empty or half full. My study revealed similar findings to the Wallerstein study: About half the families had bad divorces that caused harm to both the children and the adults. The other half of the families had good divorces that preserved family ties and provided children with two parents and healthy families.

There is little to be gained from focusing only on the bad models, except perhaps dramatic media coverage. Good models, though, provide direction for divorcing parents. These models show them how to divorce without destroying their children. Good models help families of divorce have a vital vision, one that maximizes their survival in a time of great disorganization. This vision is what I hope to provide in the chapters that follow.

What You Ask For Is What You Get

At the time I began my Binuclear Family Study, I noticed that most researchers of divorce usually asked questions with negative assumptions, such as, "How do you think the divorce harmed your child?" In order to provide a more balanced picture, I decided that each time I asked a negative question, I would also ask the positive counterpart. So, for example, in addition to the above question, I also asked, "How do you think your child benefited from your divorce?" In most cases, the positive question was asked first.

Almost everyone interviewed mentioned how rare it was that anyone ever asked something positive. Many told me that never before had anyone elicited what was good, perhaps even better, in their life after divorce. Almost everyone responded to both questions, revealing both the up and down sides of the aftermath of divorce.

I am reminded of one colleague's story. He was supervising a student in how to administer and interpret psychological tests. The student was learning a projective type of test designed for use by young children. Giving the child a piece of paper, the psychologist asks, "Draw me a picture of a person." Who the child draws, what expressions the child puts on the person, the size and proportion of the figure, and so on, become the subject of subsequent interpretation.

The student psychologist had tested five children that week and brought the drawings to his supervisor. The supervisor started with the first child's drawing, a figure of a very minuscule person. The supervisor and trainee discussed possible interpretations and pondered over the types of personality disorders this constricted type of imaging might suggest. Turning to the next drawing the supervisor was surprised to see that this child, too, had drawn a very tiny person. He then looked at the other three drawings and noticed the same unusually small drawings. Puzzled by the surprising uniformity of these five children's pictures, he asked the trainee to tell him precisely how he gave directions to the children. The trainee said, "I asked them to draw me a *little* figure of a person." The children obediently did as prescribed and drew little pictures of people.

So it's easy to understand why we know a lot about the down side of divorce. When people are queried only about the negatives, their answers are skewed in that direction. When asked exclusively about problems, dysfunctional and negative emotions, that will be the only information we get. Just as the drawings had lost their ability to be diagnostic tools so does asking questions in one direction give us only one aspect of the total outcome. How can we then understand the complexities?

A Less Tidy But More Realistic Package

In the Binuclear Family Study I tried for as full a range of response as possible, within the limits of my sample. Especially I gathered data on those exspouses who were parents. Did they continue to have a relationship? If so, what was it like? What happened to these families over time? What kinds of decisions did they make? How much of a kinship network did they establish and maintain?

In answer, I got a normal range of response. I found good and I found bad. I found healthy situations and unhealthy ones. I found some divorced parents who continued to share child care and some who didn't. I found fathers who saw their children more frequently after divorce and those who rarely saw their children; fathers who promptly paid their child support and others who were delinquent.

Counter to the bleak stereotype, I found there's as much variation in exspouse relationships as there is in marital relationships. Not asking for drawings of little people, I found postdivorce families of all sizes, shapes, and styles—some happy, some not.

The Binuclear Family Package

Most families continue to be families after divorce, even if they don't look quite the same as the families we're used to. Instead of all living under one roof, members of divorced families span two or more households. These maternal and paternal households, which may or may not include stepparents and half and stepsiblings, form a *binuclear* family. Although divorce changes the structure of the family from nuclear to binuclear, families continue to do pretty much the same things they always have: care for and socialize children, form close personal bonds, and take care of their members' financial needs.

In married families, the spouses are the architects of the family; when spouses become exspouses they are still the architects of the family. Kinship and functional responsibility transcend divorce. We all know of loving and compatible marriages; we also know of marriages that make us cringe when we have to be in the presence of both spouses. Divorced spouses show the same range. Human nature also transcends divorce. Dysfunction exists in married as well as divorced families. The way a family functions, the psychological health of the children, depends hugely on the way the spouses—or exspouses—get along.

Recent research, comparing children from high-conflict families of marriage with children from a full range of families of divorce, shows that the children in the high-conflict families suffered more distress than the children in families of divorce. In fact, a new study from England shows that when children go into a divorce psychologically okay, they come through it that way too. It is the bad marriage prior to the divorce that causes most of the psychological problems that children experience. In the past their problems were attributed to the divorce because the marriage and the children's adjustment prior to the divorce was not studied.

You may be surprised to learn about the wide diversity of ways exspouses continue to be family for many years after their divorce. Many of the common myths about exspouse relationships will be dispelled by the findings presented here.

Healthy Role Models for Divorcing Families

Although in this book I use examples from all four of the exspouse groups, I pay special attention to Cooperative Colleagues and to those who make the transition from Angry Associates to Cooperative Colleagues. In this way, the book will provide a road map—one with alternate routes to the same destination. Understanding that there are normal predictable crises in the process of divorce helps us deal with the transition from marriage to divorce in a more orderly and less destructive way.

Divorced families now make up a major part of our society. All the evidence points to the fact that the binuclear family will be the predominant family form in the twenty-first century. The time has come for us to stop resisting the tides of social change. Binuclear families are normal. They need to follow models that minimize stresses, that maximize their level of functioning and contentment, both during and after divorce. We need knowledge, inspiration, and vision so our families can usher in a sounder, more balanced view of divorce. We need to free families to find their strengths in our increasingly complex society.

But to do so—to truly value the strengths of binuclear families—we must first free ourselves from the heavy weight of myths surrounding divorce—myths based in our history and in our wish for simple solutions.

2

What Divorce Is and Is Not
TRANSCENDING THE MYTHS

SAY THE WORD *divorce* out loud. What images come to mind?

At my lectures, I hear two very different sets of responses to this question.

"Pain, grief, anger, loneliness, and loss," along with "relief, freedom, strength, joy, happiness, and courage," answers one group.

"Broken homes, latchkey children, the women's movement, irresponsible fathers, the lack of family values, lack of commitment, and the 'Me Generation,' " says the other group.

Which group do you suppose includes divorced, separated, and remarried people, and which includes those who are single or married for the first time?

If you haven't lived through divorce, it's hard to think of it personally and humanly. And it's easy to dismiss the millions of people who have lived through it with the simplistic negative judgments derived from noticing only Fiery Foes.

Take the grandmother in one group I spoke to. She summed it up as follows:

"Divorce is just too easy to get nowadays. It's a sign of the breakdown of our society. People just don't take their vows as seriously as we did. They're too lazy to work on their problems. In the thirty-five years my Bernard and I have been married, we've surely had our share of problems, but we never thought of taking the easy way out! My father used to say, 'You made your bed—now lie in it.' And he was right. If everybody acted like us, the world wouldn't be in the shape it is today."

Someone says something like this at nearly every lecture I give. People with long-term marriages stand up and harangue the divorced, picturing themselves as virtuous and steadfast and the divorced as irresponsible and immature. They have stayed the course; understandably, they're proud of earned achievement. Their testimonials are usually punctuated by applause. After, the audience begins to buzz; hands fly up. "Our family values are eroding," I hear. "Too many women are working outside the home." "Divorce is a sign of failure," someone else may assert. "Not just personal failure," adds another, "but society's failure." Understandably, the first divorced person to speak usually is quite shy. I tell him or her to go ahead, that there are probably at least one or two other divorced people in the audience. After a few responsive chuckles we hear quite a different kind of story.

"My parents were married for forty years. It was terrible. They fought every day, constantly." The speaker gathers courage before continuing. "We were miserable. They had three kids, and we all carry the scars. I don't agree that divorce is too easy to get. It's the hardest thing I've ever, I mean *we've* ever, done. Every day, my ex and I work hard to give our kids a sense of family. And I think we're doing okay. In fact, we're better parents now than we were when we were fighting." The speaker's voice hardens. "I'm sick and tired of this holier-than-thou attitude. And I'm sick and tired of being blamed for taking a step I think was healthy for me to take! Don't we want things to change? Don't we want our children to have it better than we did?" After another burst of applause, the debate is off and running.

The issue of divorce is so value-laden that when we even hear the word, our knee-jerk response is: "children," "family," "breakdown." We immediately overlay this chain of thoughts with social panic. "Ugh. It's a plague. Stop it quickly before it spreads!"

From the podium at my lectures, time and time again, I say the word *divorce* and watch the emotions rippling over the faces of my audience. What I then hear is the careful question, "Why is divorce so common?"

The answers people commonly give to this question reflect a fascinating range of misconceptions. From half of my audience I hear the astounding assertions that everyone wants a divorce these days. That some people take the easy way out. And that we could solve the whole problem with just one simple, elegant solution—make divorce harder to get. Accept divorce? No way. That would be the same as accepting the total breakdown of civilization as we know it.

The other half of my audience argues back equally passionately. Such simplistic solutions, they say, penalize the innocent. The individuals who divorce are not the problem. Why not blame society? Divorce is part of a big picture, they say, not the single cause of society's demise. If we could indeed stop divorce with legislation, surely we as a society would have already done so.

The discussion could go on for hours—indeed it often does. The conclusions are usually similar. That there's one cause for divorce is a myth. If there's a single cause there would be a single solution. That there's a single solution is another, even more misleading myth.

If instead we view the current divorce rate as a *result* of social change rather than as a cause, a very different picture emerges. We can begin to see how complex factors—political, economic, social, and personal—work together today to make divorce a normal response. We can see how divorce is an integral part of the way families have been changing for centuries. Divorce is not a sign of individual sickness or abnormality, but a reflection of resilience. Our families are trying to survive and evolve within a rapidly changing society.

Myths of Divorce

Myth: What Keeps People Married Is Love Alone

We've had a recent rapid shift in frequency of divorce, and a more recent, less rapid shift in our attitudes toward divorce. There has been an even more dramatic shift in our attitudes toward marriage. For centuries marriage was based on economic and social position. It is only since the beginning of this century that we shifted the foundation of marriage to love. With the coming of industrialization and urbanization in the 1920s, work was no longer centered in the home, and the family was functioning less and less as a discrete economic unit. Couples then began to expect marriage to be a source of personal satisfaction, romance, and intimacy. By the time we reached the 1950s, our romanticized notion of marriage became the cornerstone of our attitudes toward family life.

But when the emotional aspects of the partnership became primary, marriage became vulnerable. When we earn money outside the home and when we expect marriage to meet all our relationship needs, then we are far less tolerant of a marriage that doesn't fulfill us. The prevalent reasons for divorce, unlike those of our elders (alcoholism, desertion) are now loss of closeness, feelings of emotional barrenness, sexual incompatibility, boredom, and serious differences in lifestyle and values.

Not only are we more likely today to leave marriages for reasons that our grandparents would have deemed frivolous, but we are also leaving more quickly than we used to. The most current figures suggest that the time of greatest risk for divorce—the modal or peak point—is around the fourth year of marriage. What used to be thought of as the "seven-year itch" is now more likely to be the "four-year itch." Although the median time of about seven years—the midpoint where half of the divorces occur before this time and half occur after—has remained somewhat stable, the median duration of recent marriages is expected to be shorter.

The initial romance, however strong, is a shaky foundation for long-term marriage. In the romance-driven marriages of the 1950s the initial romance often died, gender roles soon became even more stratified, motherhood was glorified into a full-time career, and the family was almost worshiped as a child-centered haven far from workaday reality. In retrospect it is easy to see how this rigid segregation of roles and functions, and the growing psychological expectations surrounding marriage and the family, led to major discontent for women as they attempted to match their inglorious reality to the glowing myth of marrying and staying married for love. Men's earning power, their presence in the work world, and thus their wider frame of political reference did nothing to dispel the popular image of the happy little woman tending the home fire, kissing cooing babies, and waiting breathlessly to hear manly footsteps on the hearth. Historian Carl Degler says it well: "The historic family has depended for its existence and character on women's subordination. The equality of women and the institution of family have long been at odds with each other."

The pressures on marriage became particularly intense during the late 1960s and early 1970s, when many couples experimented with different forms of relationships. Open marriage was sometimes seen as a way to expand a spouse's autonomy by integrating infidelity into marriage. Unfortunately, many who experimented with open marriage ended up as casualties. In theory it seemed like a good idea, but in practice the partners' needs soon began to conflict, jealousy reared its ugly head, and many marriages collapsed under the pressures. Other marriages simply died through the waning of interest. Subtract romance or chemistry from marriage—as well as economics, family, and social position—and not much is left.

Myth: You're Less Likely to Get Divorced if You Cohabit First

Cohabitation also became popular at this time. This choice was often seen by the participants as at once more sensible and more romantic than marriage; it could also be perceived as a testing ground for marriage—a deterrent to divorce. It came as a big surprise when researchers found that cohabiting for a year did not solve the problems of the first year of married life. In fact, recent research reveals an even higher divorce rate for those who cohabit prior to marriage than for those who don't. Why? One hypothesis has to do with the type of people who cohabit—they tend generally to be less religious, more liberal, and less likely to be bound by societal rules than are people who don't cohabit; these individuals may be more likely to accept divorce.

I feel that many cohabiting couples have the same types of problems as do many married couples: communication problems, differences in values, opposing temperaments, disparate levels of commitment. And many of these couples expect these problems simply to disappear when they marry. Add to this the problem that cohabitors are often not accepted as legitimate or serious couples by the world around them. They can use this as a bond of identity—they are rebels struggling against the outside world—and then, when they marry, they may find both their individuality and this cohabitation identity stripped from them all at once. Cohabiting for love only is just as problematic, perhaps even more so, as marrying for love only.

Myth: The Longer Your Marriage Lasts, the Better It Is

The rapid rise in the divorce rates that began in the late 1960s can be illustrated by the following calculation: nearly 30 percent of couples who were married in 1952 were divorced by their twenty-fifth anniversary; couples married in 1956 took only twenty years; those married in 1962 took fifteen years; and couples married in 1967 took about ten years. Those 1952 marriages that reached the divorce courts did so in the late 1970s, a time when divorce hit an all-time high.

Social outrage over divorce in the 1960s and 1970s by those who had married in the 1940s and 1950s does not mean that the earlier marriages were any happier or more viable; rather that starting in the 1960s and 1970s, society awoke to a new concept of marriage. I remember the night I told my mother that my husband and I were separating. She was outraged. "But nobody in our family gets a divorce. Not even your Aunt Eva and Uncle Meyer!" They were the miserable couple whose bedrooms—and daily lives—were as far apart from each other as possible. "But Mom," I protested, "Aunt Eva and Uncle Meyer haven't talked to each other in ten years! They've got a horrible life!" "Maybe so," my mother responded with disdain, "but that's no reason to get divorced." To my mother, any marriage was better than being single; any divorce was shameful and sinful.

Myth: The Rise in Divorce Means We Don't Like Marriage

All this doesn't mean marriage is no longer a viable institution. Statistics for the 1990s show otherwise. The number of marriages in the United States reached an all-time high in the 1980s; in 1990, 95 percent of men and 94 percent of women between the ages of forty-five and fifty-four had been married. In fact, we like marriage so much that many of us will do it two, three, or more times. Remarriages now make up about half of all new marriages each year. Although marriage rates have fallen in some countries in recent years, generally speaking, marriage remains as popular today as it ever was. While marriage rates have remained fairly stable, divorce rates have steadily increased; the number of divorces in the United States has increased 71 percent since 1970, while the number of married couples increased only 19 percent. People are postponing marriage much longer than they used to; many are choosing to forgo marriage altogether.

But people now seem to be recognizing the true and tricky nature of romantic love: as powerful, generous, and creative a feeling as it may be, romance does not necessarily have one-to-one correspondence with marriage. We are also recognizing that reasons for marriage in earlier times, such as social status and economics, do not quid pro quo mean marriage either.

Interestingly, as we move into the twenty-first century, there are some indications that we are becoming less romantic and more practical about marriage again. The ancient practice of matchmaking is back in vogue. The popularity of singles groups that bring together people of similar interests, ethnicity, and education suggests renewed valuation of the importance of background and compatibility.

Our behavior suggests that, instead of viewing divorce as a sign of failure, we are moving toward placing a higher value today on forming successful marriages than did earlier generations. We are more knowledgeable about the many factors that go into marriage; as a society we are getting more flexible about accepting individual reasons for marriage. We expect more from marriage and are less willing to tolerate bad marriages. Slowly, we are moving toward accepting divorce as a solution to unbearable or unfulfilling marriages. And because most people prefer marriage to being single, even the pain of divorce and all of its accompanying social pressures do not today, and will not in the future, stop people from marrying again and again. As Samuel Johnson has said, "Remarriage is the triumph of hope over experience."

Myth: Divorce Is a Modern Affliction

History informs us that, despite our belief in the newness of divorce, our society evolved ways of dissolving marriages in tandem with ways of making marriages. Divorce is today as woven into the fabric of society as is marriage. History clearly reveals patterns that show us divorce is here to stay.

Despite the doom-and-gloom interpretations about the decaying American family that many special-interest groups place on minor fluctuations in divorce rates, as important as our personal values are, we cannot and must not cut the data to fit. History shows otherwise.

The first self-help book about divorce, *How to Get a Divorce,* was published in 1859 in New York. The first recorded divorce in the United States occurred more than two centuries earlier.

In 1639, in a Puritan court in Massachusetts, James Luxford's wife asked for a divorce because her husband already had a wife. The divorce was granted. Mrs. Luxford's bigamist husband was fined, imprisoned, and then banished to England. The next recorded divorce occurred four years later, in 1643. Anne Clarke asked for a divorce because her husband had deserted her and was living with another woman. In those days, adultery was the only grounds for divorce, and only under specific conditions. A man was permitted to divorce his wife if she committed adultery (and if she had, she was shamed, banished, or put to death), but a woman needed additional grounds. In the cases of Mrs. Luxford and Mrs. Clarke, those additional grounds were bigamy and desertion.

As early as the late 1700s, Timothy Dwight, then president of Yale University, decried the high divorce rates he saw around him. He found it inconceivable that fully one in every hundred Connecticut couples had dissolved their marriages. Only fifty years later, the fact that Andrew Jackson was married to a divorced woman created a huge scandal when he ran for president, but it didn't stop him from being elected in 1828 or reelected in 1832. Social reformers, such as Robert Owen and Elizabeth Cady Stanton, pleaded with mainstream society again and again to liberalize divorce, to make it more egalitarian, and to allow people to leave bad marriages.

Myth: Strict Laws Curb Divorce

Should a couple, or shouldn't a couple, be allowed to divorce?

In Puritan America, in the 1600s, divorce was governed by the church, as were other family and social matters. Between 1600 and 1800, this responsibility shifted to the state. Secularization became a cornerstone of the new United States; it legalized religious and social freedoms and created the Constitution. In these two centuries divorce became legal in America and in most of Western society.

The shift toward making family matters part of civil law did not come easily. Those who believed that family should continue to be governed by the church believed as passionately then, as do their counterparts today, that allowing divorce to spread would destroy the American family. Divorce must not occur, they felt and feel, except in the most extreme cases—desertion, failure to provide, bigamy, and in some cases, impotency.

Although early American divorce laws were very restrictive, as we have seen, even in early times the Scandinavian countries were more liberal. As early as 1734, incompatibility, ill treatment, drunkenness, and hatred and bitterness between spouses were all grounds for dissolution of a Swedish marriage. In 1796, Denmark allowed three years of separation to entitle one to get a divorce. Further south, in Prussia, "deadly and notorious hostility" provided grounds for divorce in 1751. In 1792, in France, if a couple could agree to petition jointly, they could obtain a divorce by mutual consent; as in today's no-fault divorces, they did not have to produce evidence. A couple did have to go through a long process in which the extended family was required to make all efforts to help the couple reconcile.

This liberalization of the divorce laws was not to last long, however. Divorce laws fluctuated with the political and religious tenor of the times. In 1816, when the French monarchy was restored, divorce was abolished. A century later, a cultural shift occurred again and divorce laws emerged in every country in Europe, with the exception of a few Catholic countries—Spain, Italy, Ireland. Today, Ireland is the one country in Western society that does not permit divorce.

In the United States the debate flourished. On Independence Day 1826, Robert Owen, the social reformer (also a journalist and congressman), publicly and strongly declared that no one should be forced to remain in an unhappy marriage. Twenty-six years later, a legislative committee liberalized the laws. Lenient Indiana statutes included only a current residency statement; a resident could get a divorce even if the whereabouts of a mate were unknown. Like its current counterpart (Reno, Nevada), Indianapolis—our moral heartland—was labeled the "divorce mecca." Like Reno, Indianapolis had a good railway station, was centrally located, had good shopping and recreational facilities, and an eager group of lawyers who courted the divorce trade.

Horace Greeley, editor of the *New York Tribune,* publicly accused Owen of causing Indiana to become "a paradise of free lovers." Owen countered with the statement that free love, prostitution, and adultery flourished in New York State because of its harsh divorce laws. Does external restriction breed inner morality or its opposite? Does external liberality breed rectitude or decay? Is this a question that can be settled by legislation?

If divorce were truly a sign of moral decay, then countries and states that were more liberal about divorce might show a higher crime rate, a lower incidence of spiritual involvement, and other signs of social dissolution. The evidence does not bear this out.

The early debates about divorce, so similar in tone to the two audience members with whom I introduced this chapter, developed two major positions. One faction—the conservatives—claimed, as they do today, that divorce threatened the basic foundation of society; they called for the return of traditional sanctity to marriage. Advocating lifetime monogamous marriage, they eschewed divorce except in extreme cases. To members of this group, divorce was a social problem. The need to maintain a rigid family organization, and harmony and stability (external at least), was more important than the marital satisfaction of individual citizens.

The other faction, comprised mainly of utopian thinkers and social activists, argued passionately for divorce reform and individual rights. To them, marriage was the social problem. Individual freedom was primary. Any effort to control that freedom would erode society from within.

Today every state has some form of no-fault divorce law. Waiting periods are short, and mandatory reconciliation counseling is virtually absent. These liberalizations generally occurred during the 1970s. During the twelve years of the Ronald Reagan and George Bush administrations, a more conservative period than the one that preceded it, the liberal laws of the earlier decade once again came under fire. Now, in the 1990s, the Clinton administration seems to be focusing more on the consequences of divorce than the causes. This focus potentially could encourage legislation aimed at improving the circumstances of divorced families, such as better child-support enforcement and welfare reform, rather than discouraging people from divorcing at all.

The pattern of liberalizing divorce laws and then tightening them, seesawing from honoring the individual to honoring the society and back again, is one that we see throughout Europe and the United States over a period of two centuries. As a society we are still ambivalent about divorce, still fearful that the family is falling apart more quickly than we can patch it together. We all agree on one basic issue: the institution of family is crucial to society (although we passionately disagree on how to define family and on which family values should be paramount).

Marriage is good—and so is divorce. It all depends to whom each happens, and why, and how—and when.

Realities Affecting Divorce

How have divorce rates changed over time? And what do divorce rates really tell us?

We've seen that divorce rates have risen in the past three centuries. However, in each decade there have been fluctuations. When charting these against fluctuations in politics and economics, we can see how divorce matches other trends.

Factors That Influence the Rise and Fall of Divorce Rates

Divorce rates tend to decline during hard times, and to rise in times of prosperity. Divorce rates decreased during World War I, increased when the war ended, decreased after the stock market crash of 1929, and stayed low during the Great Depression and World War II. When the war ended, the rates shot up once again. They peaked around 1946, stabilized, and declined a bit during the 1950s. The decrease in the 1950s is the sole exception to the economic theory of shifting divorce rates; and the fact that most of those adults had matured during the 1930s and 1940s perhaps means that their inner reality still reflected the dynamics of those depressed times. It is interesting to note that when the children of these 1950s marriages—baby boomers—matured, they divorced in record numbers. Between 1965 and 1980—prosperous years—the divorce rates more than doubled. By the late 1980s, as the economy dipped, the divorce rate declined slightly and has leveled off at our current rate.

Politics affect divorce rates too. In times of liberalism and social experimentation, divorce rates generally rise, as they did in the late 1960s and 1970s. In more conservative times, divorce rates decline somewhat, as they did in the 1980s. From the 1960s onward there has been a rapid and dramatic increase in divorces in every country allowing the practice. England's rates doubled between 1960 and 1970, then more than doubled between 1970 and the early 1980s. In France, divorce rates more than doubled between 1970 and the early 1980s. In Sweden and Germany, the rates doubled between 1960 and 1988. Today, the numbers are still highest in the United States, although it is likely that the other countries will catch up.

Each time there's a small surge in divorce rates during liberal times, conservatives respond with deep concern about the demise of the family. Many of the reforms are then repealed, only to pop up in even more lenient form the next time the cycle comes around. This does not mean that families are more content and more stable during conservative times, or even that there's a reduction in separations during those times. It just means that these already difficult times are made even harder by adding restrictive laws to economic misery.

The Probability of Divorce

The probability of divorce is associated with a number of demographic factors. Age is the strongest predictor. Those couples who are twenty years old or younger when they marry have the highest likelihood of divorce. People with less income and education tend to divorce more than those with higher education and incomes. An important exception to this principle relates to women: well-educated women (five or more years of college) with good incomes have higher divorce rates than those who are poorer and less educated.

Geographically, there are some differences as well. People in the western part of the United States have higher divorce rates than those in the Northeast. This may be due partly to the fact that the average age is lower in the West. Also, there is a higher concentration of Catholics in the Northeast.

There are also significant racial differences. Divorce rates for the black population are two times those of whites or Hispanics. Although the explanations for the higher divorce rate among African-Americans vary, socioeconomic differences seem to play a part. On the average, blacks are less educated, poorer, and more often unemployed than whites.

Religion also plays a part. Catholics and Jews have a lower divorce rate than Protestants. Since Catholicism is the religion of traditional Hispanics, part of the explanation for the racial difference in divorce rates may be attributed to religious affiliation. Although Catholics have a lower divorce rate, their rates have risen just as rapidly as the general divorce rates.

A sixfold increase in cohabitation since 1970 has also impacted divorce rates. In some European countries, a recent decline in divorce rates can be attributed to the increase in informal cohabitation arrangements. In Sweden, for example, this increase in cohabitation has decreased the marriage rate as well as the divorce rate. Breakups of these informal unions, of course, are not included in the divorce rates.

Trends and Projections

Demographic trends suggest that the current divorce rates in the United States are now fairly stable. Demographers predict that 40 percent to 60 percent of all current marriages will eventually end in divorce. Those who predict the lower rates say that the divorce rate will decline as the baby boomers age; that those boomers who wish to divorce have mostly already done so, and those that haven't are past the stage of life when the odds of divorce are highest. Those who predict an increase, whether large or small, say that women's and men's roles will continue to change. That change, plus the increasing financial independence of women—historically the less satisfied party in marriage—will continue to push the rates upward.

Women's increased economic and social independence, our increased life expectancy, the continued acceptance of divorce as a fact of modern family life—and history—all lead me to believe that the rates are likely to increase slightly or stabilize at the current level, with only minor fluctuations. One major factor that must be figured into any projection is the rate of redivorce. Most divorced people remarry and over half of those who do will redivorce; some of those will remarry and redivorce again. One factor that will help balance the rates is the reduction in the marriage rates. If fewer people marry, it reduces the potential pool for divorces. Women today have more options in life and more women may choose not to marry. Some women may choose career over marriage, may choose to cohabit instead of getting married, and may choose to parent without a husband. As we have seen, women are waiting longer to get married and in so doing also limit their chances of marriage because of the "marriage squeeze," a shortage of eligible partners due to a declining birth rate. The percentage of thirty-year-olds who have never married almost doubled between 1970 and 1990.

The Family Values Issues Raised by Divorce

Has divorce gained popularity because our attitudes toward marriage have changed, or have our attitudes changed in response to the increasing rates of divorce? Which came first, the chicken or the egg? Our attitudes and the phenomenon have evolved together.

Were Families Better in the Good Old Days?

Very few of us are immune to the pull of nostalgia. The older generation looks back fondly on depression families, when because everybody was so threatened and broke, kinfolk were more dependent on one another. In the glow of the cloud's silver lining, they minimize the fact that it was a thunderhead: the hardships shattered the hopes and dreams of the majority.

The middle generations look back fondly to Ozzie and Harriet and Ward and June Cleaver as the golden age of families. They forget the rigid segregation of roles and the narrow assumptions of homogeneity, the "hide the problem and it's not there" mentality that contributed to the major problems we have today. The mores of the time made many problems private, secret, invisible—kept within the family. These problems were never solved, merely hidden until they erupted later on. We know today that these family secrets—alcoholism, incest, child and spouse abuse—were present and their repercussions affected the next several generations.

As a country we look back fondly to the time of our grandparents and great-grandparents, having grown up hearing stories about the warmth and stability of big families. But if we really could turn back the clock, if we could choose to live in the good old days, most of us would shudder and flip the channel. I know I have very fond memories of visiting my grandparents at their apartment in Brooklyn. So many people were crowded into their four rooms, there was always someone to shower affection on me. But I also know that I would have hated living a married life like theirs.

My grandparents' marriage was arranged in Poland. My grandfather, eighteen years older than my grandmother, was a widower with three daughters, one of whom was only seven years younger than my grandmother. With his three children, one more of their own, and one on the way, they left their families in 1910 and emigrated to the United States. Two more children soon arrived. The family of nine plus the various other assorted relatives that were always there on a temporary basis lived and ran a business in those same four rooms.

Until my grandfather died at the age of ninety-five, my grandparents remained married. Never once did I hear them talk about love or communication or intimacy, nor did I notice any marital affection. They fought in Yiddish. They lived in separate spheres, my grandfather studying Talmud in the front room, constantly praying; my grandmother running her cottage-industry hair goods business from the back room, running out to scream at a child or stir the goulash burning on the stove.

We hear lots of romantic myths about the multigenerations of loving kin, snuggled happily together under one cozy roof. But in fact, high mortality rates, poverty, sixteen-hour workdays, overcrowded living conditions, and the lack of birth control determined most families' lifestyles back then: in reality, the three-generation family was quite rare.

My mother, who grew up in that golden time of America's families, does not speak with any nostalgia about her childhood. She recalls crowding at night into bed with six other children; she remembers parents who didn't have enough time, money, or affection to go around.

And that other golden age, the 1950s, was my era. As Betty Friedan showed vividly in *The Feminine Mystique,* all too many families of the time, beneath the roofs of their tidy homes in leafy suburbs, were much more unhappy than they seemed. I married in 1956 at age nineteen, and looked forward to raising children in the suburbs. I was close to the norm: in 1955, the average age of marriage was twenty, four years less than it is today. At twenty, I quit college to have my first child. Again, that was typical: in 1950, only 6 percent of women completed college. By 1961, my husband and I had two children, a house in the suburbs, and two cars in the garage. My husband trotted off daily to work, and I labored at home. By 1963, I was still typical: depressed, unfulfilled, lonely, and terribly guilty about having all these feelings. Although many women felt this way, we didn't talk about it. These were family matters, and besides, we felt too much shame.

The so-called traditional nuclear family of the 1950s was very short-lived. By the late 1960s, women began to go to work in droves. By the 1970s, the dual-earner family had already begun to replace the traditional nuclear family. Today, the percentage of traditional nuclear families (homemaker wife, breadwinner husband) has dropped to less than 15 percent of all American families. Among the people in my Binuclear Family Study, my clients, and the audiences at my lectures, the golden age of families is a fond part of all of our dream lives, but not a current practical option.

Can the High Divorce Rate Be Blamed on the Women's Movement?

It is indeed true that the women's movement has had an important impact on divorce rates. One of the factors that keeps women in unhappy, miserable, and even violent marriages is a lack of money. Research shows that women's greatest fear of leaving bad marriages is that they won't be able to support themselves and their children. And it is true that the higher a women's education and her income, the greater is her economic independence, the more likely she is to get a divorce.

The surge in divorce in the late sixties and early seventies occurred at about the same time as the women's movement gained momentum. Entering the workplace in large numbers, women challenged the inequities in the labor market and on the home front. Between 1960 and 1988, the number of women working outside the home increased from 38 percent to 56 percent. The Department of Labor projects that 60 percent of women and 75 percent of men will be in the work force in 1994. In 1991, more than half (58 percent) of mothers with children under the age of six were in the labor force; about two-thirds of these women were employed full-time. Projections for 1995 show that two-thirds of preschool children and three-fourths of school-age children will have mothers who are employed outside the home.

Today, record numbers of women have options for the first time in their lives. One enormous option is to leave a marriage that doesn't meet their needs. As we have previously seen, two-thirds to three-quarters of divorces in Western society are initiated by women. Studies in the United States and Britain show that married women with jobs are much likelier to divorce or separate than are those who stay at home. Gary Becker, winner of the 1992 Nobel Prize for Economics, believes that economics play a powerful role in marital and family decisions. "We're going to have a high divorce rate—there's nothing we can do about that. Women are working, they're more financially independent. Why should a couple who don't like each other stay together when they have thirty or forty years still ahead of them." He also notes that economics affect birth rates as well. The better the opportunities for women to earn, the greater the costs of giving up work to have children.

Even though more women than men initiate divorces, women's economic independence also makes it easier for men to initiate divorce. If a man knows that his wife can support herself, that he will not be abandoning a helpless victim, he is less likely to feel guilty about leaving. He knows he won't have to be her sole support postdivorce.

So, can the high rate of divorce be blamed on the women's movement? For many, the temptation to blame working women for all the ills of the family is impossible to resist. In this view, a woman's success at a career means that her child must go home to an empty house after school. And because she's successful, her parents and her in-laws will have no one to look after them in their old age. The public schools will fail because she's not as active in the PTA and she'll get a divorce and wreck her family. But I rarely hear anyone complain about working fathers. Nor have I heard proposals for a "daddy track" that would allow men to pursue a less strenuous course at work in order to be more available to their families. Women still carry the major responsibilities for the home and family, even when they share equally in the economic support. When the conservatives say that families do not now meet children's needs, you can be sure that *family* is merely a code word for *women.*

The message is clear. Traditional thinking implies: If mothers would just tend the family fires all day and night, we wouldn't need to change society at all to accommodate dual-worker families. If mothers took control of their families, our social problems would all magically disappear.

But it is very unlikely that women will reensconce themselves by the stove. They've learned the economic lesson that it's wise to stay employed and to keep up career mobility. It's a good insurance policy in case of divorce, among other things. Studies show that the women who are most hurt by divorce are displaced homemakers—the women who selected homemaking as their career. In marriage, two may be able to live as cheaply as one, but when divorce halves the cash flow, the unemployed women will suffer, sometimes for the rest of their lives. Some of the poorest of the poor will be elderly women whose marriages broke up in middle age—especially if they stayed home to care for the children.

Are Our Family Values Really Eroding?

When people complain that our family values are eroding because of divorce, what do they mean? A typical understanding is shown in a letter published in the "Letters to the Editor" column in response to one of my articles on divorce, which appeared in *Family Therapy News,* a publication of the American Association for Marriage and Family Therapy.

> We do not have to look high and low for our solutions to our family's problems or crises. If we are willing to return to the basics, such as faithfulness to one's spouse, love of children, spending more time at home, thrift, and self-reliance, we would do much . . . to solve the social woes that are plaguing our families.

It is true that we are seeing a shift in some of our basic values. It is also true that the so-called basic values of yesteryear may be more myth than reality. And, to blame divorce for these changes is misguided. We must acknowledge the wider societal rifts that undermine family life in general in the United States.

Are We Less Faithful?

Take faithfulness. This is a fine value, one to which most of us aspire. People seem to be quite faithful when their marriages work well. But as history clearly shows, infidelity, desertion, and divorce have been around as long as marriage. Since people tend to be deceitful about affairs, statistics about how many they've had and how long they've lasted are very iffy. Recent estimates suggest that somewhere between 50 percent and 70 percent of married men and women have been unfaithful. Perhaps that's an increase over past years—perhaps it isn't. In any case, for many people, divorce makes it possible to leave a marriage from which one or both have already physically or psychologically departed.

Are We Less Apt to Protect Our Children?

Now let's explore the very basic value of loving and unconditionally protecting our children. So many of us hold this dear, yet as a society we routinely fail to meet the needs of children. Why is it that we claim to cherish our children, yet we pay schoolteachers and day-care workers extremely poor wages? Why—until Clinton's election—has the United States been the only industrialized country in the Western world without a parental leave policy? Even today we are still far behind other countries—we only provide *unpaid* leave. Most other nations have better child-care policies and programs.

Economist Sylvia Hewlitt, in *When the Bough Breaks: The Cost of Neglecting Our Children,* notes the United States has a twin deficit in terms of our children: resources and time. In 1987, less than 5 percent of the federal budget was devoted to programs that benefit children. Other countries, such as Great Britain, France, Sweden, and Canada, spend two to three times as much as we do on families with children. The growing time deficit is evidenced by the increasing amount of time parents work. Since 1973, the average American workweek has increased by six hours (from forty-one to forty-seven hours), and for professionals it has increased even more (to fifty-two hours). Thus, in addition to having less time for leisure or community involvement, parents have less time to spend with their children.

Hewlitt notes that, "An anti-child spirit is loose in the land." It's always been there but it's getting progressively worse. The United States has never done more than give lip service to the high value we place on children. The current economy—with its high unemployment and alarmingly high incidence of poverty—and the conservative political climate, with the decrease in governmental support to institutions that serve children and families, have only exacerbated the problems.

Even if you do not equate adult caretakers' wages with valuing children, you may equate our ability to protect children from psychological and physical harm with valuing them. As a society, despite our good intentions, our children have always been vulnerable to parental abuse. In the good old days from which our traditional values sprang, child labor laws had to be enacted to prevent parents from economically exploiting their children. Indeed, we had laws to protect animal rights before we had laws to protect children. In modern times, child abuse laws have arisen to prevent parents from physically abusing, neglecting, or abandoning their kids. Incest, family violence, and alcoholism have plagued children for centuries, even in what many of us think of as the best old days—biblical times.

Do We Spend Less Time at Home?

Another cherished myth is that if we only spent more time at home our families would be more stable. Families did indeed spend more time at home in the 1800s and early 1900s, but those hours were consumed with labor and survival, not with sitting around the fire telling stories. Except in very rich families, in which the parents could afford to hire housekeepers, nannies, and laundresses (who then had to leave their own children in order to work, or who were children themselves, some as young as eleven or twelve), the consistently childcentric, well-ordered, leisurely home was as much a dream then as it is today.

When we reflect on parents spending more time at home, we don't mean parents, we mean mothers: fathers never have. In the 1950s, when the workweek was somewhat shorter, fathers were still virtually absent from families. They may have had more leisure time but they didn't spend that time in child care. Today, with most mothers employed outside the home, family time is scarce, but putting mothers back in the home full-time is not the answer. Parent activists have concentrated their energies on encouraging new corporate policies, like flextime and leaves for both fathers and mothers—trying to make a world in which everyone has the chance at a job, and everyone has the chance to be home with their children.

Are We Less Thrifty?

Thrift has been taken care of by inflation and recession; and self-reliance is practically impossible, by definition, for the nuclear family. The scattering of generations and of services has equally scattered what were once familial tasks over the face of the earth: education, food production, child care, religion. Only wealthy families, the larger religious organizations, corporations, and the government can afford to buy all these services separately. Poor and lower-middle-class families simply cannot afford the services, or the loss of income entailed when one parent stays home to take care of children.

Is the Family Eroding . . . Or Diversifying?

The problems are not caused by families, divorced or not. Families are reactors to—even more than they are initiators of—social change. Pessimists say that the family is eroding. Optimists say that the family is diversifying. Both points of view are right. Families are more diverse, and they are in trouble, but not because of their diversity. The families of today—whatever their size or shape—are in crisis because our economy is failing, our national resources are shrinking, and our governmental policies to support them are inadequate.

Is Divorce Too Easy to Get?

It's easy to understand why some people feel divorce is too easy to get. Our current divorce laws are much more liberal than they were in the past. When I got divorced in the mid-sixties, the option of a blameless divorce for "irreconcilable differences" wasn't available. So, after waiting almost two years, I stood before a judge and stretched and molded the truth into a claim that my husband had treated me in the requisite "cruel and inhumane" ways. It was a mortifying experience. My lawyer, the judge, and I all knew I was magnifying petty incidents into major abuses, in order to concoct sufficient evidence for that type of case.

Today, spouses don't have to fight in court about who did what to whom, because no-fault laws in almost every state have removed the need to place blame. They also don't have to spend the time and money my exhusband and I did. Today, anyone who wants a divorce can get it over with relatively quickly and inexpensively, compared to the good old bad old days. In Tennessee, a "drive-through divorce" is available for $300. In Los Angeles, one legal firm advertises low-cost divorces on TV and on bus-stop benches.

So it's true that divorce is easier to get. But whether that's an incentive to divorce is questionable. Most historians of divorce agree that liberalizing the laws did not cause the increase in divorce rates. There was a surge in the year following the initiation of no-fault laws, caused only by couples who postponed their divorces to take advantage of the newly instituted laws.

Tightening the laws, then, would be an exercise in hypocrisy. As we saw earlier in the chapter, people are parting and will part, regardless of the laws. The major advantage to easing the laws is, it's helped reduce some of the stigma around divorce, making the process a bit emotionally easier—that's all.

As we will see in later chapters, the process itself is still plenty difficult and adversarial, if not because of the laws governing divorce, then because of the emotions fueling it. Instead of fighting over blame—"just cause," as the old laws put it—the fight now revolves around splitting up money and property and determining custody of the children.

One couple from my Binuclear Family Study illustrates how costly and painful no-fault divorce can be. Janet and David spent two years and $45,000 in adversarial divorce proceedings. On our second interview, three years postdivorce, they were still escalating their battle. Said Janet, "*No-fault* divorce? What hogwash! For the past six months all we've done is find faults! The final straw was when he accused me of being a lousy mother. That did it. And after all those years of his not giving a darn about the kids, now he wants joint custody. No way. He's such a cheapskate, I know he only wants it so he can dodge child support. Well, he's in for a battle. I'm not giving."

Except perhaps for a rare couple, I've never heard anyone who's been through a divorce say that it is too easy to get, either in regard to the external process or the internal. The laws are certainly more liberal now than they were a century ago, but the legal system is still embedded in the old moralities. Emotionally, legally, and socially, divorce is difficult to get.

To Transcend the Myths, We Must Accept the Facts

Divorced Families Are Not Deviant

When I divorced, my older daughter was one of only two children in her class whose parents had split. I had only one friend who shared my plight. My daughters and I were deviants, and felt the stigma that deviants feel. We felt different from and lesser than others. Ashamed failures.

Now, almost thirty years later, the picture has changed dramatically. In most American classrooms, one can expect one-third to one-half of the children to be living in a family of divorce or remarriage. In most demographic reports, children from divorced homes are counted along with children born to unmarried mothers, all included in the category of single-parent families or mother-only households. In this larger group, the 1991 statistics show 20 percent of white, one-third of Hispanic, and one-half of African-American children live in mother-only homes. The number of mother-headed households has almost tripled since 1960, and doubled since 1970. About half of America's children will spend some portion of their growing-up years in a "single-parent family," most as a consequence of divorce.

Even though divorce, clearly, is no longer deviant in the statistical sense, it still remains socially and psychologically deviant. Our bias toward nuclear families is so embedded in our culture, so inherent in our policy, that we still ostracize other family forms. We thus feel ashamed and less than normal. We have the painful sense that we've failed in life.

It's troubling that those who today profess to be pro-family advocates, who pride themselves on their family values, promote this nuclear family bias. In a highly publicized article in the *Atlantic Monthly* (April 1993), Barbara Defoe Whitehead, historian and research associate at the Institute for American Values—a conservative think-tank—strongly affirms the belief that two-parent married families are the best way to raise children. Titling her piece "Dan Quayle Was Right," Whitehead paints a picture of how awful life is for children living in mother-headed households. Her data are not always correct or complete; her knowledge of the social science research is superficial. Nevertheless, Whitehead makes a convincing and passionate argument.

It's not that I don't agree with some of the findings indicating that children from single-parent families have more difficulties than children raised in two-parent families. It's that I believe parents should not be blamed. Nonnuclear family forms must not be labeled inferior. If they are, we will label more than half of American families failures. As a society we must not send the message to the children in those families that they are doomed, deviant failures. To me, this message does much more harm than good. What would be helpful, instead, would be to create a new constructive public image—to normalize instead of stigmatize this half of America's families.

Yes, it's more difficult for one parent to shoulder all the responsibility for child rearing. Yes, it's certainly arduous for one parent to earn as much household cash as can their two-worker, two-parent counterparts. And yes, it's clearly grueling to do so in a society that offers no support—institutional, economic, or social. But to continue to scapegoat these adults and children as failures only creates more problems.

Divorced People Are Not Failures

Judith Stacey, noted sociologist and author of *Brave New Families,* makes an incontrovertible point. "The election of a President who was reared, as was George Washington, by a single parent provides an excellent opportunity to end the scapegoating of unconventional families and to begin rebuilding public responsibility for all of our children, and for their kin."

In spite of the escalating family values debates between the nuclear family advocates and the family diversity advocates, children today talk more matter-of-factly about their living arrangements than did my daughters in the mid-1960s. I recently overheard one nine-year-old child nonchalantly say to a friend, "If you come over this week you'll have to come to my daddy's house, but next week if you come, I'll be at my mom's."

At the same time, singles clubs have mushroomed in every city and town, in large part because the divorced population is attempting to disembarrass itself. Even the churches and synagogues have gradually come to accept divorced congregants, now that there are so many of us. In large cities, some congregations consist entirely of singles, the majority of whom may be divorced. Others, I noticed recently, publicly note that their congregants include singles and divorced families. Many Catholic churches, traditionally the staunchest opposers of divorce, have groups for single parents, and support groups for the divorced. We all knew that Nancy Reagan was Ronald Reagan's second wife, although it's true that they never spoke of their marriage as a remarriage; George Bush's daughter remarried during his presidency.

All the same, we still hear messages from the pulpit about the evils of divorce, about "broken homes." There's still a strong message that divorce is bad, and that somehow if you'd been a better person you could have avoided this situation.

The noted anthropologist Margaret Mead was interviewed before her death about her long and interesting life. She was married and divorced three times. When the reporter asked her about her "failed" marriages, she quickly replied, "I didn't have any failed marriages. I've been married three times and each marriage was successful." She went on to explain that she had gone through several very distinct life stages and had at each time chosen a different mate, one who could meet her needs and priorities of that time. She also suggested in her writings—over twenty-five years ago—that her own pattern of serial monogamy was the wave of the future.

Longer Lives = Serial Marriages

Although Mead's contemporaries thought her vision was immoral, the reality in the 1990s is that a significant proportion of the adult population will have serial relationships, just as she did. There's a good reason for this trend. In 1776, a child born in America could expect to live to age thirty-five. A century later, life expectancy had increased to age forty, and by 1989 it had jumped to age seventy-five. In two hundred years our life expectancy has doubled. By the year 2040, most people will live well into their eighties and even nineties. Not surprisingly, the average length of a marriage has increased, too. A century ago, the average marriage lasted a little over thirty years; today, if you don't divorce, it's forty-five years. These days, if you marry young enough and stay married, you can anticipate celebrating your sixty-fifth or seventieth anniversary.

When life was so much shorter, there was barely time to live out one's adult life with a single mate. Today, the thought of twenty, thirty, or even forty years in a bad relationship can be a very weighty factor in deciding to leave. In 1990 in the United States, 134,000 couples married twenty years or longer got divorced. That was 12.4 percent of the total divorces. It represents an increase of more than 10 percent in that age group since 1975.

As our life expectancy increases, so does our need for growth and change. Because the population over age fifty has grown so rapidly, there is now greater public and private concern about how to make those extra years satisfying. Years ago parents didn't have to cope with an "empty nest" when their children left home; at the turn of the century, the average couple could expect to live only a year or two beyond the time when the last child left. Today, fifteen or thirty years of empty-nest marriage is becoming the norm. The average couple can now expect to spend decades of postparenting together.

Neither intellect nor vigor necessarily declines with age. Ken Dychtwald's *Age Wage* and Betty Friedan's *The Fountain of Age* show us that creativity, productivity, and personal fulfillment can all increase as we age; Maggie Kuhn, the gray-haired lady in tennis shoes who founded the Gray Panthers, shows us that the aging are as ready to combat negative stereotypes as are other populations of the divorced. The media now present images of gray-haired adults having fun, being active, being romantic and sexy. Why should the divorced elderly be any different?

With longer life, we have the time and resources to live many incarnations during a single life span. For some, divorce now acts as a functional substitute for death: ending one type of life and starting another. It is indeed a lucky and hardworking couple who develop in tandem over a period of decades, and we cannot count on being part of that particular lucky few. Just as it is no longer uncommon to change careers two or more times during our lifetime, it is no longer uncommon to change mates.

A friend of mine announced at age seventy that she was going to divorce her husband of forty-five years, well known in the community for his alcoholism and womanizing. I knew the marriage had been bad for a long time, but I asked her, "Why now, after all these years?"

She explained: "A lot of things hit me all at once. I've seen two of my children get divorces and watched how they survived. I talked with them a lot. They were truly supportive. As much as they love their father, they could see the pain in our relationship. As I imagined being seventy next month I thought, 'Why shouldn't I make the remainder of my life better?' "

My friend is not alone in her decision. In the past two decades the rate of divorce among the elderly has increased three times as fast as the rate of growth of the older population. However long each of us has to live, we each have to decide for ourselves what will make the rest of our years happy.

Longevity is probably the single most powerful reason why divorce rates are unlikely to decrease appreciably in the future. Even if we could turn back the clock, would we want to?

"She married and then divorced, and then she married and divorced, and then she married and lived happily ever after."

Drawing by W. Miller; © 1993 *The New Yorker* Magazine, Inc.

Divorce Is Normal

Our current divorce rates should not be viewed with doom and gloom. Families are amazingly resilient. Divorce is one way that families are adapting to current realities.

What we must change is our outdated ideals about marriage and family. We need to stop clinging to our myths, to our nostalgia for vanished or fictional good old days. We must stop expecting families of today to look like families of yesterday. Within the proper human limits of relationships—families should be nurturant, affectionate, and as stable as possible within our unstable world—we must encourage and expand the real kinship networks that people have already begun to develop.

Since divorce today is intrinsically part of married life, we need to stop loading it with negative judgments and to explore ways to improve families' quality of life, postdivorce.

Too many people persist in viewing the unstoppable phenomenon of divorce as a social plague that needs to be eradicated instead of as a practical problem. Divorce cannot be cured. It is here to stay. Half of our marriages each year are remarriages. Divorce and remarriage are as institutionalized today as are first-time marriage and single life. We must make the difficult but necessary shift in our perceptions, and realize that marriage and family are no longer synonymous. That's not necessarily what many of us would have wanted if we had sole choice, but it is the reality.

Everyone I know would prefer to live in a vital love relationship. Every divorced person I know feels divorce is a last resort, used only when all chances of happiness in the marriage are gone. Almost every divorced person I know wants to recouple or remarry. The current remarriage rates show 89 percent of men and 79 percent of women remarry within five years of their divorce.

Instead of wasting our energy on futile regrets for a golden age that is unattainable, and that only existed by common social consent, we'd be wise to accept divorce as one viable way to end dissatisfaction in marriage. Once we do, we'll be able to turn our efforts to keeping what we can of our kinship networks, to respecting the struggles of the divorced to remain viable families.

We must stop looking for causes and shift our priorities to prevention—not of divorce but of its negative consequences. The real consequences of divorce fall upon the children, who like their parents are labeled as deviant. The projections are that well over half of America's children will experience life in a divorced family for some of their dependent years. By not pathologizing it, and instead accepting the current realities, normalizing divorce would mean that these children would not have to live with painful stigma, nor would they have the realities of their family life cast in the shadows. The negative effects on children would be minimized if they could be assured that their family life was not dependent on their parents' marriages. Children could expect that their parents, with the help of social institutions—schools, churches or synagogues, and social agencies—would work to provide the security, love, and support of family life. Children could count on not just one kind of family structure, but any structure that would meet their particular family's needs. The self-esteem of these children of divorce, even the adult children of divorce, would benefit greatly from knowing that binuclear families are just as good, just as real, just as normal, as nuclear families.

3

What's Normal in Divorce
CREATING A NEW VISION

IF I HEAR 'broken home' one more time, I'll scream. This spring my son is graduating from Harvard. He's got good friends and a nice girlfriend, and he's reasonably happy. But, since his father and I divorced when he was six, all I've heard from people—my family, his teachers, even my rabbi—is: 'It's surprising how well James is doing.' Why is it so surprising? His father and I are good parents. He's got two nurturing grandmothers and a bunch of cousins he's close with. He's not different from his friends. Sure, we had a couple of really bad years during the divorce, but we got through them. The truth is, life was actually better afterward than it was before Don and I split up. I wish everyone would stop making my divorce this massively negative thing that ruined James forever."

This statement, coming from a colleague, has an all too familiar ring. Not only do I remember so many times in my own past hearing this message, but my research participants and my clients echo the same feelings. Sarah, a teacher and divorced mother of three whom I interviewed for my study, was tearful as she told me how bad she felt about the stigma her children bear. "It's as if they're second-class citizens because their father doesn't live with us. Why is this shameful? Why is it a cross they have to bear? Sure, it's sad sometimes, especially at Christmas, but most of the time their life isn't that different."

A student of mine recently said to me: "Whenever I tell a new friend that my folks are divorced, they give me this troubled look. Just the other night four of us were sitting in the Commons talking. Then I asked them about their families. It turns out one kid's father is an alcoholic. And another kid's mother has been on antidepressants since the kid was born, and another said how she stayed away from home because her parents were always putting each other down. So what, they're married? I don't know, I think their families sound much worse than mine."

What my colleague, study participant, and student have in common is their growing puzzlement and anger. Their experience of divorce simply does not fit society's consensus. They (like many divorced parents and their children) question why others assume—based on family structure alone—that, of course, divorce has destroyed them and their families.

In Chapter 2, I identified the stigmatizing myths and stereotypes that show families of divorce as nonfamilies. Now I'll counter these myths with facts. In showing the true diversity of families of divorce, I hope to challenge you to look beyond our society's current limited picture. I hope that you will then start to share in, and even help to build, a new vision: a vision created by looking at healthy and enriching family models.

Wherever you are in the stages of divorce, you can benefit from hearing about healthy models. Whether you're just making the gut-wrenching decision to part; whether you're facing the painful reality of the physical separation; even if you've completed the legal divorce and weathered many years since—at each stage you can further strengthen your family in ways that work for you. A new vision, one incorporating many options, each of which leads to a positive outcome, is absolutely central to a good divorce.

The Real Relationships of Divorce

Our new vision acknowledges the real relationships of divorce. We've seen how the existing negative role models won't teach us anything—how they've kept us in a relative vacuum. They've told us how we *shouldn't* behave, and how we would have behaved if we fit some mythic mold, but give us no direction for how we should behave as real divorcing or divorced couples. We've thus felt a lot more anxiety than we've needed to, and have been more likely to experience debilitating crises during the necessary transitions of divorce.

This new vision both describes divorces and provides road maps necessary for change. Many exspouses, through trial and error, through the example of friends, have been able to find their own way into a well-functioning binuclear family.

Positive Models, Fewer Crises

In the Binuclear Family Study, the questions that most preoccupied the adults were: "How can we get through this without destroying the children? How do we get from this awful place of feeling shattered to some semblance of order? How do *other* divorced families manage to have a normal sense of family?"

Jessica, a thirty-five-year-old legal secretary, remembered her terrible feeling of doom when she and Craig started seriously considering separation right after their tenth wedding anniversary. "Night after night I sat in my rocking chair in Timmy's room, long after he was asleep, crying, trying to imagine what our lives would look like. I just couldn't get a picture. Everything looked so bleak. I knew Craig would continue to be in our lives, but how? Craig and I were having trouble even being decent to one another—how were we going to figure this out? In the midst of one of our screaming battles, he warned me that if I tried to push him out of the kids' lives, he'd take the war to court. I knew that would be a horror for all of us.

"Just trying to picture the holidays was enough to throw me into a deep depression for days. Thanksgiving. Christmas. How could we divide them up? The kids had a friend whose parents were divorced and her whole family—not only the parents, but both sets of grandparents too—spent Christmas Day together. Craig and I couldn't do that! I couldn't imagine it! How were we going to spell out every occasion when we could hardly talk to one another without a fight erupting?"

A year and a half later, Jessica and Craig were no longer Fiery Foes. They'd agreed on a joint-custody arrangement. The children spent the weekdays with Jessica and spent most of the weekends with Craig. For the most part, both parents (now Cooperative Colleagues) thought things were working out pretty well, although they still occasionally screamed at each other about discipline and wrangled over the holidays. When we interviewed them for the third time, five years after their legal divorce, they were feeling pretty resolved about most of the issues. Their new feelings of cooperation allowed them to be more flexible about the children's schedules. Now twelve and fourteen, the children still lived with Jessica most weekdays but occasionally would spend a couple of nights during the week with Craig, as well as some part of every weekend.

With some surprise in her voice Jessica said, "I never could have imagined we'd end up being able to do this. It's been a tough few years, and we've made some bad mistakes, but we came through it pretty well, I think. In fact, I've invited Craig and his new wife for Thanksgiving dinner. How civilized can we get!"

Like Jessica and Craig, many couples wend their way from separation through divorce without the benefit of role models. By trial and error, some manage to reorganize their families in ways that provide children with the security of having two active parents. Others, unfortunately, remain stuck in unresolved battles that perpetuate the distress of the early separation, and perhaps of the marriage as well. As the range of positive role models becomes part of our culture, it's likely that more exspouses will reorganize their families in ways that better meet children's needs. And they'll do so sooner, reducing the prolonged distress experienced by families of divorce.

Exspouse Relationships: The Foundation of the Binuclear Family

When I presented my first paper on divorce at a professional meeting in 1978, I told my audience, "The time has come for us to move beyond asking *whether* exspouses should relate and start looking at *how* indeed they do relate." Almost two decades ago that seemed like an unusual suggestion: at the time there was no published research that focused on the exspouse relationship. It's hard to believe, but even today, we still know very little. Besides my own research, only a few small studies have attempted the subject.

We still hold the assumption that divorced couples must be antagonists; otherwise, why would they divorce? Society still assumes that divorced people are amputees, that the relationships surrounding the married couple are dissolved along with the marriage, that friends of the couple now will have to choose one partner and reject the other.

This view puts forth the belief that when spouses become exspouses they have two options: either they hate one another or they have no relationship whatsoever. Margaret Mead said, "It's as if any contact between divorced people somehow smacks of incest." Actually, aside from this Dissolved Duo option, and the dramatic Fiery Foe option so loved by the media, there are three other distinct options, plus all the shades of gray.

In Chapter 1, when I introduced the major findings from the Binuclear Family Study, I noted that one of the biggest surprises was that almost 50 percent of the exspouse couples we interviewed had relationships that defied our stereotypes. They weren't filled with anger and bitterness, but rather their feelings toward one another (not about the divorce itself, however) were more ambivalent. For the most part, they acted civil, even amicable, and sometimes downright friendly.

Although the ninety-eight pairs of exspouses could be placed on a long continuum from the stereotypical rageful warriors to the highly suspect best friends, most found their places somewhere in between these polar opposites. This range of role models is helpful in the early stages of uncoupling by providing exspouses with good, workable models from which to choose. For those who are already divorced—even those divorced for a long time—these models can also be useful. Suppose you are still angry, still fighting, or have no contact and are sad about it. When you and your ex have children together, you are linked together for life. Like other relationships in our lives, the exspouse relationship is dynamic and has the possibility for change, even many years after divorce. You still have the option of bettering your relationship.

How the Typologies Were Formed

Forming typologies entails seeing how people cluster together based on their similarities. Once they are grouped, the next step is to look for the things that differentiate the groups from one another. In this way, large amounts of information can be pulled together in ways that are understandable and useful. But it is important never to lose sight of the fact that typologies are merely tools for helping us to organize and summarize information. They are not discrete nor are they mutually exclusive.

What you are likely to find as you read about these typologies and try to place yourself is that on some dimensions you fit into one category, while on others you may be more like the people in another category. Use the typologies to help you form a general picture of your relationship, to better understand how you interact, and to find some helpful ideas on how to relate more constructively. Remember, the types may not fit you exactly. Also, you'll likely change types at different stages of your relationship.

In the in-depth interviews my assistants and I asked participants numerous questions about their current lives, as well as questions about their past marriages. We then selected a series of thirteen detailed questions about their current relationship. I assessed the exspouses' degree of conflict about parenting with questions such as these: "When you and your former spouse discuss parenting issues, how often does an argument result?" "How often is the underlying atmosphere one of hostility or anger?" "How often is the conversation stressful or tense?" Other questions assessed the amount of inter-parental support: "When you need help regarding the children, do you seek it from your former spouse?" "Does your former spouse go out of the way to accommodate any changes you need to make in the visiting arrangements?" "Do you go out of the way to accommodate your former spouse?" Still other questions determined whether exspouses had a relationship that wasn't related to the children: "How often over the past several months have you and your ex talked about old friends in common?" "About your families?" "About new experiences you're having in your present lives?"

My assistants and I then quantified the answers to these questions, and used the numbers thus obtained in statistical analyses. As we had interviewed each former spouse separately, we combined their scores to form a typology of couples. Once we established the typologies, I examined issues such as living arrangements, specifics of the legal divorce, child-rearing responsibilities, remarriage, rules, rituals, and other topics. I looked for similarities and differences among the groups.

The Typologies: Diversity and Change

Based on our initial interviews (one year after the divorces) the relationships of the ninety-eight couples divided almost equally into good (Cooperative Colleagues and Perfect Pals) and bad (Angry Associates and Fiery Foes) models. (We had no Dissolved Duos in the initial study.)

Perfect Pals

Perfect Pals (the high interactors–high communicators) comprised a small minority of the sample, about 12 percent. For them, the disappointments of a failed marriage didn't overshadow the positive elements of a longstanding relationship. Most explained that the strength of their marriage had been that they were basically best friends, and they still called themselves good friends. They spoke with each other at least once or twice every week and were interested in each other's current lives. They asked each other how their work was going, what they were doing that week, and even how they were feeling. They trusted one another, asked for advice, and helped each other out, as friends do. One couple still owned and operated a business together. Another lived a block apart; both exspouses continued to mingle with the same social group. Although a few exspouse pairs continued to be affectionate, only one couple reported ever engaging in sex.

Perfect Pals stayed well connected with family and old friends. Because they hadn't had an angry adversarial divorce, women and men were both still very much a part of each other's extended family.

Marisa, divorced from Joel after nine years, explained it this way: "Joel's mother has always been like a mother to me. My mother died when Joel and I were married only a year, and Joel's mother was so caring and available to me. There's no way I will ever stop loving her."

All of the Perfect Pals had joint custody arrangements. They weren't all equal time arrangements but both parents assumed child-care responsibilities and stayed very involved with the children. These are the couples that you hear about who spend holidays together, and have certain times that they and the children share a meal or an activity as a binuclear family. One couple, who we'll learn more about in Chapter 5, had the unusual arrangement of the children staying put in the family home, while they took turns living there with them. Other couples had more usual arrangements, but all shared decision making fairly equally. It's not that they didn't argue: they did. But occasional disagreements did not result in extended, angry disputes.

If all this sounds too good—or too weird—to be true, remember that it works only for a small select group of people. And then, it is likely to work best at the early stages of divorce—before individual lives differentiate. In fact, at our next two interviews (two and four years later) many of these Perfect Pals had moved on. About one-third of them became Cooperative Colleagues. These couples still remained friendly, but they talked to each other less often. Their lives were less entwined, although they continued to relate very well as parents. Another third, though, became Angry Associates. Usually, some incident—sometimes related to a new partner—had erupted, which was not easily resolved. This created an angry distancing, although the custody arrangement and the amount of time each parent spent with the children remained quite stable. One couple plummeted, however, into being Fiery Foes. It turned out that the exwife had not wanted the divorce, and had nursed some unrealistic hopes of reconciliation. When her ex remarried, she became very angry and punitive.

The fact is that the few couples who remained Perfect Pals five years after their divorce (and a few earlier Cooperative Colleagues couples who later became Perfect Pals) had not recoupled with new partners, or had recoupled for a brief period and then split up again. It seems clear that it would be difficult, and perhaps even detrimental, to the new relationship for the exspouses to continue to hold on to each other with the same degree of frequency, intensity, and intimacy.

One question that often arises about these friendly couples is: Why did they divorce if they get along so well? Julie, a thirty-seven-year-old chemist, said what other couples also noted: "We really get along better now. We don't live together well—we don't feel romantic about one another. I'm much happier living apart from Chuck. Yet, we have a long history, and two wonderful children. There's no reason we shouldn't continue to be good friends." Although many divorced spouses can't imagine having this kind of relationship with their ex, it can be an effective, supportive option for those who choose to live this way.

Cooperative Colleagues

The largest (38 percent) and most diverse group were the Cooperative Colleagues (the moderate interactors–high communicators). Unlike Perfect Pals, they didn't consider each other to be close friends but for the most part they cooperated quite well around issues that concerned the children. Some of the couples talked fairly frequently, while others had only minimal contact. For the most part, they usually were able to compromise when it came to dividing up the holidays and vacations, though they were more likely to split the time rather than spend it together. Some couples, however, did spend occasional time together— usually special occasions such as birthdays, school plays, or parent-teacher conferences.

When Cooperative Colleagues discussed issues other than the children, like the Perfect Pals, they talked about extended family and friends they had in common. Some of the couples spoke about their work or other such nonintimate issues, but only a few couples got more involved in each other's lives than that.

Ken was typical of many of the fathers in this group. "I'm not entirely happy with this setup but it's probably the best solution, for right now, at any rate. I'd rather see the kids more but they have stuff with their friends that they want to do. So sometimes I pick up just my youngest on Saturday morning and then come back in the afternoon to get my older boy. Frances and I get along all right—except for a fight we had last Christmas when I wanted to take the kids skiing—as long as we stick to talking about the kids. Our kids are just great, and Frances is good about telling me special things they did in school, or making sure I know about school events."

All the couples had some areas of conflict. Some managed disagreements better than others. For the most part they didn't end up in vicious battles, but rather they either resolved controversial issues or avoided them. Peggy, a high school teacher who'd been Harry's spouse for twelve years, explained how she dealt with volatile issues: "There are just some things I tip-toe around. Money, for example. I'm real careful not to get caught into talking about how I spend my money. He'll drop a comment like, 'Looks like you really spent a mint on that suit.' I used to snap back, 'It's none of your business.' And we'd be off on a stupid fight, even in front of the kids. Now, I just let it go by."

The children's living arrangements and custody agreements were quite varied. Some Cooperative Colleagues had joint legal custody, but few split the time fairly equally. Usually one parent's house was considered "home." Most often mothers were the primary parent; dads tended to see their children almost every weekend and usually one night during the week.

In a few cases, the fathers were the primary parent. The mothers in these families were responsible for the children about a third of the time. Monica was one of these noncustodial mothers. As she explained at her initial interview, "Stan was better equipped to be the full-time parent. It was my choice to leave, not his, and I wanted to go to graduate school. His life was more stable. He could afford to keep the house, and even though he was angry with me, I knew he wouldn't stop me from seeing the kids. People are always surprised when I tell them—it's always as if they think something must be wrong with me. But it really works best for the kids, and in truth, it does for me too right now. I see the kids several times a week and call them at least once a day. Last month when he had to go away for five days, I came and stayed with the kids at the house."

A common denominator for Cooperative Colleague couples was the ability to compartmentalize their relationship: they separated out issues related to their marital relationship from those related to their parenting relationship. Their desire to provide the best situation for their children took precedence over their personal issues. Unlike the Perfect Pals, most of the Cooperative Colleagues said they wouldn't have much, if any, personal contact with their exspouse if not for their children.

Five years postdivorce, at our third interview, the relationships of about one-quarter of this group had deteriorated and the exspouses were now Angry Associates. Arguments, particularly about money, had increased. The exspouses of this minority tended to blame their expartner's remarriage for the increasing problems, either because the new mate galled them, or because the change affected the earlier pattern with which they'd become contented.

However, the vast majority of Cooperative Colleagues—about 75 percent—remained Cooperative Colleagues, even though most had remarried or were in serious new live-in relationships. It's promising to see that three-quarters of the divorced couples were this flexible. They continued to cooperate despite a lack of positive reinforcement in society. Who can say what percentages of exspouses would be equally cooperative after five years if they had such reinforcement?

Angry Associates

Angry Associates (moderate interactors–low communicators), on the other hand, felt angry almost every time they communicated—which they only did in order to make plans for their children. The major difference between Angry Associates, who made up about 25 percent of the initial sample, and Cooperative Colleagues was in the way they managed conflict. Instead of being able to compartmentalize their anger, they let it spread into related and even nonrelated issues. With each other they were generally tense and hostile, or even openly conflictual.

"Every time I need to change any plan, try to discuss anything, all I hear is her constant barrage of 'What a lousy father.' It's a strain not to respond to her sniping but she usually carries it one step too far and then I explode. I know now to just wait a few hours and call back again. But it's awful for the kids. They get caught in it. Waiting for me, they must be very anxious. Is Dad going to be allowed in the house to pick us up? Or, if we're still fighting, will I have to wait in the car and they sort of sneak out?" For the fathers in this group, situations like Steve's were all too common.

The mothers' perspectives were a bit different. Bonnie, Steve's exwife, blamed their bad relationship on him. "He's always trying to get out of something or manipulate plans the way he wants them. He calls up very friendly-like and then asks me if I can switch days, or can he have the boys for an extra day next week, or why didn't I buy the boys a computer given how much child support he pays. I try to control my temper but he just pushes my buttons and we end up screaming and I just hang up. It wrecks my day and I know it upsets the boys."

Angry Associates all had some form of sole-custody arrangement, with the nonresidential parent (almost always the father) spending a range of time with the children—as often as two to three days a week and as seldom as one day a month. Five years postdivorce, almost all had recoupled. Some had returned to court for changes in child support or visitation orders. Both mothers and fathers were dissatisfied with how things were going.

By the time of our third interview (five years postdivorce), the initial group of Angry Associates had split evenly in three ways. A third were still Angry Associates. Another third had deteriorated into Fiery Foes or Dissolved Duos, and even though they had less contact, whenever they did, they screamed at each other and stayed furious for months and years afterward. The last third had improved their relationship, and were now Cooperative Colleagues. They'd moved on to other spousal relationships and reduced their anger. Some went to counseling and worked things out; most learned how to better manage their disputes.

Fiery Foes

Fiery Foes (low interactors–low communicators) made up about 25 percent of the sample. These exspouses rarely interacted and when they did talk they usually ended up fighting. Their divorces tended to be highly litigious, and their legal battles often continued for many years after the divorce. Each change brought further anger: they were not able to work out arrangements for the children without arguing. Many relied on a third party (i.e., a lawyer, friend, or child) to settle their disagreements over each issue as it arose.

Fiery Foes were unable to remember the good times in their marriage. They clung to the wrongs done to each other, and even exaggerated these wrongs for effect or in order to keep building their case. Like couples in a conflict-habituated marriage, the Fiery Foes were still very much attached to each other, although they were quick to deny it. They simply could not let go.

Almost two-thirds of the couples who were Fiery Foes when we first interviewed them continued to be at their subsequent interviews. The good news, though, is that more than half of the remaining one-third had become Cooperative Colleagues. Joe, a noncustodial father of three, was typical of this latter group. "We don't fight as much because there's less to decide. But, I think, it's also because she's remarried and feels better about her life. When I remarried, she hit the roof—and pretty much stayed there for the next three years! But now, she just seems happier in general, and is even more willing to let the kids spend more time at my place."

At the initial interview Fiery Foes tended to have the most polarized arrangements in all categories. Many of these exspouse pairs exchanged their children, saying not a word to each other at the door. Others had ongoing escalations that went as far as kidnapping. Still others were unable to manage any visitation at all. By five years postdivorce, though the exspouses' relationships were still hostile, the custody arrangements had become formalized. Contact between noncustodial fathers and their children had diminished considerably, with some fathers noting that they hadn't seen their children in the past six months. A few couples were still calling their lawyers frequently, arguing over child support and visitation, but most had withdrawn into no interaction at all with one another.

Dissolved Duos

Since an initial criterion for participating in the Binuclear Family Study was that the out-of-home parent had seen the child at least once in the prior month, there were no Dissolved Duos in my study. Dissolved Duos are exspouse pairs who entirely discontinue contact. They garner a disproportionate amount of media attention, especially in those cases in which a noncustodial parent kidnaps a mutual child from the noncommunicating custodial parent.

It is common for one partner of a Dissolved Duo to leave the geographical area in which the family lives. There are isolated cases in which one partner, usually the man, actually disappears, leaving the other partner to carry the whole burden of reorganizing the family postdivorce. In these cases the marriage has often been so stressful that the only way of coping was for one partner to try to psychologically eliminate the other by totally withdrawing. The Dissolved Duo family is a true single-parent family—in which there is no further presence of the former spouse, except in memories and fantasies. Occasionally, at some later date, the absent parent may return and even reclaim parental rights. Such was the case in the movie *Kramer vs. Kramer,* when the mother, played by Meryl Streep, returned after abandoning her son. The father, Dustin Hoffman, refused to give up custody, and after a long, painful hearing, he won.

As we've seen, membership in these categories is not static. Many exspouse relationships changed over time. Others stayed the same over years. Many times, the key for these changes in postdivorce relationships seemed to be the introduction of new members into the binuclear family, or the approach of a milestone celebration in one family member's life. One exspouse's fortieth birthday, the graduation of a mutual child from college, and the financial success or remarriage of one exspouse all marked changes in exspouse typologies.

Exspouses and Rites of Passage

How might one's exspouse relationship affect behavior at a milestone celebration, such as the high school graduation of a child?

The Perfect Pals would plan festivities to celebrate the graduation together as a family unit. They might plan a lunch or dinner together, sit together at the graduation, and perhaps even give a mutual gift. The Cooperative Colleagues would be less likely to plan the festivities together, but both would attend them. Perhaps Mother would plan a dinner and invite Father to join them. They might sit together for the graduation, but interactions would be more strained and formal.

The Angry Associates would celebrate separately with the child, perhaps one taking the child to dinner the evening before and one having lunch after the ceremonies. They would sit separately at the ceremonies and avoid contact with each other as much as possible. It is very likely that in the Fiery Foes one parent would be excluded from the celebrations surrounding the event and might not be invited to the graduation. The excluded parent would be aware of the event and feel angry and hurt to be left out. In the Dissolved Duos the noncustodial parent would probably not even be aware that his or her child was graduating and, if he or she was aware, would not acknowledge it in any way.

How each of these possible scenarios would affect a child is quite obvious. A child with Cooperative Colleague or Perfect Pal parents would be free to enjoy the occasion, surrounded by family without feeling caught in a tug of war. If his or her parents are Angry Associates, loyalty conflicts would likely emerge, and issues of which parent to greet first, who to spend time with, and whose feelings are hurt would overshadow the joy of the event. For a child whose parents are Fiery Foes or Dissolved Duos, the absence of one parent is likely to be remembered with sadness or anger for many years afterward.

Coping with the Structural Changes of Divorce

Suppose you are caught in the throes of a messy transition, and you can't decide to which type you and your ex belong. Or, more importantly, suppose you can't decide what's the best model you can realistically expect to follow.

Structuring the good divorce requires that families let go of familiar patterns and establish unfamiliar, current ones. New rules need to be established, roles need to be shifted and redefined, and new rituals need to be created. It is in working out these new rules, roles, and rituals that you will find typology almost clarifying itself. As your new rules, roles, and rituals become established, the ambiguity will eventually disappear.

Truth Is Stronger Than Fiction

Divorce makes for interesting storytelling. Today's sitcoms abound with strange families. Daytime soaps present revolving-door marriages in which so many spouses come and go that they begin to run together. But Cooperative Colleagues began to appear in the 1980s. "Golden Girls" and "thirtysomething" presented divorced lead characters in civil, even tender, relationships with their exspouses. Movies of the 1980s and 1990s show divorced couples who are funny, angry, sensitive, and even realistic.

The raging, vengeful duels between Michael Douglas and Kathleen Turner in *War of the Roses* permit the divorced and nondivorced to laugh together at how ridiculous, humorless, and hateful we can be when we try to "get" another person. *Hannah and Her Sisters* shows Woody Allen's character marrying his exsister-in-law, still keeping a close relationship with Mia Farrow's character—the exwife and mother of his children.

In *Second Time Around,* the middle-aged Gene Hackman character falls in love with a younger character, played by Ann-Margret, and leaves his "displaced homemaker" wife, Ellen Burstyn. Devastated at first, the exwife character gradually gains independence, and by the last scene, she's able to speak with her ex. This interaction is a clear sign that she's made a new life.

In *Mrs. Doubtfire,* Robin Williams portrays a noncustodial father. Through an absurd, though humorous, disguise as a housekeeper, he gains daily access to his children. The importance of this film for families of divorce, though, is in its conclusion. Sally Field, as the angry but caring exwife, realizes how important Williams is as a father to his three children, and they work out an unusual but mutually satisfying parenting plan. From Angry Associates we see them move to being Cooperative Colleagues. Williams tells the children (and the audience) that even though they're not all living together under one roof, they are indeed still a family.

We also have nonfictional Cooperative Colleagues. Many of today's public figures are divorced; some of them have good divorces. When we have Princess Diana, stating for the newspapers that she "will spend only enough time with Prince Charles, heir to the throne, to give her two sons 'as normal an upbringing as possible,' " we can confidently state that divorce has come of age. When Sarah Ferguson tells Diane Sawyer in a December 1992 interview, "Andrew and I are best friends. Given the kids, it's the best way to do it. We have a straightforward family life. They love their papa. He's a lovely man and he deserves that," we've begun to institutionalize and accept Cooperative Colleagues.

We have writer Kati Marton and ABC News anchor Peter Jennings, who give us an example of a tasteful way to announce a divorce. "After fifteen years of marriage and two children, writer Kati Marton and ABC News anchor Peter Jennings have separated. This action was taken 'with great sadness on both parts.' Marton and Jennings have asked us to stress that there is no third party involved on either side."

We have columnists such as Dr. Joyce Brothers advising splitting couples to try joint custody of mutual friends. "Those who have been good friends to both of you in a less intimate way can be shared if they're willing. It might sound odd, but you and your husband might pave the way by sending out a simple printed announcement."

We have the role models of Audrey Hepburn's exhusbands and her entire extended family gathering in a spirit of generous mutual acceptance at her funeral. Her companion of twelve years, Robert Wolders, her second exhusband, Andrea Dotti, her sons Sean Ferrer and Luca Dotti, and her first exhusband, Mel Ferrer, all attended and none of the 120 guests batted an eye. "Mother believed in one thing above all," said Sean Ferrer: "She believed in love." This graciousness has come to the good divorce.

We have James Farentino saying of Michele Lee, his exwife, "There is a closeness that we never lost." An article publicizing their 1992 TV movie *When No One Would Listen* stated: "Michele Lee and James Farentino had a stormy fifteen-year marriage. Their divorce, however, has been a rousing success."

Joyce Maynard, editor and publisher of *Domestic Affairs Newsletter,* sums it up beautifully in a "My Turn" column in *Newsweek:* "If there's one thing I feel sure of, it's that I'm doing a good job as a mother, and that our children are happy and well in the home we've made here. (That they love and need their father too was never a question in my mind.) . . . I'll always regret that my children's father and I failed to provide them with the model of two parents raising them together and loving each other as well as them. I take comfort, though, in the knowledge that we did not do what my own parents did: stay in an unhealthy situation, tacitly conveying the message that pain is a fact of life and change impossible."

Yes, it is possible today to find role models, fictional and nonfictional, for almost every facet of the good divorce, from healthy parting to mutually raising the children to participating in the entire extended family. Besides finding role models, we can find comfort in the fact that we are not alone.

Roles

There are two distinct stages of role-changing after divorce: coping with role losses, and establishing new roles.

Each of us implicitly and explicitly accepts numerous roles at any given time in our life. Some roles—parent, child—are biological. Others—boss, employee—are professional. Still others—friend, spouse—reflect personal choices we've made. Each of these roles gives meaning to our life, adds richness and challenge as we try to fill the new expectations. When our roles conflict, and they often do, we experience the stress associated with what sociologists call *role overload.*

To shift a role, to lose a role, brings stress in and of itself—and that's before we add the demands of any new role. Just as when we retire, we lose our worker's role and we feel that loss keenly; just as when a parent dies we may be surprised to find we miss being someone's child (a role we have long thought we resented), now when the nuclear family splits into two nuclei we mourn the loss of role of spouse, no matter how unworkable our marriage may have been.

Difficult as role losses may be, when they come at the usual developmental times, we can prepare for them. The painful loss of a parent due to old age can be anticipated and even grieved in advance; we can plan for retirement. It is the role losses we don't anticipate, and the ones that occur prematurely, that are the most difficult to integrate. And what if the spouse role has been central to our life?

For women in particular, the two roles of wife and mother traditionally provide a central core of identity. Often the two roles have become enmeshed. As a therapist and researcher, I have often heard exwives say, "He left us." It's not surprising that some women find it difficult to disentangle themselves and separate motherliness from wifeliness, even in the face of divorce, even in the throes of creating a whole new family structure.

Charles and Maureen, a couple I interviewed for this book, separated right after their thirty-second anniversary; they had four children, ranging in age from twenty-two to thirty-one. Theirs was the typical midlife divorce. When the children left home, the already failing marriage collapsed, and Charles set out to begin a new life. Maureen was devastated—not the least by the ensuing disorganization. "When Charles moved out," she says, "I was furious. Everyone told me he was just having a midlife crisis, and I should just wait it out, but I knew there must be somebody else, someone younger, prettier, better educated. I immediately changed the house, got myself a perm, enrolled in a class, and tried to be nice. When Charles would come over, I'd ask him to lunch, even to dinner. But it all fell apart the day he wanted to move ahead with the divorce. I flew into a rage, threw a book at him, and told him never to set foot in my house again. That was it. From that day on, we have never had a conversation."

Maureen forbade "her children" to mention their father's name. Overwhelmed with hurt, panic, and loss of identity, her loss was so great that she was not able to accept her exhusband's role as the father if he was no longer her spouse.

When a husband leaves, the wife may feel she's lost her identity, especially when she has had no separate sense of self. Such was the case with Brenda, a fifty-six-year-old client, who became severely depressed after the breakup of her three-decade marriage.

Brenda's husband Fred was a star surgeon, and Brenda had spent most of her married life living in his shadow. Her social life revolved around being Mrs. Doctor. Though Fred and Brenda's marriage had deteriorated into a hollow shell of convenience for at least a dozen years, Brenda's role and status had remained stable. She volunteered four days a week in the hospital where Fred worked, chaired the local association for doctors' wives, put on benefits, worked in the hospital gift shop, and entertained Fred's colleagues lavishly. Fred was rarely home; he even slept at the office several nights a week. But when he asked for a divorce, Brenda was devastated—not because she loved Fred so much, but because she felt her identity slipping away. Ashamed at work, she quit volunteering, quit going to the hospital, or going out at all: she stayed in her bedroom for almost a month.

"I feel like I don't exist," Brenda told me. "I don't have a place in the community anymore. Everything I looked forward to is gone. Even my family. I so looked forward to being a grandmother." Brenda had three adult children, two of whom had recently married, so clearly, in all likelihood, she was still going to be a grandmother some day. But this fact seemed to elude her. Finally she murmured, "I can't see being a grandmother without Fred as the grandfather. I can't be a grand-mother alone!" Though Brenda's premises were fallacious, that didn't make her sense of loss any less strong.

Men's role loss after divorce may be less pronounced than women's. Although gender roles are shifting, men are still more likely than are women to define themselves by work, and to more narrowly define their role as spouse. Think of how many of us define the role of husband as "provider" and, perhaps, "handyman." The role of wife usually encompasses much more territory—"homemaker," "social planner," "nurturer," "caretaker"—and its borders are not as sharply distinct from the woman's other roles.

If a man's major role has been that of breadwinner or provider, his role stays intact postdivorce. The more demanding and compelling is his work, the more he can throw himself into it to fill up his time and thoughts, anesthetizing the pain of separation. If his fathering role has been limited to his children's bedtimes and weekends, that role may also not change drastically after divorce; these days, though, it's likely he's been more involved and feels the loss of his fathering role quite sharply. Studies show that men suffer at least as much as women do in the first year following divorce. Even if a man finds most of his rewards in work, even if he initiated the divorce, he may be surprised to find how ill prepared he may have been, and how devastated he feels.

Married to Rebecca for twelve years, Jack, an engineer and a study participant, became acutely depressed when he and Rebecca separated. "I never really knew how important coming home was to me. Rebecca always complained that I was never there, that I didn't enjoy it when I was. We argued all the time about how much I should do around the house, and she'd stick me with chores. I'm a doer. What I wanted was to take the kids to games, or play hockey. Anyway, when we split, I moved into this furnished apartment and felt lonelier than I ever have in my life." Jack was experiencing the loss of his spousal role. "The hours between six and eight were especially bad." For most married people, that's the time when work is done for the day, and the family sits down to dinner, and later, puts the kids to bed. Said Jack— as do many newly separated adults—"I'd do anything to avoid going back to that apartment. I'd go to happy hours, to malls, to every one of our friends' houses for dinner, to every movie in town."

To insulate ourselves from the pain of role loss, many of us rush right into another relationship. It's not unusual to see women and men frantically dating in the first year after their separation, trying to fill the void with an intense new love or even with just another warm body. Although many profess not to be looking for a new mate, becoming single again is profoundly difficult. Over 50 percent of men and 33 percent of women remarry within a year after the legal divorce; 75 percent of women and 83 percent of men within three years. Add to this the number of people who find serious relationships or cohabit, and the figure will be closer to 90 percent. But assuaging the pain of role loss is not a good criterion for choosing a new mate. One of my favorite cartoons shows a beaming bride in a flowing white gown, at the altar. Her groom, clad in a fancy tuxedo and beaming just as broadly, is the *devil*.

Exiting any role requires a struggle to incorporate past identities into present conceptions of self. Often there's a "hangover identity," a residual feeling of still being a vanished self such as wife or husband. The process will be easier if one has the cooperation of significant others—family members, co-workers, friends—and if a new role can be visualized.

It is often difficult for the long married to visualize themselves as single. Singleness feels so odd. As I said in Chapter 1, *exwife* and *exhusband* are negative words with no specific, clear, or positive social function. There's not much incentive to label oneself an "ex"!

According to sociologist Helen Fuchs Epstein Ebaugh, in *Becoming an Ex: The Process of Role Exit,* the change in roles will be made harder or easier by where the person falls along a spectrum of certain factors. How voluntary is your role change? What degree of choice and control do you have about the role exit? How central is the role to your perception of self? How long have you fit the role? How socially desirable is it? How institutionalized is the old role? The new? For some role exits society has evolved names: widow, alumnus. In other cases, the person is simply known as an "ex." If there weren't any other reasons for creating new language about divorce, this would certainly be sufficient.

As time passes, you'll adopt new roles—hopefully appropriate and enviable ones—and the anxieties of spousal role loss will lessen. Separating your role as spouse from your other roles also helps greatly. Some roles are defined flexibly and many of the functions filled by the spouse can temporarily be occupied, if not comfortably filled, by another. People need time to redefine themselves. They need the willingness to pattern new habits, and to decide which roles they now wish to accept.

Rules

In order to function, any system needs a set of rules. Complex systems need complex rules; some of the rules may be widely acknowledged, while others may be unspoken. Most families spell out who takes out the garbage or whether the family eats meals together. But the rules about who sits where at the dining room table, or what constitutes acceptable conversation, or whether the toilet seat goes up or down, are often known to all without anyone articulating them.

One major role in the good divorce is to reorganize each one-on-one relationship in the family system so that the new needs of individuals and of the now-changed family group are met. The main purpose as a binuclear family stays the same as what it was for the nuclear family: to provide security, nurturance, and value fulfillment for each family member. But individual needs may now overwhelm the group feeling as each person (spouses, children) goes through the necessary realignment involved in such a major transition.

Some degree of orderliness and predictability is required in all social groups. Some families need less; some need more. Most families fall somewhere between the loose organization formed by a planeload of passengers on a transcontinental flight and the tight order of the army. Whether your nuclear family was tightly or loosely organized, your family of divorce will now be different, and there will be a period of relative disorder while the new structure forms.

When one household becomes two, many of the rules built up in the marital system become instantly obsolete. You now need to consciously construct a whole new set of rules: rules that will define a new set of relationships. Will your exspouse be welcome in your household? Will you continue to celebrate holidays together? How much time will the children spend with each of you? Will you be flexible or rigid about the schedule? Many once-implicit, daily interactions will now need to be spelled out and may even need to be written down in a formal agreement, depending on your postdivorce relationship. Everything is now open to question: family values, time, money, friendships. As familiar rules fall by the wayside, your entire family is likely to feel anxious and in flux.

Depending on your couple style, you may choose more or less explicit negotiation. Fiery Foes may need a very clear set of rules, requiring as little negotiation as possible. Perfect Pals are able to negotiate efficiently at the time of the transaction. But whatever the style of interaction, a new set of rules must be formed. Even when divorce occurs after a long-term marriage, and the children are older, even when the parents believe new rules are not necessary (it's not unusual for them to say, "The children can decide for themselves!"), this is true. Even adult children will find a lack of family rules distressing when they try to play catch-up in the midst of an angry divorce. Charles and Maureen, the couple I spoke about previously, are a case in point. She'd immediately set her children the new impossible rule of never mentioning their father in her presence. And soon she set other rules, all reactions to her immense pain. No holidays would be spent together. There would be no contact whatsoever. Every negotiation would be handled by a lawyer.

And what about the children? They were caught in the middle. They loved both their parents and wanted to maintain relationships with both. Although Charles would ask the children how their mother was doing, they now began to feel disloyal to her if they told him. Maureen's mother and sister, although close with Charles in the past, never spoke with him again. Now the children felt they constantly had to choose, even though they no longer lived with their parents. If they chose Maureen's for Thanksgiving, Charles felt hurt. If they didn't, Maureen, who remained angry and depressed, would be devastated. When Stan, the youngest, got married, he bravely invited both parents to the wedding. They sat at opposite ends of the church and put a damper on the wedding; Charles left early because of the discomfort everyone felt.

Even a decade later, even after both Charles and Maureen remarried, the new system of rules held firm. Maureen still didn't want to be in Charles' presence, didn't consider Charles or his wife members of her family, and grudged the children any fleeting moment of contact with their father. The reasonably loving couple had become a Dissolved Duo.

For Ted and Martha, a midlife couple I interviewed recently, the rules were not all spelled out during the change—they felt able to carry on negotiations. Says Martha, "At first we seemed to go over and over the same things. He couldn't understand how I could decide it was over after all these years. He thought I wasn't playing fair. After a couple of months, though, he accepted that it was inevitable. Then we started to talk about *how* instead of *why*."

Cooperative Colleagues, Ted and Martha spelled out a short list of explicit rules. The children could talk freely about their parents; both parents were willing to mutually attend celebrations at each child's home. The business was settled with a brief financial agreement.

Five years later, Ted had remarried and Martha remained single, but both had resumed full and active lives. Each of their lives was extremely different from what it had been during their marriage, but both Ted and Martha were satisfied and neither was bitter. Where Charles and Maureen's rigid rules of separatism had left their children sad, upset, and trapped, Ted and Martha's flexible system had allowed their children to maintain unconflicted relationships with both parents. No one was left out of the family, and no significant emotional cutoffs occurred. Of course, there were times in Ted and Martha's binuclear family when people argued and felt left out at holidays, or when Ted griped about having too little time with a child, but everyone was able to talk about these feelings. The resolution didn't always please everyone, but everyone was satisfied that it was fair: they'd all agreed on the rules.

Ted and Martha's redefinition of their family through a flexible system of rules led to far fewer personal losses than did Charles and Maureen's. The difference was that Maureen allowed her spousal anger and hurt to dictate rules in another area entirely—parenting—and Charles (perhaps taking what he thought was an easier way out) allowed this. Ted and Martha allowed their parental generosity to dictate the overall system of rules. As they had each realized early that they were no longer spouses, they dealt with their hurt themselves.

Rituals

Rituals mark important transitions and events. They solidify, solemnize, and publicize our values. They also quell our anxiety by showing us how to behave in the face of the unknown. At weddings, for example, rituals help the bride and groom through their nervousness. The rabbi or minister tells them how the processional should go, when to exchange rings, even when to kiss. And what about funerals? The ritual of accepting condolences in a private room, the ritual of going out of the ceremonial service first and privately—all these help the newly bereaved. Not only do rituals make occasions more comfortable for a family, they help the community around them as well.

Although plenty of rituals exist that help people enter a marriage, welcome a newborn, start a new job, or retire from one, there are no socially accepted rituals to mark the end of a marriage, the announcement of a divorce, the construction of a binuclear family, or the acceptance of new and sometimes instant members into a family of remarriage. No rites of passage exist to help mourn the losses, to help healing, to help solidify newly acquired roles. Entire sections of greeting card stores are given over to reminding couples and those around them that it is time to celebrate another year of togetherness, but only a few stores offer cards designed to cheer up those who have parted ways.

Generally, any news of divorce is greeted with discomfort. Even the simplest ritual opening to an exchange—"How are you?"—becomes fraught with awkward emotions when the answer, instead of "Fine," is "I just got divorced." What do you say? "I'm sorry" or "Congratulations"? There's no *easy* way to know what the divorce means to the people involved, so there's no easy ritual answer. One wouldn't have the same problem in speaking to a friend whose mother had just died, who'd just lost a job, or who'd just had a new child. Unlike other important transitions, divorce lies in a zone of ritual ambiguity.

Many members of our society feel the gap in rituals acutely, and some new public rituals are springing up. These help the celebrants to define the change in family and social roles. If they were to gain more visibility and credibility, these rituals could become socially important to the healing process. The most popular of these rituals is a reversal of the marriage ritual. Vows to release and forgive one another replace the traditional wedding vows to honor and cherish. As an ending to the ceremony, the couple then gives back their wedding rings, placing them in their exspouse's right hand.

Another wedding ring ritual was developed by an artist in Albuquerque, New Mexico. Lynn Peters, founder of Freedom Rings: Jewelry for the Divorced, totes a sledgehammer to carefully set up parties at which the newly separated may bash the most symbolic memento of their marriage. Ms. Peters performs a ceremony aimed at the participants' celebrating their new life. "When they hit the jewelry with the sledgehammer, there's a release. They say, 'I feel so much better.'" Later Peters crafts a new piece of jewelry from the ruined metal. One of her clients noted: "It was great—it was very symbolic. I wanted to make something beautiful out of something tragic, and she did it." Quite a few rituals now occur; in time we shall see which ones are incorporated into public usage.

I'd like to see us get to a time when a parting ritual for divorce is part of our culture. Couples would have a brief, quiet gathering involving the children. They could speak about the good things the marriage brought them, and the necessity for parting now. Each person could say what they wanted from their new situation, if this were possible to do without too much bitterness, and pledge that they will try not to bad-mouth one another. The children could be told this was not their fault. Most importantly, these parents would say to themselves, their children, their friends, and extended families, as well as to the community around them, that they are committed to continuing to raise their children in a healthy family, albeit one in which they each live in a different household.

While leaving its participants in a void with respect to public rituals, divorce also impacts the *private* rituals so central to family life. Daily rituals such as opening the mail together over coffee, or walking together to get the newspaper, are seamlessly woven into the texture of group and individual life; the more elaborate rituals that many families construct around birthdays and holidays will also disappear or change, leaving gaping wounds. These private rituals help define our lives, make sense of our history, partially determine our future, and help us to connect with one another. When we dismantle our nuclear family in the wake of divorce, we also dismantle what we may have thought was a permanent point of view on this portion of our past, present, and future. For a divorce to be a good divorce, family rituals around birthdays, holidays, dinnertimes, and vacations need to be redesigned to accommodate the new binuclear family; and the loss of this portion of our lives must be balanced by its satisfactory reconstruction.

Study participants Joseph and Marilyn, for example, had always celebrated birthdays with lots of fanfare. The birthday person chose the dinner menu and the entire family got dressed up for a special dinner. A few months after her parents' separation, daughter Amy turned ten. "Amy said she wanted a family party as usual," Marilyn told me. "I couldn't pretend we were one big happy family and cook dinner as usual. It just felt too difficult, the thought of sitting around that table together again. Joe felt the same way, but we agreed we could take the whole family to Amy's favorite restaurant."

By the following year the divorce had been finalized. Marilyn and Joe were both in less pain and feeling more amicable. Marilyn decided to have Amy's eleventh birthday dinner party at home. She invited Joe, and they and their children celebrated in the grand old style. "We were uncomfortable at first, a little more formal than in old times. The kids seemed a little scared. Our six-year-old, Jason, kept trying to get Joe and me together, by insisting on holding both our hands. But within an hour, we were all laughing. I even felt a little nostalgic, but then Joe's selfish habits of making long-winded speeches—always needing to be center stage—reminded me why we got divorced. The nostalgia passed. By the end of dinner, I was glad not to be living with him anymore, but I was still able to kid him about next year being his turn."

Joe and Marilyn were able to maintain one of their most important family rituals by being flexible enough to change it during a period when the old way felt uncomfortable—and then they were also flexible enough, once their relationship improved again, to bring back the original ritual, which had worked so well for their family. By the time Joe remarried, two years later, Marilyn felt sufficiently comfortable to include his new wife.

Continuing the old rituals will not work for every family of divorce. Some couples, especially Angry Associates and Fiery Foes, need to develop new rituals to reflect new realities. They may opt to divide up holidays, perhaps allocating Christmas Eve to Dad and Christmas Day to Mom. Or they may opt, especially when they live far apart from one another, to alternate holidays.

Holidays—especially the first ones after the separation—are painful times when the losses are felt most acutely. The old rituals no longer work and new ones have not yet been developed. They can be especially problematic when exspouses differ fundamentally in values or religion. Exspouses, even if they're angry, must not force the children into choosing one ritual or religion or value structure over the other. Setting up such guilt-provoking loyalty conflicts does nothing to promote the joyousness of anyone in a family, nuclear or binuclear, and it's worse in a season that was once celebrated in mutual joy.

When I interviewed Josie and Bennett, they were getting ready to spend their first Christmas apart, after fifteen years of spending the holidays together. They had decided to split the day. Josie would take the children until midafternoon, when Bennett would pick them up and bring them to his mother's for dinner.

Josie wanted to make this Christmas feel different so that they all wouldn't feel quite so sad. But she also wanted to make it feel like Christmas, and that meant including some of the old rituals—hanging up the stockings on Christmas Eve, opening presents on Christmas morning, having home-baked honey buns—which they'd all enjoyed as a nuclear family. She suggested to her children that instead of having the usual big brunch, why not all go down to the local mission and bring food to the homeless? They did. Instead of becoming a lesser replay of the past, they'd established a new Christmas ritual at Mom's house.

What roles, rules, and rituals each family chooses to establish will vary depending on individual preferences, sometimes on ethnic background, and certainly on the particular life stage of the family. They need to be flexible enough to change over time, according to the needs of the children and the adults. The Three R's are dynamic processes, rather than static, one-time decisions.

The Individual, Family, and Social Vision of Divorce

Thus we see that a good divorce is good on many levels. Individually, we accept role changes and set up new rules and satisfying rituals. If you are a dissolved or fighting couple, you may be able to restructure your binuclear family into at least an angry-but-speaking or even an amicable-and-cooperative form. We've seen that a family of divorce is not static in society, and that society is in the process of changing its views on these families. We've begun to establish a new vision of a good divorce.

In the next chapters, we'll explore specifically how to set up a road map for a good divorce, and how to effect the necessary changes.

Development and Change

A working binuclear family is dynamic. The family, and each of its members, must adapt to one of the most grueling demands that any person or group can encounter: the loss of an environment once felt to be permanent. The stresses of losing roles, rules, and rituals in one fell swoop; the ambiguity that is perpetuated by the lack of adequate role models; the physical and financial stresses; the nonrecognition by society—all these make constructing a binuclear family an enormous, frequently overwhelming, but sometimes exhilarating, challenge.

Accepting the binuclear family means accepting divorce at any developmental stage in life, within every ethnicity or religious context in which it is possible, and making provisions for it. Issues associated with constructing a binuclear family cut across every age group, every economic class, every ethnicity. Although family customs may be different within a matriarchal family or a patriarchal one, within a Christian family or a Jewish one, within a politically liberal family or a conservative one, although the society as a whole may treat each of these families differently, in each of these families divorce is a very real possibility. In the process of setting up a binuclear family there are many more similarities, cross-culturally, than there are differences. The inexact language, misunderstandings, and losses affect every family of divorce. Each family goes through a partially uncontrollable period of dissolution, followed by a partially controllable period of reconstruction.

Most couples go through long periods of trial and error in reconstructing their family postdivorce. Understanding the process of uncoupling—emotionally and legally—is critical to being able to cope with the transitions as effectively as possible. To know that there are universal predictable stresses—to be able to anticipate the rough times—increases the likelihood of managing them better. And when they are managed better, when the potential for debilitating crisis is lessened, couples have the opportunity to make decisions that will serve the family's best interests.

4

The Emotional Process of Divorce
LETTING GO WHILE HOLDING ON

No MATTER HOW you cut it, divorce is painful. Whether you're old or young, woman or man, rich or poor, the one who leaves or the one who's been left, uncoupling is disorganizing, unsettling, and extremely stressful.

Major decisions involve ambiguity. Changing jobs, moving to a new city, or ending a relationship requires us to abandon the known. We cling to the comforts of the old while we agonize over the new and unknown. How can I tell if I'm doing the right thing? Will I regret this later? How can I hang on to my security in case this doesn't work?

For most people, ending a marriage is the most traumatic decision of their life. The usual ways of coping aren't likely to work. People act in ways that no one around them can make sense of—not you, nor they, and certainly not their spouses. As Abigail Trafford says in her book *Crazy Times,* "Divorce puts you on the edge of sanity."

Transitions: Creating Order from Chaos

Transitions are turning points. They're uncomfortable periods that mark the beginning of something new while signifying the ending of something familiar. Although we may anticipate changes with puzzlement and foreboding, we may also approach them with exhilaration. Transitions are times when we're more personally vulnerable, and paradoxically they're also the times when we're most likely to personally grow.

Usually when we think of transitions we think in terms of the bio-logical-developmental clock: adolescence, midlife, or aging. All of these developmental transitions are stressful not only for us but also for others involved in our life. We know, for example, that the transition to adolescence is characterized by unpredictable behavior; teens can swing from childlike moods one day to mature behavior the next. We also know, as Gail Sheehy has shown us in her book *Passages,* that the seemingly irrational behaviors of some people in their forties and fifties are common and normal ways of coping with that difficult transition. The aging transition, defined until now by mainly negative stereotypes, is being transformed by new research indicating that learning continues as we age. In *The Fountain of Age,* Betty Friedan challenges and discards old stereotypes by providing new role models of active, engaged, and wise people who are eighty years old and even ninety.

In defining biological-developmental transitions, in outlining typical themes, common feelings, and experiences, we normalize situations that otherwise would feel, and appear to be, abnormal. Knowing what to expect doesn't take away all the pain or upheaval, but it does help us cope better with our own transitions. There's great relief in being able to place oneself within a natural progression that has a beginning and an end. We feel less crazy when we know we're not alone, when we have a common language, when we can identify with others who have similar experiences.

Defining the Transitions of Divorce

Unlike these other transitions that occur, more or less, on pre-dictable chronological timetables, divorce is an unscheduled transition that can occur anytime during the adult life cycle. Even though not everyone experiences divorce, it's similar in many ways to the biologi-cal-chronological life transitions. For many of those who do experi-ence it, divorce *is* a developmental transition. It marks the end of one distinct stage in one's personal life and the beginning of another.

A number of years ago, based on my research, I identified five dif-ferent component processes that together form this giant transition we call divorce. By breaking down the process into common developmen-tal steps, I could then explore the ways we choose to adapt at each of these distinct stages. I realized that as with the biological life transi-tions, knowing where they fit along the spectrum of normal divorce would make my clients more comfortable. Their path from one stage, marriage, to the next, divorce, could be made more orderly and less debilitating. Although—as was the case with the exspouse typologies—these transitional processes were originally named with social scientific names, I have replaced those terms here with simpler, more straightforward, language.

The first three transitions—the *decision,* the *announcement,* and the *separation* (originally termed individual cognition, family metacognition, and systemic separation)—are the subject of this chapter and the next. The latter two transitions—the *formal divorce* and the *aftermath* (systemic reorganization and family redefinition)—are material for the chapters that follow.

The most grueling disruptions occur during the first three transitions. Deciding to divorce, telling your spouse and your family, and leaving your mate form the core of the emotional divorce. These three transitions are characterized by ambivalence, ambiguity, power struggles, soul searching, and stress. Even childless partners feel out of control and crazy during these initial transitions. For couples with children, they're even more complex and difficult.

The fourth transition—the formal divorce—can be every bit as emotional as the decision, the announcement, and the separation, but it doesn't need to be. If the early emotional tasks of uncoupling have been settled, the divorce transition can be contained within its proper limits: terminating the marriage contract legally in a fair and equitable manner. I will discuss these issues separately in Chapter 6.

The last transition—the aftermath—infuses life for many years. Well after the legal divorce is completed, you'll still be building your postdivorce binuclear family. Just as issues emanating from our family of origin become woven into our personality and lifestyles, so do the issues and relationships that were created in our former marriages. Chapter 7 will show how remarriage and divorce are intertwined.

In divorce, as in any human relationship that involves a large personal transition, there are changing currents of parting and rejoining, misunderstanding and understanding. At each transition there are also changes of social role, relationship rules and rituals, and appropriate coping behavior.

Although I discuss the five transitions sequentially, in developmental order, they usually chronologically overlap. Divorce is a very complex and individual experience. There is no neat rule for when a particular transition will occur in a particular individual or couple, or for how long that transition will last. What we do know, from studies in the United States and the findings of our cross-national study, is that regardless of cultural or national differences, it takes most people between one and a half and two years to stabilize their feelings after the initial separation.

Along the way, important marker events occur. These marker events spark common, predictable feelings in the participants. You can identify where you are, either from stepping back from your feelings for a second, or by moving the marker point. For example, if you're furious enough to leave, you might be approaching physical separation; if you know you're about to separate, you might expect to feel fury, confusion, loss. I call all these transitions *crisis points* because at any one of these markers the situation has the potential to become volcanic; a full-blown, debilitating crisis may erupt. But if the process is understood, couples can be shielded with knowledge, options, and some good models. They will then stand a very good chance of surviving the ravages and of growing stronger. They will also begin to evolve the vision we spoke about in Chapter 3—to see the forms their family might take at later stages. Recognizing the normal feelings, identifying the marker events, it's more likely that you can set up a clearly designated path to a good divorce. As impossible as this might sound, it means having to look to the future at a time when the present is overwhelming.

Each time we face change, we tend to clutch more tightly to what we know. In the case of divorce, each transition is heralded by increased stress. At the end of each transition, the stress tends to plateau or to decrease.

Even through the pain of the earliest transitions, couples can set the groundwork for a good divorce. They can begin to identify where to let go, and they can begin to see which part of holding on is due to insecurity and the desire not to face change.

Stress, Crisis, and Adaptation

Stress, crisis, and adaptation are three concepts often used in understanding how people cope with a myriad of bad things, such as chronic illness, death of a loved one, and unemployment, in addition to the breakup of a marriage. Stress occurs when there is an imbalance (perceived or actual) between what is actually happening—the *stressors*—and what a person feels capable of managing. Crisis occurs when the stress exceeds the ability to effectively handle the stressors.

We all have different levels of tolerance—*breaking points*—beyond which we are no longer able to cope with the situation. When too many things hit us all at once, when stressors pile up, *system overload* sets in. When your father is ill, you've lost your job, and your husband says he wants a divorce, that's system overload and it's likely to plummet you into a crisis. When your reservoir of coping behaviors become depleted or outmoded and you don't know what to do to pull yourself out, or what new behavior to invent, you're in a crisis.

In my study, Alice and Chuck, Cooperative Colleagues, said they were "good friends" at the initial interview, as they had been in marriage. Just before their second interview, their five-year-old daughter broke her leg. That same weekend Chuck announced he was remarrying. Alice, who was studying for her final exams in law school, reached her breaking point. She wanted Chuck to take over care for their daughter; he had just moved in with his fiancée and her kids and wasn't able to do so. Unable to complete her exams, Alice felt abandoned and betrayed by Chuck. By the second interview, she and Chuck—now Angry Associates—were barely speaking.

The way out of system overload is *adaptation*. Adaptation requires change—restructuring or reinventing some portion of life, changing the way stressors are perceived or managed, learning new skills, and finding new resources.

By their next interview two years later, Alice and Chuck were again Cooperative Colleagues. Alice realized that, although Chuck was generally quite supportive, she needed to expand her personal support system and be less dependent on Chuck. When she did that, she became more realistic about her expectations of him. Her anger at him also decreased and she now had several other people she could request help from when she needed it.

Divorce is ranked at the top of the list of stressful life events. Many stressors overlap in the divorce transitions. Said Joanne at her second interview, "It was all too much coming at me at once. I was in a panic about how I was going to survive financially, I had to decide on where to live, what—and when—to tell the kids, when to tell my boss, which lawyer to go to. All this in the midst of not knowing what I even felt anymore about Jim and at the same time feeling insanely jealous of him. All I could think about was finding a way to escape. I started reaching for the wine the minute I walked in the door. It was the only way I could make it through getting dinner, helping the kids with their homework, getting them ready for bed, throwing in a wash.

If my sister hadn't arrived when she did, I don't know what I would have done."

Joanne's feeling of being overwhelmed, her system overload in the early transitions, is common to most of the mothers I interviewed.

One mother said, "It's like being shot out of a cannon. All of a sudden you're on a new planet. You have no idea what's happening or how you'll make it through to the next day." All of our normal coping abilities are taxed by all the rapid personal changes and are further shaken by the general social misunderstanding of our predicament. When we add the lack of good role models, no clear-cut rules or rituals for managing this new and unfamiliar stage of life, and the lack of external resources, such as community support and positive social sanctions, crisis is certainly one predictable outcome.

How can you avoid a full-blown, debilitating crisis? Understanding the process, knowing that your feelings are normal and that the chaos is only temporary, helps to at least reduce the intensity and duration of the crisis. It's amazing how naming something we feel and identifying its causes immediately helps us to cope. You know it's temporary and it's not all in your head. You can plan when to rest and when to go on. With knowledge of what to expect, which decisions need to be made immediately (and which can be put off for a while), and what kind of new rules need to be established, we will feel more in control of our emotions because we can plan—even if only for the next day. At times of system overload, finding good role models will dissolve some of the ambiguity, a big contributor to the stress.

Turning to some social support—perhaps a family member, a close friend, a support group—also helps. You may feel like a pressure cooker, so you'll need to let off some of the steam at different points, thereby preventing the pressure from building up and causing you to explode. When my friend Barry was having trouble with his boss at work, was exhausted after a bad case of flu, and was the primary support for his seriously ill father, he knew he couldn't also deal with requests and complaints from his exwife. "If she calls and starts in on me for something or another, I know I'm going to blow it and start screaming at her." He decided that he couldn't tolerate any additional stress and decided not to answer his phone for the next few days. His answering machine picked up all his incoming calls and he could then choose how and when to respond. He then spent an evening playing bridge with friends; the next night he crawled into bed right after dinner. Just by reducing the amount of input, by getting additional rest, and by diverting his attention and absorbing himself in a card game, he began to feel more in control. Sometimes even small changes like this are positive adaptations to stress.

Acrimony Takes Its Toll

There is no way to talk about divorce without talking about anger. It's a universal reaction and it's inevitable. But that doesn't mean you should feel free to express your anger without restraint. Anger takes a terrible toll. If you throw more fuel on the inner fires, they'll flare higher and higher and you'll be stuck with the damage. When we focus on our rage, we stifle our ability to get on with life.

In the Binuclear Family Study it was clear that those who stayed angry—Angry Associates and Fiery Foes—stayed mired in the past instead of moving on to the present. As we saw in Chapter 3, some continued to do so even five years later, with no indication that they ever wanted to change. In a real sense, they were actually more attached to their exspouses than were Cooperative Colleagues. Their ex became the target of any situation that created anger. Every time they felt hurt, they blamed it on their ex. "If it weren't for the divorce, I wouldn't have to date, or work, or take care of myself." Bad day? It's was their exspouse's fault. Messy apartment? Burned dinner? Broken zipper? Child failing school? The holder of injustices—or the hostility junkie—needs to place blame on something tangible. The ex is an easy target, a habitual target, even a socially sanctioned target.

Continued, unrelenting hostility and anger are a clear indication that the losses that are an inevitable part of any divorce haven't been mourned. Rage wards off not only the fears of facing sadness but ultimately the sadness itself. What almost always lies beneath rage is grief. If the loss of one's dreams was allowed to surface, was felt and accepted, the rage would dissipate and life would go on. For many people, maintaining the continuing anger acts as a defensive shield.

Unfortunately, anger all too often leads to system overload. The anger itself becomes a stressor, either turning inward (the angry person can get ill) or outward (the angry person can hurt someone). At the breaking point, spousal violence is not an uncommon occurrence. In fact, 62 percent of the participants in the Binuclear Family Study said there had been at least one violent episode at one time or another in their relationship. Half of these participants noted that the violence had occurred in the last six months of the marriage. A quarter of this group also said the violence continued even after they were separated. One year after the divorce, almost all of these couples were Angry Associates or Fiery Foes.

I am not suggesting that we should all repress or deny anger. But neither do I suggest that we should freely vent anger whenever—and on whomever—we wish. In general, the research on expressing anger indicates that it is healthiest when we can identify our anger and acknowledge it. Then we can manage the situation rather than being controlled by the anger.

Learning how to manage anger is a major key to having a good divorce. One striking finding was that Cooperative Colleagues and Angry Associates both had about the same levels of anger. What differentiated the two groups was that the more cooperative group *managed* their anger better. They accepted it and diverted it, and it diminished over time. One man spoke for a lot of others in this group when he summarized his reactions several years postdivorce: "There were times I was so enraged at her I wouldn't even trust myself to see her. I didn't always handle it well. I drank too much. I took it out on the kids. I finally got some help from a support group. And when I could let myself cry, I felt less angry. Even now, she says things which infuriate me, but I hold my tongue, knowing . . . this too shall pass."

Most of the Cooperative Colleagues successfully managed their anger when they interacted by avoiding highly controversial subjects like money, by monitoring their responses when they felt they wanted to make an angry retort, by setting up a special time in a public place—like a coffee shop—to discuss specific things, or by writing letters to one another when they had to make decisions that usually provoked arguments.

The couples who stayed Angry Associates five years after the divorce, however, couldn't—or wouldn't—let their anger go. They held on to it like a child holds on to a beloved blanket or teddy bear, stroking and nourishing it, finding protective comfort in it, until it became the structure for their life. Joanne, five years after the divorce, was still stuck in her anger. "I can't stop thinking about how he got all our good stuff. He lives in this nice house, has this young wife and her two kids. It just makes me fume. I can't stand it. So whenever I know he wants something real bad, I don't give it to him. He really wanted to take the kids to his new in-laws over Christmas. I made sure they had other plans. It's the only way I can get back at him."

Sometimes anger is appropriately related to the specific act at hand. Often, though, an incident touches off unresolved anger from previous transitions, causing even more rage than the situation actually justifies. Commonly—not just in divorce—our intimates bear the brunt of unresolved angers either from our family of choice or our family of origin.

Divorcing spouses are often nasty and hateful to one another. They may each do things that seem unforgivable at the time. When the participants in my study told us about the few months prior to their separation, many of their stories were full of times where they screamed angry insults, called vile names, told hurtful lies. There's so much pain, so much grief, so much loss, that all we want to do is lash out.

Understanding that the lightning bolts hurled at each other during the divorce storm were situation-specific—not a longstanding characteristic of either the mate or the marriage—opens the door for forgiveness. As time passes, exspouses can heal some of the past wounds by forgiving the other as well as themselves. Notes social worker Beverly Flanagan in her important book, *Forgiving the Unforgivable*, "To forgive, one must remember the past, put it into perspective, and move beyond it. . . . It is too difficult to go through life feeling 'not right' about enemies, let alone someone you have borne, married, raised, or held in your arms and cried with."

The Goal: A Harmonious Relationship

Clearly I'm not suggesting that harmony is always possible—or even appropriate—at all the transitions of divorce. But I do feel that you should choose your battles. And, at some point, to lay down the swords and make a peace agreement will benefit you greatly. In addition to helping your children, cordiality will heal you. Over time, being able to integrate our past history into our present life provides a wonderful sense of wholeness. Those who adapt well to the stresses of divorce, and develop amicable relationships with their exspouses, are better able to appreciate their own history and to understand how it has prepared them for the present.

Some couples are able to maintain that basic link throughout most of the divorce process. Others need time and distance—need to pass through several of the transitions—before they can reach out to make the final adaptation.

A friend of mine, Sylvia, who has been divorced for over twenty years, recently celebrated the baptism of her first grandchild. Her ex came from across the country to join in the celebration. The next day, at Sylvia's suggestion, she and her ex took a long hike alone together. As they walked, they discussed their eighteen-year marriage, what had gone wrong, what their current lives were like, and how proud and pleased they were to have raised their four children. Sylvia called me the next day: "It was so good to talk about our history, to apologize for the awful stuff we'd done during the divorce, and to compliment ourselves. After all, our marriage couldn't have been all bad if we raised such kids—four of them, and each so wonderful! We also talked about aging, and about the many other occasions—both happy and sad—we plan to share. When Don left I felt like we were old friends. We may not speak often, but I know if the need arises we'll be there for each other." I remembered Sylvia and Don's divorce, and how angry they had been with one another for many years. It was wonderful to hear that at this time of their life they were able to heal old wounds and reclaim their kinship.

Connection with one's ex—at whatever transition it happens—provides a sense of continuity. Even a relationship that starts poorly can change enough over the years to become supportive at critical times. Recently, the fifteen-year-old son of a client developed a terminal illness. My client and her exhusband had been distant for a few years, but the moment she was told the diagnosis, she called him. After the shock of hearing each other's voices—they'd had a bitter divorce and separation—they cried. Then they spoke together to the doctors, planned finances and personal care during their son's long hospital stays, and comforted each other as they watched their son's condition worsen. The one person who had shared this child from birth was the only one with whom my client could totally mourn this tragic loss.

Many study participants told stories of making peace at different transitions. One woman told us how in the midst of an angry custody battle, the sudden death of her mother-in-law made her and her ex realize how important family was. They then were able to compromise for the sake of maintaining their family relationships. Another participant told us how, several months after their separation, he and his ex were escalating their battle over who gets the house when she was diagnosed with breast cancer. They stopped the negotiations withdrew their divorce petition. They remained separated but without legally divorcing. That permitted her to remain on his insurance policy while she was undergoing treatment. Three years later, they resumed the divorce; by then, the property settlement was easily resolved.

Many exspouses want to stay connected. I asked couples in my study—all parents—if they didn't have children, would they still want to relate to their ex? One year after the divorce, 40 percent said yes. Two years and four years later, almost 33 percent still wanted some kinship. "I can't just forget fourteen years of intimacy," one woman said. Another expressed it this way: "I know why I married him. I know why I divorced him. And I know why I'm still fond of him. He is very much part of my family."

Perfect Distance, Perfect Closeness

All relationships, no matter how deep and enduring, have limitations. Some friends have annoying habits and others we see infrequently but that doesn't prevent us from being friends. For exspouses, the link may be of the same magnitude as that with distant cousins, with siblings, or with college roommates twenty years later. Even when there's infrequent contact, the sense of a shared history can remain current.

But how about those cases in which friendship is impossible? When there has been no friendship in the marriage, there is no basis for it afterward. If there's a long history of betrayals, lack of trust, or abuse, the potential for further harm overrides the need for interconnection. When there are no children, that relationship can be neatly severed. But, when there are children, you must negotiate a divorce that permits parenting to continue with as little contact as possible between the exspouses.

Being peaceful, even friendly and comfortable, with one's exspouse is more possible than most people think. Some exspouses feel defensive about having a good relationship. Friends and family tell them they're not letting go. But, in fact, forthright coordination is what's healthy. Once again, it deserves repeating that one of our best hopes for increasing the proportion of good divorces to violent ones is to replace the old negative images of warring exspouses with new ones that normalize and support basic interconnection. When people change their expectations, their behavior usually follows.

It's a Dynamic, Circular Process

Thus, letting go while holding on is a dynamic, circular process. How stressful the separation is—and whether or not the stress blows up into crisis—depends in large part on how angry and vengeful the exspouses feel. In turn, the way exspouses cope with the transitions changes the nature of the relationship. A couple may start out as Cooperative Colleagues, and under the stress of the legal divorce become Fiery Foes. Fiery Foes can duke it out for years, and then at some crisis point pull together and become Cooperative Colleagues.

That relationships change over time is not exclusive to divorce. Parent-child relationships, sibling relationships, friendships, and marital relationships all change character throughout their chronological-developmental transitions. Perhaps in childhood you were archrivals with a sibling. Some incident caused a disagreement that blew up into a crisis. You hated your sibling, only to be reunited again a few years later, perhaps when you both lost a parent or celebrated some family milestone. Your currents of interconnection with an exspouse, the partings and rejoinings, may have roots in your other intimate relationships.

Wherever you are in the divorce process, you can identify your own system overload and avert or shorten your own crises. More importantly, you can find and take all possible opportunities to heal past wounds. Without giving up any of your hard-won individual gains and without denying any of the pain or work you've been through, you can aim at developing a mutual understanding that meets the needs of your own binuclear family. This is true at each of the five transitions. Because divorce forever remains a part of your life, it's never too late for exspouses to search for a new, more productive level of communication.

The Decision

The decision to end a marriage is usually far more difficult than the decision to marry. The dread of negative repercussions, of an uncertain future, of painful losses, all combine to make the first transition a wrenching and internally violent one. Very few people make the decision lightly. If you obsess about your marriage, vacillate, anguish, get depressed, see a therapist, or have had an affair, you may be entering the stage of decision.

The first step toward divorce is rarely mutual. It begins within one person, often starting as a small amorphous nagging feeling of dissatisfaction. The feeling grows in spurts, sometimes gaining strength, sometimes retreating, flaring up, and again moving forward. For some, this private simmering of unhappiness goes on for years. For others, a few months of depression may be more than they can bear.

The Erosion of Love

When one begins to question, *really* question, one's feelings for his or her mate, a passage of emotional leave-taking begins. This erosion of love starts slowly. It may be barely noticeable at first. Behaviors that were acceptable for years now become annoying. Habits that were tolerated become intolerable. Gradually, the partner who wants out collects more and more evidence that the other partner is too rigid and tiresome, too despotic and swaggering, too defective and ruinous and spoiled. In this manner the leaver builds a case to justify the decision to leave.

Such rationalizations are rarely clear-cut. One day it's all over; the next, an anniversary celebration is being planned. Ambivalence—wavering between the pain of leaving and the pain of staying—is disquieting, but very normal.

In her first interview for the Binuclear Family Study, Susan, a thirty-eight-year-old mother of two, married for ten years, was typical of many in the throes of the decision. A sales manager in a computer firm, Susan privately questioned her marriage to Brian as early as two years into the marriage. She repressed these feelings. "It was so scary to think that maybe I didn't love Brian. I couldn't possibly have made such a big mistake! He's Mr. Strong-and-Silent, and I'm Ms. Social. Of course, even then I recognized how different we were. I could see that even on our first date, a Sierra Club hike, when he wanted to go slowly and I wanted to forge ahead. But I was twenty-eight, tired of the singles scene and dying to get married, and here was this nice, sweet, appropriate, and very handsome man—and he was ready and willing."

As Susan recounted her first two years with Brian, she slumped, fidgeted, and used such words as *bored, depressed,* and *lonely.* "I really didn't look forward to coming home to him each night, but told myself, 'That's marriage!' I told myself I was being childish, expecting some romantic fairytale. And then I would initiate lovemaking to reassure myself that I was still deeply in love."

Joseph was born during the fourth year of their marriage. Susan hoped that the baby would bring her closer to Brian. For the next year, sinking under the triple load of Brian, Joseph, and her job, she tried not to obsess about her pent-up, accumulating wretchedness. "I remember so many times sitting in my rocking chair, feeding Joseph, and weeping. I thought it must be postpartum blues. Brian was really a nice guy, a good father. Then why were we growing further apart? Was this the way life had to be? Was I going to spend the next fifty years empty, irritated, and dissatisfied? I must be spoiled and unappreciative. What was wrong with me?"

When Joseph was two, a second son, Andy, was born. Susan hated her relationship with Brian, but she still thought she should settle and make peace with it. But she found herself exploding. "Brian wouldn't fight. He wouldn't even argue! When we first met I thought his calmness was wonderful—my parents used to fight like cats and dogs. But now I would test him, saying things just to get a rise out of him. When he didn't respond, I would seethe inside. Before long, everything he did drove me insane. He liked sitcoms. He saved his napkin after a meal. And his 'yups' and 'nopes'! I tried to tell myself, 'Accept who he is! It's better than Mom and Dad.' And then the fantasies started. About another kind of life—a life without Brian. I felt scared. How could I manage alone? What would my parents say? Would my unwillingness to settle totally devastate Brian, and Joseph and Andy too?" Susan had reached her breaking point, and these fantasies were a way to rehearse possibilities for future adaptations.

Although the particulars of each person's story are different, most leavers experience a long first transition. Terrified and guilty, they identify their feelings, then quickly deny them, not wanting to face the possibility of divorce. Some describe this time as being on a roller coaster. Others describe unbelievable despair, a time when your whole foundation feels like it's crumbling.

The most commonly stated reason for divorce is incompatibility, both in my study as well as most other studies. To most of us, though, incompatibility seems like a flimsy excuse to end a marriage, especially when we have children. We then succumb to the temptation to look for so-called better reasons. It's easier to divorce an ogre than a decent human being. Even though the legal reforms of the past decade, such as no-fault divorce, have removed the necessity for finding "just cause," psychologically we still feel obligated to search for real evidence to rationalize what we fear is an irrational decision.

Again, our language has misled us. "Incompatibility" is a small label for what may be a very large and complex set of feelings and responses. As I said in Chapter 2, our reasons for marriage today are much more developmentally oriented than they used to be. Today we tend to choose a partner with whom we think we can develop in a certain way over a lifetime. When we say we are incompatible, we may mean that our development is now blocked by constraints that we feel we've irrevocably outgrown—constraints we permanently built into our marriage. If we let those old and now empty constraints rule us, we will stress ourselves, our mate, and our children. Divorce is one escape valve for such incipient system overload.

The "Leaver" and the "Left"

Although a divorce often ends up being a mutual decision, at the early stages there is one person who harbors the secret desire to leave and one person who is initially unaware of that desire. Both partners may have had similar fantasies, but one person usually takes the first step and begins the process.

At the outset, the leavers and those who are left can expect to have quite different feelings. The leaver has had the advantage early on of wrestling with his or her emotions, has already started grieving, and has already detached to some degree. The person being left is the victim. Immediate reactions range from disbelief and shock to outrage and despair. The partners have unequal power at this point. The person being left is more vulnerable. Having had no time to prepare—to adapt to the overwhelming threat—the one being left is more likely to experience crisis at this point. He or she demands justifiable reasons. Meanwhile, the leaver has been rehearsing reasons for some time, trying to find the most palatable way to tell the person being left that he or she isn't loved anymore.

Over time, many leavers and lefts switch roles. My research shows that (at the five-year interviews) many of the couples who originally clearly identified one or the other as leaver and left changed their account to say that the decision was mutual. One man, after a bitter divorce, reflected on his decision this way: "In the beginning I was furious. Morally outraged. How could she break our commitment? I also remember having been miserable for years, constantly fantasizing about not being married. Yet, when she said she wanted a separation, I flew into a rage. I know now that it was as much my decision as hers. She just got it started." Another participant (not his wife) corroborates: "It seems so strange now that I didn't realize back then that it was my decision as much as his. For a couple of years I had withdrawn. I wanted out. I even had a brief affair. But I was too scared to say I wanted to leave. Yet when he did, it still took me by surprise. I think I didn't want to be responsible, so I got into blaming him instead."

How can those who leave avert crisis at this marker point? Many leavers keep their decision-making process a secret until they are ready to split. They are often perceived by their partners to be leaving without any warning at all, although the leaver often reports that he or she has been sending clear messages of dissatisfaction. When leavers share their doubts with their partners, in the months or years prior to making the decision, it is more likely that the decision will eventually become more mutual.

Leavers and lefts both have bruised egos that they need to protect. They both defend themselves against the outer world. No one likes being the bad guy. Some leavers are so uncomfortable that they subtly try to get their partner to assume the role of leaver. They may stop the little rituals that characterized the marriage: the goodnight kiss, the daily check-in phone call, holding hands. They may subtly change the rules of marriage without warning. Others are more bold. They stop making love; they blatantly take on a separate life. The spouse usually notices changes in rules, roles, and rituals but avoids a confrontation by pretending to be oblivious. The marriage is teetering, but on the surface all is as usual. This use of denial as a coping mechanism allows the spouse to minimize the problems and his or her own fears.

Many leavers in the study shared an early hope that they would make their spouse miserable enough to do the leaving, so they wouldn't feel as guilty. It is very common to have elaborate fantasies of how your spouse will die; widowing is a far more socially acceptable way out of marriage than is divorce.

Leavers do pay a stern price: the disapproval of society. Friends and family demand to know why they're leaving, especially when the marital distress has been kept secret. Children want reasons. The spouse wants reasons. The community wants reasons. Everyone looks for tangible evidence. The leaver, who more often than not is still lost in a morass of feelings, begins to develop an account of the deterioration of the relationship. It's not enough to say, "We grew apart," or "We're not compatible." To most outsiders these motives seem vague, shadowy, weak, and insufficient. So leavers have to find personally justifiable and socially substantial grounds for divorce that vindicate their own uneasy sense of wrongdoing.

What about the one who's been left? Rejection can put some on what they feel to be a moral high ground. "She's the one with the problems," sniffed one Angry Associate husband at his first interview. "Why she chose to dump us I simply do not know." By his second interview, this man's position had hardened further. "She hurt me and damaged the kids," he said, his eyes filling. "She's going to have to pay for this—but good." He had changed his role over time from being pure victim to being the righteous martyr. Thus she could become the villain and he could become the committed one, the responsible one, the representative of society. And all the while, he'd denied the one glaring fact that he'd been just as miserable in the marriage as had been his wife.

For some, the victim role is comfortable and it gives them power, both in the financial negotiations as well as in the continuing personal argument with the leaver. Most often, though, being left ravages one's self-esteem. In order to protect their public image, as well as to get over the very personal, intense blow to their ego, the ones who've been left often develop their own self-exculpatory account. Over time, they make the leaver into a despicable character. However, they do not feel better. When spouses assassinate the character of the leaver, paradoxically, they are also maligning their own character as well. If the leaver is so awful, why did you ever marry the person in the first place? And if you made the mistake of getting married, why did you ever stay in the marriage this long?

Developing an account of the breakup is important to both the leaver and the left. That the accounts rarely agree, however, is a fact of life that everyone should acknowledge. The leaver's account, as we have previously seen, is equally exaggerated. Especially in Angry Associates and Fiery Foe couples, the stories can develop over time into destructive myths that take on a poisonous life of their own. Sociologist Jessie Bernard noted the importance of recognizing that "his" marriage and "her" marriage are often quite different; the same holds true for divorce.

The degree to which the accounts of the spouses differ is often a good indicator of what type of relationship they will have as exspouses. The fewer discrepancies, the higher the likelihood of a cooperative relationship. Cooperative Colleagues have fewer extreme differences in perceptions. Though they maintain a healthy difference, they often check their stories against their exspouse's reality.

Though much of the process of developing an account occurs after the second transition—the announcement—the future story has its roots right here in the decision transition. Whether you're the one who leaves or the one who's been left, you may well be able to avert more than one painful future crisis by seeing your ex's account in a more forgiving light. Doing this right at the beginning will undermine your pure villainhood to the other party.

It's a fact that both stories are part of an important healing and reindividuation process. They are one form of response to the continuing shock of parting. Both stories—if they can be grounded in reality—will probably alleviate more suffering than they will cause. Both stories—if you and your ex can root them in a common vision of a binuclear family—have the potential to heal, instead of to hurt, yourselves and your children. As they develop over time, both stories become part of a larger whole—your binuclear family's account of its formation.

Gender Differences

In my Binuclear Family Study—as in most research studies in the United States and Europe—the issue of who takes the role of leaver, and who takes the role of being left, is often related to gender. The findings are that between two-thirds and three-quarters of all divorces are initiated by the wife.

The numbers are inexact because, in most studies, the question—"When and how did your marriage end, and who ended it?"—was often posed differently and thus answered differently. Was the moment of decision measured as the day someone moved out? Was it measured by the first suggestion of separation, by the first time a partner saw a lawyer, by the date of the earliest legal papers in the divorce file? Or was it measured by who first betrayed the trust of the other, perhaps by having an affair?

As it turns out, regardless of the question used as the standard, women initiate divorce more often than men. This was not always so. Researchers agree that a larger percentage of women are leaving unhappy marriages today than in the past.

One of the biggest factors leading to this statistic is the increase in women's economic independence. It's not that women used to be happier in marriage than they are today, but often they felt they wouldn't survive outside of marriage without their husband's money. Even today, the lowest divorce rate occurs in traditional marriages with breadwinner husbands and full-time homemaker wives.

Not only have women's economic opportunities expanded, so have their social opportunities. They have cars, support groups, job networks, personals ads, and the gym. They can travel comfortably alone and eat dinner at a fine restaurant without a male escort. Even though we are still a very coupled society, it is much easier today than it was in my mother's time (or even in the mid-1960s when I first divorced) to live a full life as a single woman. All this has made getting out of a bad marriage a better possibility for more women.

Even so, many women still say that they left because they had no choice. Stories of years of abuse, betrayal, or absenteeism by their exhusband are rife. Many women say they just put in time, waiting until they could make it on their own.

Women's assumption of power in choosing the role of leaver seriously affects their husbands. Not only do the men who are left suffer a devastating blow to their self-esteem caused by the rejection, but they also tend to feel completely powerless. This sense of powerlessness gathers throughout the time the women are deciding to leave. It may surface during the decision, or at the time of the announcement, but recognizing the gender differences at this marker point may avert many a future crisis.

The way gender differences are handled during the decision transition may affect a father's future involvement with his children. Many of the noncustodial fathers in my study talked about how used they felt; the wife's leaving had heralded their own breaking point. David, a Fiery Foe, spoke eloquently in his first interview about the bitterness he felt. "Not only did I lose my wife, but also my kids, my house, and a big chunk of my money. She took matters into her own hands for once, and the first thing she did was cut me off at the knees. Then she wants me, get this, to go back and talk to her about it. What was I going to do, go back and beg for the goddess to hand me whatever scraps she had left over?"

Underlying many women's decisions to leave their marriage is their frustration with their men's communication style. That women in general want to talk with their men more, to share more of their feelings, while men hear women's words as complaints requiring immediate solutions rather than as avenues toward intimacy, is an all-too-familiar pattern. When recounting their breakup, women often insist that for years they tried to get their husbands to talk. Their husbands withdrew, didn't take them seriously, or told them to quit complaining. Commonly when the women ultimately left, the men were totally surprised, shocked, and indignant. The women often responded: "I've been telling you for years. You just didn't listen."

Coping During the Decision Phase: Some Examples

Denial ("Nothing's wrong!"), projection ("It's his or her fault!"), and avoidance ("They have the problem—not us!") are common ways of coping with crisis. These patterns of coping were similar for many of the leavers in the study. Many leavers first tried to confront their spouse with small complaints. Their attitude was that a few improvements would repair their marriage. But, the petty complaints generally escalated into a blowup, or else the spouse withdrew from the onslaught and turned off. In reaction, these leavers often tried to accept their state by looking elsewhere to fill their needs.

Other leavers tried to alleviate the discomfort of ambivalence by projecting blame directly onto the spouse. From them I heard a chorus of: "He's changed!" or "She *hasn't* changed."

Still other leavers blamed the economy, or avoided the problem. They blamed anything except the marriage for their unhappiness. They bought summer homes, took trips, had babies, or switched jobs. But their marriages did not magically improve. Their problem couldn't be avoided. The first transition was occurring already. Bits and pieces of new evidence came in daily. The leaver was beginning to find reasons why the marriage was no longer viable. Uncoupling began.

A couple I recently interviewed had a very typical pattern of decision. Maria, a teacher married for fifteen years with three young children, left her husband after nine years of painful soul-searching. Maria had developed extraordinarily since she married Manuel. She'd attended night school for eight years, gotten a college degree, found new friends and new interests. It is a common situation: one spouse blossoming, the other remaining static. "I just didn't love Manuel anymore. That was so hard to face. We'd known each other all our lives, since our families were neighbors in Mexico City. I felt so awful, knowing that it was me who'd changed, me who kept nagging him, picking on him. After a while, no matter what he did, I was thinking, 'He's coarse, he's rude.' He was so small town. Things I used to like now annoyed me. He's a cuddly guy who uses baby talk. I used to like it; now I kept telling him to grow up, be a real man. And he'd hit the roof."

Maria struggled for years with her ambivalence and guilt. Although at one level she knew Manuel wasn't at fault, she still found herself blaming him for being who he was. Their Hispanic culture puts family before everything; their devout religious practice made it excruciating for her to justify (to herself and their families) wanting to end the marriage. She tried for many years to deny that love was important; she spent more and more time with her friends from work. Finally, she fell in love with a fellow teacher. This new mate's support helped her to see divorce as an option.

In my Binuclear Family Study, the participants were asked what and who was most helpful to them during the decision transition. Where did they find support? They mentioned lawyers, family, friends, books, counseling, and new partners. Although many said their friends were most important, most cited the new partners. As in Maria's case, a new love gives the leaver the support and courage necessary to make the final decision.

Ending any marriage, even an abusive or violent one, is very difficult. We so fear the unknown that we will tolerate even the most destructive situation, if it's familiar, in preference to facing this anxiety.

Sometimes, when the system overload has been severe, the decision will bring less stress, not more. Marsha, a lawyer in my study, spent seven years being beaten by her husband, David, before she found the courage to leave. "After he punched me out, he'd feel so bad. He would abase himself, apologize, bring me gifts, seem to change. He'd be so sweet for several days. It wouldn't happen again, he'd promise. I kept hoping that was true. But then he'd hit me again. And I'd cry. He refused to go for help, saying it wouldn't happen again. For several years, my whole family begged me to leave him, but I kept defending him, saying he really didn't mean it. Then my sister dragged me to her therapist. It took two years of individual therapy for me to come to know I could make it on my own."

When denial, projection, or avoidance fail, the leaver often sets up a crisis, a situation that will decisively shatter the marriage. The leaver may fall in love, allow an affair to become known in a particularly humiliating way, or create sufficient anger to erupt into violence. Sometimes the leaver hesitates until some other life transition, perhaps a biological one, sparks the departure. The loss of a job, a geographical move, a serious illness, the death of a parent or a child, a momentous birthday—all can catalyze the decision to move on.

One such catalyst is facing one's mortality. In our first interview, Paul, a chemist, was fifty-one. When he spoke of leaving Julie, his wife of twenty-six years, it was clear that he'd long been ambivalent. "Turning fifty was hard. My older brother died suddenly. And my father had died at age sixty-one. Suddenly I realized how depressed I'd felt for years. I got jolted out of my complacency. Was I going to have only eleven more years? How was I going to spend them? With Julie? Forget it! I'd always told myself I couldn't leave till the kids were grown. But now my kids were grown. And Julie got this great job. I told myself that now it was okay for me to have my time. And I started not feeling guilty about the thought! I even started to feel entitled."

Unlike Paul, some people never find the courage. They just can't cope with the unknown, possibly negative, consequences. Months become years, and lifeless relationships continue because ironically it is easier that way.

Among the wealthy, or those who hold public office, these loveless marriages survive because partners can lead separate lives while the marriage remains intact. In some cases, people formally separate, without going through a legal divorce. Think of Prince Charles and Princess Diana, whose highly publicized separation was preceded by years of news reports portraying their devitalized relationship. Early intimate snapshots of the pair were replaced with pictures showing them side by side, looking increasingly more uncomfortable, until one day they looked disdainful.

Among the rest of us, the most frequent excuse used by couples for staying together in a loveless arrangement is the children. Lawyers and judges tell a story about a couple in their nineties who filed for divorce. The judge, shocked by the decision, asked them: "Why now, after seventy years of marriage?" The couple replied: "We waited until the children were dead."

Approaching the Announcement: Making the Decision Known

After months or years of building stress, it suddenly becomes clear to the leaver that hints, nagging, withdrawing, or fantasizing are not going to work. The revelation bursts into consciousness that the partner is truly not going to be the one to make the decision. The system overload of this marriage has escalated to the breaking point, and what has been a private struggle within the leaver, and an even more subconscious struggle in the one who will be left, is not going to come out into the open. How this is handled will affect the rest of the divorce process.

At her first interview for my study, Jennifer, married for four years, could not accept responsibility for her choice to leave. Nor could she be honest with her ex about things she needed to communicate. "I couldn't tell him how I really felt, or what I'd done—go off and be with another man. I knew he was going to blame me for wrecking the marriage. He was the reason I was leaving—there was no way I was going to tell him all my secrets." By the time of her second interview, Jennifer and her ex were Fiery Foes, engaged in an all-out custody battle. He'd found out about her affair from a friend, and had unilaterally decided she was an unfit mother.

Accepting responsibility for one's decision does not mean that the leaver accepts having broken up the marriage. Both partners were responsible for that. It means that after painfully wrestling with the pros and cons, the leaver has decided to do something different. Most likely the feelings are not all resolved; most likely the decision to divorce is not yet firm. No matter how protracted the decision transition has been, the leaver at this stage commonly believes that he or she wants only a trial separation.

When feelings during the decision transition are shared, instead of being withheld as secrets, each partner gives the other one some time and opportunity to come to terms. This greatly lessens the likelihood of a crisis at the end of the decision transition.

The Announcement

"I just couldn't say it," says Joanna, a mother of three in my study. "'Honey, I've decided we need to live apart.' I knew he'd be shocked. Furious. Devastated. I kept saying it to myself again and again, trying to figure out some way to break the news. Finally I called him at work and told him over the phone."

Proclaiming one's desire to separate from one's partner is no easy task. But for some couples, the announcement is as far as their divorce will go. Sometimes the moment of confrontation creates an opportunity to actually improve a marriage. The announcement can be a call for help, a plea for attention. It may be the moment the husband does listen to his wife's complaints and needs, or the moment the wife perceives her husband's vulnerability for the first time in years.

For other couples, the announcement is the first step in a tangled or escalating series of confrontations and reconciliations. For still others, one day they're married and the next day they're not: the announcement can also be a clear, direct, and sometimes almost instant path to separation and divorce.

Before the announcement, days, months, even years, can be spent rehearsing the words and the scene. Though most of us hope that the decision to end the marriage can be a rational, mutual one, we realize that more often than not, at the beginning rationality and mutuality may not be possible.

"When Bill told me that we had to sit down and talk, that we both knew our marriage wasn't working and he felt he had to do something about it, it was a shock," said Elizabeth, a forty-year-old housewife and mother of two in my study. Elizabeth and her ex started as Cooperative Colleagues and have remained that way. "I knew for years our marriage wasn't perfect, but I thought his problems with me were a little silly. Okay, so I don't enjoy sports, so I wasn't going to be a good tennis partner in his retirement years—so what? I called him all sorts of names and went out and got drunk. Then I took some tennis lessons, which I hated. But over the next few months I realized his objections weren't as stupid as they seemed."

One common reaction to an announcement, even to one in which the decision to divorce has been building for years, is to call the partner's reasons frivolous. Denial may follow any big shock. It's not uncommon, in the early phase right after the announcement, to think that a few minor changes—becoming more attentive, or more attractive—will help what seems to be an anomalous outburst to blow over. And sometimes a new wardrobe, flowers, extra telephone calls, and so forth, do help—especially when the potential leaver is still very ambivalent, or is merely serving notice or issuing a threat.

But the example of Bill and Elizabeth is far more common. "I'd spent months figuring out how to tell Liz," said Bill, forty-five, in his first interview. "It wasn't just the tennis—it was the whole issue of retirement. I knew living with her full-time would be boring. She's so involved with her church activities, and her gardening, and the kids. I had to figure out what would keep up my energy for living, and it just wasn't her." Because Elizabeth, like most people being left, was unaware of Bill's months of soul-searching, she felt his announcement was a cruel, unprovoked blow that he'd inflicted for trivial reasons.

The accounts of those in my study who were left reflect shock, hurt, and outrage. However, the leaver's account almost always portrays a long, painful process of leave-taking. The other person is coping not only with rejection but with having to develop an account after the fact. In these first two phases of the process the leaver commonly feels guilty; the left feels angry. Rarely is the process symmetrical, let alone rational or mutual.

So what's the key to defusing crisis at the time of the announcement? For the leaver, it's accepting responsibility for the decision. Bill came close to this when he said he felt he had to do something about the bad marriage. For the one who's being left, it's the quality of his or her coping skills. Elizabeth demonstrated an imaginative variety when she tried surface solutions first, and then searched deeper. The degree of rejection also matters far more to the one who's being left than to the leaver. After a bit of hesitation, Bill made it clear that he didn't think Elizabeth was awful—merely wrong for him at this stage of his life.

Affairs: Creating a Crisis

In many cases, the announcement seems spontaneous, as much of a dreadful surprise to the leaver as to the left. In these cases, often the discomfort is so severe that the leaver (either consciously or unconsciously) resorts to setting up a situation that will bring the issue into the open without anyone having to accept responsibility. The disowning of responsibility sets up trouble. The leaver may get forgetful and leave a lover's letter on the dresser, or stay out all night, or arrive home with the proverbial lipstick on the collar. Once discovered, the objects or events provoke a crisis momentum, and it's over. The couple can then fight about whatever issue got raised in the crisis, rather than dealing with the long-term issues of their distressing marital relationship.

Two years after his divorce from Susan (the computer programmer with two children whom we met earlier as she wrestled with her decision), Brian still remembers every detail of the one horrible night he says ended it all. "Susan was out shopping and I'd just put Andy to bed. I was looking for a letter I'd received a week before and started to rummage through a pile of mail on Susan's desk. I came across the phone bill, which she usually takes care of. Man, it was huge! So I scanned it. There were fifteen night calls to Chicago, all to the same number, and we didn't know anyone in Chicago. I called the number and got some guy's machine. I don't know quite why. There was something about his voice. Suddenly I found myself frantically searching Susan's drawers. There it was, under her sweaters, a box full of letters . . . and pictures. That's when Susan walked in. She started yelling at me for invading her privacy. What a bitch! I still can't believe it—*her* being angry with *me*? We fought until 4 A.M. Finally, she yelled out how they'd met for the first time two years ago at a conference. And every two months, since then, on her business trips to one city or another . . . I remember thinking, was that about the time that she stopped wanting to have sex with me as often, was it when I thought she was caught in a snowstorm, was it when she suggested I go on a skiing trip with my brother Jeff?"

Susan and Brian stayed together for three months after that, but all they did was fight over her affair. He wanted to know every detail. "I couldn't trust anything she said. I started to feel crazy. I would go from rage to tears, calling her names, then feeling ashamed." It was Susan who finally walked out, saying she couldn't take the fighting.

Creating a crisis makes it possible to shift the blame. Affairs can be a big smoke screen. Susan had been miserable for years, wanting to leave and unable to muster the courage. The exposure of her affair created a crisis in which she could scream at Brian—and then run away.

The Cycle of Deceit

Betrayals rarely come in ones. And crises can become an addictive substitute for responsible adaptation.

It's a common misconception that when affairs are first disclosed, the betrayed kicks out the betrayer. More often, the betrayer walks away. "His recriminations! His pain! And those endless discussions!" sputtered Susan in her first interview. "He kept calling me names." System overload gives the betrayer plenty of surface reasons to escape—a poor substitute for accepting responsibility and making a positive adaptation.

Society contributes to worsening this particular type of betrayal. Extramarital affairs are far more common than we as a society have been willing to acknowledge. Current statistics suggest that well over half of those married have had at least one extramarital affair. Society denies this. Drumming into our ears the wish that marriage should be a monogamous and lifetime union does nothing to make this wish come true. Judging from the statistics, many couples must cope with the sudden disclosure of an affair. Because of their personal beliefs and because of society's belief in happily-ever-after, a sexual betrayal is the one symbolic act that these couples can't or won't tolerate in an intimate relationship. Trust once broken is difficult to regain.

What is worse than the affair itself, more difficult to cope with, is the protective web of lies. In both my research and in my clinical practice, I find that affairs themselves are not what creates the devastation. The lies are. As each lie gets uncovered, or explodes during a battle about the affair, the betrayed spouse begins to question the entire history of the relationship. The whole marriage and the role of each partner in it seem like lies. The betrayed questions the betrayer closely, sometimes obsessively, trying to separate truth from fiction. "When we made love last week, had you slept with her the night before?" "When you said you were in Denver, was he with you?" "When you said you loved me last week, how could you have meant it?" "Were there others?" "What does he look like?" "Is she a better lover than I am?" The questions are endless and the answers rarely satisfy, because it's the uncertainty that is the plague.

The seemingly endless recriminations that Susan complained of in Brian were quite normal. The betrayer and the betrayed rarely see eye-to-eye on how much talking-out is needed. For a myriad of reasons, it's difficult for the betrayer to be completely truthful. Perhaps he or she wants to hold on to both the lover and the spouse, or wants to protect against the possible legal ramifications, or doesn't want to inflict more pain. The betrayed senses that there's more and keeps pressing, trying to get to the bottom of things felt to be the betrayer's responsibility. The betrayer complies for a while, then usually grows impatient with the constant focus and repetition. The betrayer thinks the betrayed spouse is "carrying this too far." Blame shifts then to the betrayed spouse for not letting go.

There are many possible scenarios after the initial crisis. When the affair has been brief, or was a one-time occurrence, or the lies were minimal, the couple can often constructively resolve the crisis and end up with a better relationship than before. In other cases, nobody learns. The partners sweep the issues (and the affair) under the rug, sometimes for a few years, and try to return to the same old relationship. In these couples the power balance may shift a bit. The betrayed may gain control by having something on the betrayer. These marriages are often very stable, continuing for years with one person taking the role of saint and the other the role of sinner. Still other couples in the face of crisis silently compromise. If the marriage has sufficient rewards, occasional transgressions will now be tolerated, from one or both partners. In this case, affairs implicitly or explicitly become integrated into the marriage contract. Sometimes neither partner has any comment about this infidelity—until the next crisis.

Common Reactions of the One Who's Been Left

Leavers aren't the only ones who fool themselves during the initial transitions of divorce. The cycle of deceit has two participants; so does the cycle of escalating anger. That there are two sets of opportunities for managing a good divorce is a fact that is too often ignored in the storm of negative emotions that assail both partners, particularly the person who's left.

Rage, prejudicial myth-making, depression, and impulsive desires to retaliate are normal reactions if you're the one who's been left. To manage a good divorce when assailed by urges to sink into victimhood, or worse, to get revenge, is not easy.

Anger plays an important role when there's a bad blow to the ego. It temporarily shields the betrayed from facing devastating emotions: grief, rejection, even self-hatred. If over the course of the marriage mutual anger has been buried, at the announcement the anger can easily erupt. All the past injustices that went unconfronted are replayed. Both the earlier denial and the current anger help the one who's been left to cope with a life swinging out of control.

Julie, the exwife of Paul, fifty-one (the chemist we heard about earlier who in midlife dealt with issues of his mortality and decided to leave his wife), had never considered divorce. When faced with it at age forty-six, after twenty-six years of marriage, she blamed Paul for destroying her whole life. "Paul and I had gone up to the cottage for the weekend. We didn't vacation alone very often. Even on the drive I could tell something was wrong. Paul was so quiet. He'd been blue lately—because of work, he'd always said. As I unlocked the front door he said, sit down, he had something he wanted to discuss. Without anger—actually, without much of any kind of feeling—he said flatly, 'I want a divorce.' "

Julie remembers going numb. "I couldn't believe my ears. I didn't say much. But I stayed up all night in the living room, drinking sherry by the fireplace and going over everything in my mind. By 6 A.M. I couldn't stand it any longer. I went right into that bedroom and let him have it. How dare he? What was this idea—leaving now? It was idiotic. Here I'd spent decades building up his business, raising his kids. Now I wanted to reap the benefits. Instead, he was scaring me like this, making me feel so unloved and unwanted and old. I was forty-six and had been married since I was twenty. I had never lived alone. What right did he have to abandon me now?"

I yelled at him. "Here I've put up with you for twenty-six years! You think I've been happy? I've had to make my peace with it. Now you're having some stupid midlife crisis and I'm the one who has to suffer? It's selfish and unfair!"

Paul and Julie stayed together for two more months. They consulted a therapist they'd seen together when one of their children was having school problems. Over a series of ten sessions, Julie's long-term unexpressed anger at Paul's preoccupation and distance came out in a series of rageful attacks. Paul was then able to express his fury and disappointment at Julie's cold withdrawal. The brief therapy helped clarify that Paul had wanted to end the marriage for years but only now—their youngest son was about to graduate from high school—had the courage to do so.

After Anger May Come Depression

Now Julie had to deal with the loss of her marriage and her terror at finding herself alone. She got seriously depressed. "The next few months were hell. I didn't know what was happening to me. There was nothing I wanted to do. I lost any interest in how I looked and spent days just going from the bed to the couch and back, not even bothering to get dressed. I felt old, ugly, and utterly alone."

With the help of a therapist, Julie mourned not only her relationship with Paul, but also her many role losses. She grieved about ending her time as a wife and as part of a couple. Other role losses were more developmental. She mourned her youth, and her children leaving home. As she grieved she found new interests, new joys in life. Her depression resolved; she and Paul were then able to resume a cordial, sometimes friendly, relationship.

Julie had gone through two of the most common reactions to being left, and discovered that where anger is mobilizing, depression is paralyzing. Anger often masks depression, and when the angry feelings abate, the depression emerges. In fact, some Fiery Foe and Angry Associate couples stay furious as a way to maintain their energy over months or even years postdivorce.

For those who have a history of depressive moods, a spouse's decision to leave can set off a serious reaction requiring professional help. This reaction is by no means limited to the decision and announcement transitions. If this occurs, the partner who leaves the marriage may feel guilty enough to reconcile temporarily. Although this situation tends only to prolong the time until the day of reckoning, it does give even the one who's being left time to adjust to the decision and announcement.

The Urge to Retaliate

When faced with the anguish of rejection, it is normal to want to retaliate, to hurt the other as badly as he or she hurt you. Impulsive revenge, however, causes extreme damage to both partners. It is impossible to get even, and revenge by one partner can spark an escalating war that will damage not only the divorcing couple, but also their children. The newspapers are filled with stories of spouses in the midst of separation: kidnapping children, stalking their ex, or even attempting murder—sometimes successfully. Fortunately, though, most couples can defuse impulsive retaliation.

Manuel and Maria (the couple we met earlier in the chapter during the decision transition) are a case in point. Manuel remembers vividly the night Maria announced she wanted a divorce. "We were at my aunt's house eating dinner. She was quiet, like she's too good to talk to me since she became such a big shot. It came out of nowhere. Suddenly she starts to cry and says, it's not gonna work anymore, she has to leave me. She says she's wanted to leave for a long time but didn't want to hurt me. I ask, is there someone else? She says yes but he had nothing to do with this. She says it's not my fault. I got so mad I wanted to kill her! I called her a whore and kicked her out. Told her to get out of my family's house and to get out of our lives. No way, I said, was she going to take my kids and ever see them again."

Manuel's impulse to retaliate is typical. Her announcement badly hurt him. He'd already been feeling lessened by her going to college, and by her other personal gains. When Maria announced that she was leaving, Manuel internally replayed every occasion, public and private, in which he'd ever felt inadequate. To protect himself, he struck back quickly. In doing so he hurt himself as much as he hurt Maria. He placed himself in an extreme, indefensible position from which he could neither back away nor compromise without further damaging his pride.

How Gender Issues Affect the Announcement

One factor deeply involving Manuel and Maria's case was a double standard. They're Hispanic, but this double standard exists in many other cultural groups as well. Over the course of the marriage, Manuel had several affairs. He indignantly noted at our first interview that his affairs were only for sex and didn't hurt the marriage. Maria had taken the first opportunity to demand a divorce. Women in Manuel's community mustn't want or have extramarital affairs, whereas men can.

In mainstream middle-class white American society, the same double standard exists. In general, men treat their own affairs less seriously than they do women's. Many men describe falling into an affair because an opportunity presented itself, perhaps at a business conference or at the office; they describe falling out of the affair just as quickly. Women, however, are more likely to fall in love with their lovers. Because once involved they tend to want to stay, and because they treat the affair more seriously, it appears to cause worse damage when a wife commits the grievous act.

Add gender expectations to the common reactions of the person left—anger, depression, loss of self-esteem, grief, and impulse to retaliate—and it's obvious why the moment of announcement is so difficult, and different, for women and men. Each partner tends to judge the other by his or her own standards. Nothing could be less useful.

When they'd moved from Mexico to the United States, Manuel and Maria had not realized the profound cultural change they would face. Maria blamed Manuel for the culture clash they were both undergoing; Manuel had felt stressed as well but had chosen to bury his uneasiness. At his moment of impulsive retaliation the rage exploded. Fortunately Manuel quickly relented, and he and Maria worked things out to some degree.

During the month after Maria's announcement, Manuel, although enraged, realized that Maria was a good mother, that she spent much more time with the children than he did, and that her philosophy was viable for the children as well as herself. He temporarily moved into his sister's house; she was a major support for both partners during the crisis. A good friend to Maria, as well as a good sister to Manuel, Lupe helped mediate. While Manuel stayed with Lupe, Maria and he moved from being Fiery Foes to Angry Associates. Since they never did look at their gender issues together, they never did resolve the clash underlying their mutual anger.

Delaying the Inevitable: Postannouncement "Bliss"

Sometimes couples scurry to reconcile immediately after the announcement. The words "I'm leaving" can spark deep probing of the marital relationship, and when that occurs, an improved marriage may result. But more often, the reconciliation is a surface illusion, prompted by fear. The couples have not resolved any of the fundamental issues that divide them.

In my Binuclear Family Study, several couples reported a temporarily terrific sex life after the announcement. Others took a trip to Europe, bought a new house, and had a new baby. But the marriage did not permanently improve.

"When Martha said she was moving out, I told her—for the first time in years—how much she meant to me," said Gary, an engineer in his fifties, during his first interview. The couple had been married for twenty years and had two children: one in high school and one just starting college. "I begged her to stay. She said she'd try again, and she did. We went out on our boat for two weeks. I made a special effort to hold her and compliment her and things seemed to be fine. But when we got back, she said nothing had changed. Within six weeks, she was gone." This time, Gary continued, the announcement was accompanied by the feeling that nothing would ever work to better the situation.

Couples often seek professional help at this crisis point. It's a common scenario: one spouse pulling to make the marriage continue, and the other saying, either metaphorically or literally, "It's over."

The one who wants out may or may not be open about it. That spouse may cover up for a time, saying he or she sincerely wishes to mend the marriage, and how puzzled he or she is that nothing seems to succeed. But this subterfuge rarely works for long. Therapists are quick to pick up the cues that show one spouse's so-called trying is designed to fail. Canceling therapy appointments, insisting that the other spouse go for individual therapy, withholding information, continuing an affair, and resisting change all signal that one partner desires to dissolve, not improve, the marriage. A good therapist can help the couple to face their divergent goals, to halt the vicious cycle of deceit that plagues many relationships at this crisis point.

The surface reconciliation has in these situations masked the fact that husband and wife now have different, and often opposite, agendas. By helping to bring these deep wishes out into the open, the therapist can assist the couple in making strong decisions based on reality, rather than on superficial impulse. The couples in my Binuclear Family Study show that wishing the marriage was blissful unfortunately does not make it so.

After the announcement transition was over, Martha and Gary said they regretted having tried so long and so hard to keep their marriage together. "We threw away thousands of dollars," sighed Gary in his second interview. "We could have been getting on with our lives. Deep down, we always knew nothing was going to help. But each of us wanted to come off better than the other." Many couples feel this way in retrospect. In fact, the "try again" periods, even the false honeymoons, provide the time many couples need to prepare for the next transition—the physical separation.

The announcement indicates that all was not well; that deep problems—which must not be minimized—exist; and that communication, attention to facts, and deep reorganization must now occur. Superficial changes, no matter how spectacular, only delay the pain.

Slowing Down the Pace

As we have seen with Manuel and Maria, the most dangerous pitfall of the announcement is impulsive, out-of-control rage. Although the leaver may have wrestled privately with the decision for a long time, the way that decision is presented to the partner in the announcement sets the stage for the next transition—separation. Consulting a family therapist at this time can be useful. The announcement transition can be slowed down so that it can come in manageable chunks. Sometimes, even a few sessions can help clarify how to de-escalate the anger whenever it occurs during the divorce process.

Additional sessions can help both children and adults defuse their terror about the major changes that divorce brings; they can start to plan.

One key to a good divorce is becoming able to see how decisions made early in the process affect the emotional adjustment of the whole family. We have seen how the one who is left may become so angry that he or she begins to obsess about revenge: straight destruction of the spouse or creative, devious destruction. When the obsessing gets out of control, it's important to find ways to vent the anger—talking to friends, a therapist, or a support group—rather than to act rashly, which will only end up creating an even worse situation. Sympathetic friends and family members can point out consequences. They may even help the angry spouse to laugh. They can often tell if the rash act would be self-destructive. Most importantly, they can create that little extra bit of time and distance which may be all that's necessary for everyone to cool down.

To avert a serious crisis requires that both partners show considerable patience, maturity, and honesty. Leavers need to understand their partner's angry reaction and give him or her time to deal with it. Being able to talk about some of the changes that can be expected during the next transitions as the marriage is being dismantled is important, as difficult and frustrating as such talk may be. The more responsibly you can plan for a timely separation, the less likely it is to break down into debilitating crisis. Being rational when you're emotionally seething, though, is often humanly impossible without help.

It's very important in crisis not to act precipitously. Sometimes it's the leaver who feels he or she can't tolerate living together and just wants to separate as soon as possible. Sometimes, though, it's the person being left who is so filled with anger and pain that he or she wants the other spouse out of sight as soon as possible. At that moment, everything propels that partner toward a quick removal of the other, and to not move in that direction requires great restraint. To ease from the transition from announcement to separation, and to minimize the crises, requires time. Couples must process what's happening and plan for the physical separation. When, after the announcement, the rage is too murderous to allow discussion, it's wise to cool down—separately or with a mediator—before running off to a lawyer, calling the moving van to pick up all the furniture, or stalking out.

The Separation

Most people remember the day they separated—not the day their divorce was legally awarded—as the day their divorce began. Separation day is one of those marker events that divorced people never forget. For children, this is the first time they realize the enormity of what's going on, even though they may have suspected or feared the prospect for some time. Perhaps they've heard arguing, even witnessed some form of abuse, or felt subtle changes such as Mom or Dad being gone more, or the lack of laughter in the house. But rarely do they get told (until the parents are definite) that their parents are now going to separate.

What is separation? It means different things to different people and may even mean different things to each spouse. For some, separation means, "It's over." For others, separation means, "Let's temporarily cool off and then see how we feel." Some couples and children feel a sense of great relief at the separation transition, especially when the marriage has become highly stressful; others are overwhelmed with anxiety and fear. For still others, it's the worst crisis point of all. Everyone experiences this transition as a time of major disorganization, when the routines of daily life go up in smoke. It's a time of what sociologists call *anomie*—normlessness. Old roles disappear; new ones have yet to form. The future of the family is unknown.

There are no clear-cut rules for separating. Who moves out? How often should you continue to see each other? When (and what) should you tell family and friends? Who will attend the school conference next week? How about the wedding of a mutual friend next month? What will you do about your season tickets for the theater? These types of questions, seemingly trivial but deeply resonant, plague the newly separated.

Many people are surprised by how ambivalent they are at this time. Even leavers, who may finally have felt clarity about their decision, are taken aback when echoes of love and need bubble to the surface. They may feel lonelier than they anticipated, and miss their spouse, no matter how badly they used to argue. They may flash back to every good time they and their spouse ever had together.

Adding to the stress is the major fact that it's no longer possible to keep the marital problems under wraps. During the first two transitions, most couples have continued to enact the public rituals of their marriage. During the separation transition, these rituals cease. No longer is the couple able to project the image of happy conflict-free parents and partners. Now, with family, friends, and the larger community, the truth comes out, and the publicity hurts.

Disorderly and Orderly Separations

Separations fall on a continuum from the orderly to the disorderly, from the anticipated to the utterly shocking. Orderly separations are the least destructive. They are more likely to occur if there's been time for some preparation and planning before the actual physical separation. Disorderly separations usually occur when the earlier crisis points have not been worked through. If a couple separates without having at least some discussion of how they will go about it, this transition will likely be chaotic and destructive. Separation involves major life changes and it requires careful planning, especially when there are children. Children have the right to be told what's going to happen in their lives, and they need to have adequate time to process it with both parents.

When the separation occurs on the heels of the announcement, it sets the stage for severe crisis. Jennifer and Bruce, a midwestern couple we interviewed in the study, are a case in point. Married for eleven years with two young children, Bruce and Jennifer had a conflictual marriage, with divorce being threatened by one or the other after every big fight. But it wasn't until Bruce fell in love with Ginger, a woman he met at his son's soccer practice, that he decided to leave. He revealed the affair to Jennifer on a Thursday night. Very early Friday, he left.

"He didn't take much," Jennifer recalled. "Just a suitcase. He said he'd be back for his clothes the next day. I couldn't believe it. I told the kids he was away on a business trip. The next day, Saturday, he called and asked if I would take the kids to a movie so they wouldn't have to see him moving out. When the kids and I came back, his closet was empty. He didn't take anything else. Not a picture, a memento, anything. I couldn't believe that, worst of all."

Bruce left as he did because he couldn't face having to deal with his family's pain. He didn't want to be responsible for his decision, or for the fallout. For several months after Bruce left, Jennifer was in shock. She kept waiting for him to return. The children too had no way to make sense of it all, no time to adjust to the abrupt loss, and their pain showed in school. They developed behavior problems. Not only had they lost their father, but their mother was too distressed to provide them with the comfort and caretaking they needed during that time.

Abrupt departures usually create severe crises for those left behind. It's the ultimate rejection, abandonment. Confusion, uncertainty, and rage are usual reactions. Any methods of coping we've developed for lesser crises are insufficient. The abandonment leaves one feeling totally helpless and frequently culminates in a severe debilitating family crisis, such as a suicide attempt by one partner, or a major clinical depression requiring hospitalization. Abandoned children regress, get depressed, or act out. The rejection is too great and sudden to cope with.

Compare Bruce and Jennifer with Karen and Jim, another study couple who gradually prepared for separation. In their twenty-second year of marriage, Karen, a journalist, and Jim, a public relations executive, had been growing further apart. Karen felt confined by the marriage. Painfully wrestling with her feelings, Karen had stayed married, hoping she could find peace. She finally came to realize that she couldn't.

Jim had seen Karen's distress growing for years, but when she presented him with her decision, he was still surprised. He communicated his reaction, and she responded. They spent many marathon evenings over the next three months discussing their marriage and ultimately— after Jim became convinced—they hashed out how they would handle the separation. They went from tears to anger to cautious hugs. Although they disagreed about such things as who would keep the house, how they would divide their music collection, and who would get certain special household things they'd collected together, they were able to resolve most of the issues before the actual physical separation.

Both Karen and Jim were very concerned about their three teenage children. Together one night at dinner they told them about the impending separation. They explained their decision as best as they could, assured the children that both parents loved them and would continue to nurture them. Although the children had no choice in the matter, they appreciated and benefited from the opportunity to understand their parents' reasons. They began to anticipate the changes they all knew would occur, and they began to adjust.

Karen had compromised. Jim would stay in the house and Karen would get an apartment. Fairly contentedly, Jim and the kids spent a few Sundays helping Karen look for an apartment within biking distance. When moving day rolled around they all helped her move. Who'd get what had mostly been settled by now; both Jim and Karen agreed that there would still be some further negotiation and some switching things around. Each wanted their share of mementos and art objects, but they divided the furniture based on what fit where. The night after Karen moved, the whole family ordered a pizza and ate together, sitting on Karen's new living room floor.

Even an orderly separation is painful. Karen remembers her departure this way. "I felt devastated leaving home, but at the same time I felt relieved . . . and excited. The separation had been such a long time in coming that I was glad to be finally doing it. It wasn't easy, but we'd sure prepared. The kids were going to be able to come and go from our places as they chose, and we knew we would all see lots of each other."

Jim's account is a little different. "It was a really hard day. We had it all planned, but I didn't expect to feel so empty. There were big holes everywhere I looked. Karen had rearranged my half of the furniture so it didn't look as if pieces had just been plucked out, but still it looked just like what it was . . . a house with missing pieces. I tried to keep things light but I could feel myself getting furious, remembering that, no matter how much I'd come to accept this choice, it really wasn't mine and I didn't like it or understand it. Most of the day I pretended to be okay, but that night I couldn't sleep. I sat in the living room for hours after the boys went to bed, listening to music and feeling dazed."

So no matter how planned and orderly, the separation still brings painful feelings. However, it does not usually bring on a crisis. Unlike Bruce and Jennifer's family, Karen and Jim did not undergo depression, rage, or adolescent regressions. Instead of acting out and further destroying the participants, at least this family made the active choice to heal.

Establishing Boundaries

Other than giving the process time, what makes a particular separation orderly instead of disorderly? That is a question whose answer is very individual to the particular binuclear family under construction. But there are two factors common to all orderly separations. These are good management and firm relationship boundaries.

We've already spoken about good management. To repeat, knowing and preparing for the transitions of divorce, averting crises by defusing tension at marker points, and giving the process just enough time so that everyone can adjust all define good management. Karen and Jim's family demonstrated excellent management.

Less easy is how to consciously establish new boundaries for your family relationships. Manuel and Maria's family, and Bruce and Jennifer's, all foundered because the partners could not define new boundaries.

The rules, roles, and rituals I spoke about in Chapter 3 will come into play here. Boundaries are simply rules for how you and your ex will now interact—and not interact. To make boundaries you will have to recognize how you have now changed roles. To keep boundaries firm you and your ex will have to make new rituals. The boundaries will give your binuclear family a common ground and a common law.

In marriage we spend years struggling with boundary issues in specific areas as we gradually trade independence for interdependence. But how much we concede remains an important dilemma that plays itself out differently at different life stages, with their different mixtures of personality and situation. How much intimacy is each person comfortable with? How much personal space does each one need? How much separate time?

Questions of how to regulate intimacy and distance arise at every life transition. They also plague the newly separated. Only now the dynamic is reversed. Instead of struggling to open up the relationship, separated couples need to find ways to reduce the intimacy and appropriately increase their distance.

There's an old adage—noted before cohabitation was commonly accepted—that the first year of marriage is the hardest. So is the first year of divorce. Instead of coming at a time of joy, these negotiations come in a time of grief.

Until the moment of actual separation, a couple is usually unaware of how interdependent their lives have become. Now they feel all the threads yanking apart. Time and trial and error may be necessary until they can establish a new comfort level.

Neil and Denise, a clinic couple, were a dual-career couple in their late forties who separated after a seven-year marriage. Each had been married once before; each had children from the prior marriage. Their mutual child, Ethan, was five years old; their other children ranged in age from eight to eleven.

Initiated by Denise after two years of painful questioning and discussion, their separation was amicable. They decided to stay friends—to get together for weekly family dinners. For the first couple of months after he moved out, Neil freely popped in and out of Denise's home whenever he pleased. He stopped by almost daily to pick up the mail, say hello to the kids, fix up the house, do his wash. Sometimes he stayed for dinner and read the kids bedtime stories. Sometimes Denise was home for the whole visit. Sometimes Denise would go out and Neil would stay with the kids until she came back.

In the beginning, they kept reverting to their old marital boundaries. On the couple of occasions that Neil and Denise spent time alone after the children had gone to bed, they ended up making love. Afterward Denise felt angry and Neil felt confused. They argued: Neil questioned why they couldn't get back together—they were so good in bed; Denise replied that she'd succumbed to his sexual advances because of loneliness, habit, and too much wine.

Soon Denise began to feel that, although she still wanted to be friends, she must make her life more separate. She suggested that they establish more of a schedule for his visits. She also said that for a while she didn't want to have any more evenings alone; she needed to master her internal struggle about sex. Establishing new boundaries wasn't easy. Neil was angry. He felt pushed away by Denise's request for more distance.

Denise and Neil tried a number of different plans as they negotiated their boundaries of distance and intimacy. After about a year they worked out a fairly stable and moderately flexible pattern that included occasional dinners together, which they had in restaurants rather than at home.

Many couples—especially those who are amicable—see a lot of each other when they first separate. This closeness is a way of easing out of the dailiness of their life together, slowly breaking some of the accustomed ways.

To be so deliberate requires being able to cope with a highly ambiguous situation, which creates additional stress for many people. The person who doesn't want the separation is apt to have the most difficulty.

Neil put it this way: "I really wanted to be with Denise. But whenever we were together, I'd get so mixed up. How could we laugh like this and yet she didn't want me? I would look around our comfortable home, which we'd built together, and feel jealous and lost. One day I walked into the living room and she'd changed it all around. She'd chucked our old couch, on which we'd made love so many times. I went home early feeling lonelier than I'd ever felt in my life. I spent my night tossing and turning, dreaming about Denise, longing for her touch, her smell, our home, our life together."

In setting boundaries, it's the seemingly simple things—when you can call or drop in on one another, whether you will help each other out in the minor daily crises, if you will spend any time alone together—that matter. The lack of clear boundaries gave Neil false hopes. It's important to know, for example, if one partner needs a ride to pick up a car at the shop, or if one partner's got the flu and needs some soup, whether the ex can reasonably help out. When expectations differ and the boundaries are unclear, it's a setup for conflict and anger. The better both partners can newly define these limits on the relationship, the less likely either will end up disappointed because the other didn't meet some need that used to be a part of the marriage.

There's no cookbook answer for how rigid or flexible the boundaries should be. This is totally dependent on the relationship; boundaries continue to evolve over the years. I suggest that couples separately list their needs and desires and work them out one by one.

Friendship is very possible after separation. I've met divorced couples who, for years, continue to help each other out in crucial ways. Bernice and George, who I recently interviewed, are one such couple. After thirty-one years of marriage, four grown children, and six grandchildren, they decided to split up. Now, seven years later, George continues to manage Bernice's investments and to do some general household repairs. When George had open-heart surgery two years ago, Bernice brought him to her house to recuperate. Some of their friends and family thought this was weird and inappropriate. Others romanticized that soon they would get back together. Bernice's response to this was, "I care deeply for George. Like my brother, or my close friend Sally. Live with them? No way! But they know I'm there if they need me. The same goes for George. We're really much better off not living together, but I'll always feel like he's family."

Boundaries are hot issues in all intimate relationships, not just separations. They touch off unresolved conflicts or crash into opposing strongly held values. Among exspouses, money and new loves often are the touchiest issues, bound to set off a bloody struggle (like Manuel and Maria) or to spark an acute wish to run away (like Jennifer and Bruce). Or perhaps there's an old repetitious fight over power that the couple has engaged in for years (like Denise and Neil).

Suppose you're talking about money, and your ex, who's just moved out, brings up your spendthrift ways during marriage. Further suppose that the argument about different spending styles was part of a greater argument, sustained throughout the marriage, about power and control. How can you establish and maintain a new boundary about such a loaded issue?

Recognize that the surface issue—money, sex, nutrition—is not the other partner's concern anymore. Nor is it the real issue. The issue is power. And an unconscious power struggle will turn almost any discussion into a fight. To avoid destructive, purposeless arguing, a separating couple needs to place sensible general limits on discussions. If either partner can't keep these limits, the discussion may be over for now. The limits include the length of discussion ("Whatever we can accomplish in an hour"), the circumstances surrounding discussion ("Only on neutral ground"), and the emotional temperature that discussions generate ("If we start yelling we'll take a time-out"). The limits may include anything loaded ("We'll talk about religion later").

Some issues are best avoided during boundary negotiations. For some couples there are many such issues; others need to steer clear of only a few key areas. If a couple wants to keep their relationship cooperative, they will scrupulously learn to dodge these issues. However, if one or both want to continue fighting, either because it feels good to remain that closely connected, or paradoxically, to get some distance, they march right into the familiar battlefield of unresolved boundary issues.

The First Three Transitions: The Emotional Fallout

These first three turbulent transitions—the decision, the announcement, the separation—form the core of the emotional divorce. The lingering feelings of attachment, the ambivalence of the decision, and the ambiguity of the future combine in complex ways to make this a time of deep soul-searching, anxious discomfort, and vacillating but intense desires.

The continuing bonds of attachment cause great emotional distress but are healthy, normal feelings. Few relationships are without some caring times, certainly few marriages, and arguably, few divorces. Seeing old photographs, or a gift the two of you received for an anniversary, or a favorite piece of furniture, is bound to evoke echoes of the good times, and intense sadness. A telephone call from a mutual friend may make one feel depressed about no longer being part of a couple. At times, most feel a sense of overwhelming personal failure, or project the failure onto the exspouse.

It's normal to feel emotional extremes during these times. This does not mean the decision is wrong, the announcement is bad, or the separation is unsuccessful. Even when a relationship has been very bad for a long time, feelings of attachment can linger for years. As the time passes, and a new life is established, these feelings diminish. Years and years after a divorce, something happens to create a reminder of a pleasant time, and instead of the accustomed rush of angst, perhaps feelings of nostalgia will bubble to the surface, a little sadness at the memories, and even some joy.

At first, though, divorcing couples—in their ambivalence—may deny any good memories about their ex. Although this wards off the pain of the immediate loss, it also requires shutting down other emotions as well. Anyone who relies on denial as a major form of psychic protection limits his or her ability to form healthy relationships in the future—the very ability needed most in this time.

A good divorce requires being able to let go of some aspects of the relationship while holding on to others. To do so means effectively managing conflict, tolerating seesawing emotions, and defining piece by piece the painfully ambiguous boundaries as you change from being spouses to being exspouses. The three transitions of the emotional divorce require a huge amount of patience, maturity, and creativity—and when that is used up, it may even be necessary to invent some more.

When there are children it is even harder to let go while holding on. Even when the children are no longer dependent, the parents are still attached, and later on most likely they will be joined together as grandparents. No matter what the future brings, the bonds of kinship remain; the good divorce will ensure that these bonds never become the chain or noose of kinship.

As you will see in the next chapter, the task involves far more than setting new boundaries for intimacy between expartners, far more than good management of oneself and one's ex. Parents must form a limited partnership, one that nurtures the parent-child relationship of both exspouses. Just as there are no easy recipes for how to separate, there are also no easy recipes for working out this limited partnership. But as former intimates and as parents, there are good options and bad ones. Once you can recognize the underlying principles, you can provide the groundwork for making the choices that best suit your children's needs.

5

The Binuclear Family
FORMING A LIMITED PARTNERSHIP

AFTER A YEAR of fighting over living arrangements, Patricia and Joseph decided upon a compromise: Their two daughters, now ages four and seven, would spend half the week at their mom's place and the other half at their dad's. On Wednesdays, Patricia dropped off the girls at Joseph's; three days later he'd drive them back. In the front hall of each parent's apartment was an identical calendar, outlining the family's schedule. Entries were color coded to show each parent's responsibilities. Patricia and Joseph kept each other updated on all the girls' appointments, homework assignments, and play dates. This arrangement lasted until the girls finished school for the year, when by mutual consent the girls alternated weeks with each parent for the summer.

Sally, in her late forties, had left Dave, in his early fifties. For a year—until they finalized their divorce—Dave kept the family house; there he took care of the couple's two sons, ages ten and twelve, during the school week. Sally rented a condo a mile away; the boys slept there on weekends. The boys called Sally often during the week, and she cooked dinner for them almost every Wednesday night. When her promotion came through, Sally was able to buy another house fairly close by. She and Dave then sat down together and developed a more permanent arrangement.

At the time of their divorce, Maribel remained in the family home and Marty rented a small house a few miles away. The children alternated weeks at each parent's house. A year and a half later, Marty's firm transferred him to another office 2,000 miles away. Although neither Maribel nor Marty was happy about this arrangement, they decided that their children, twins Ben and Betsy, age twelve, and Lisa, age ten, would spend alternate years with each parent. School vacations would be divided equally. The children and the nonresident parent would write and call each other frequently. This arrangement lasted for three and a half years, until Marty's next transfer relocated him back to his old hometown, 85 miles from Maribel.

For eight months after Belle left Jim, the couple took turns living in their beautifully decorated, comfortable family home. They also rented a small, convenient apartment about a mile away. Every other Friday, Belle packed her overnight bag and moved out of the family home; Jim moved in. The next Friday they'd switch again. Matthew, age three, Bobby, age five, and Jeremy, age eight, stayed put, feeling secure in the familiar, cozy surroundings. A family appointment book, kept by whatever parent was resident, tracked schedules, shopping lists, chores, doctors' appointments, and after-school activities. The financial responsibility for both residences was divided equally between Belle and Jim.

What do all of these binuclear families have in common?

Their stories are all drawn from interviews of Cooperative Colleague and Perfect Pal couples in my study—exspouse pairs who achieved successful divorce arrangements. Also, from the first day of the first transition of their parents' divorce, and throughout the subsequent transitions, the children of these families felt secure that they'd be allowed to maintain meaningful and unobstructed relationships with both parents. These arrangements were all temporary. They were explicitly worked out as interpersonal contracts—limited partnerships—and were again worked out by common consent once the temporary arrangements were over. By the time of their third interview (five years after the legal divorce), each of these exspouse pairs established a more permanent arrangement.

What is a limited partnership? Simply, it is much like a business partnership. It's defined by a set of rules—rules that limit the boundaries of the partnership—worked out by mutual consent between two adults. Some of the rules are conscious. Some, as we have seen in Chapter 3, are implicit. But all the parameters of the limited partnership have a single purpose.

The eight adults in these study families all shared this purpose: to keep, and even to strengthen, kinship bonds with their children and with each other, as over a period of years they transformed their families from nuclear to binuclear. The limited partnerships they worked out with each other reflected this commitment.

None of these contracts were written in stone. As the children's needs changed, and as the parents' lives and work schedules also changed, the agreements in these four families were revised. Sometimes the changes occurred easily. At other times they required considerable negotiation and many compromises.

The Best-Case Limited Partnership: Egalitarian Marriage, Egalitarian Divorce

Patricia and Joseph, Sally and Dave, Marty and Maribel, and Belle and Jim, all fit along a continuum of successful, but nontraditional, postdivorce limited partnerships. These families may seem odd to members of traditional nuclear families, and even to many divorced people. They don't fit our stereotypes of families of divorce—children living with their mother during the week, whose fathers visit on the weekends, if at all. These families were egalitarian during the parents' marriage, and they were also egalitarian during the parents' divorce. After divorce, their solutions were consonant with the way they shared parenting when they were married.

I have chosen to begin this chapter with best-case scenarios because they show how complex it is to set up even the simplest limited partnership. Two things must be established when you and your ex begin: ground rules and a list of the problems at hand.

In the four limited partnerships described, the ground rules were simple. Discussions would be open. Exspouses would put themselves second and their children first.

In each of these families, both parents wanted to be with their children as much as they possibly could. Neither wanted to be a visitor. Neither wanted to give up watching their children grow and change. Each wanted to be the best parent he or she could be. Each wanted his or her children to have healthy, nurturing, continuing families, as minimally interrupted by the divorce as was humanly possible.

The problems at hand were also relatively clear-cut. Since the parents put the children first, they decided to work out temporary living arrangements right away. By the time they separated, all these families moved straight into their new situations. At this point they had to deal with the reactions of outsiders.

Friends and extended families tend to think these families—and others like them—are strange. For example, when Belle's mother came to visit she was appalled. She told Belle and Jim they'd carried this "sharing the kids thing" too far. She was convinced that her grandchildren's lives would be ruined because their friends would make fun of them. She also thought they'd end up confused about whether their parents were divorced or not.

Jim's mother had a similar reaction. She was sure her son and daughter-in-law were sleeping together and would remarry. She, too, worried about the effect on her grandchildren of this bewildering situation.

Both grandmothers were right to be concerned. Given that traditional nuclear families are the norm by which we judge other family patterns, the kids in nontraditional families may indeed be laughed at by their friends. Shame is an all-too-common feeling for children living in families that deviate from the idealized norm. Kids in gay or lesbian families, single-parent families, and interracial families all share this problem. The kids wonder what's going on, and feel embarrassed that their family is so weird. This is a real problem in setting up cooperative limited partnerships: as we've already seen in Chapter 2, society expects the partners to be bitter and noncommunicative. The exspouses in these partnerships must together address this problem; they must speak about their arrangement with friends and family.

The long-distance parents, Maribel and Marty, also faced the problem of being misunderstood by their immediate society, and the problem of how their divorce would bounce back through their kids. The schools, their extended families, and their friends all thought the idea of changing schools each year was rash and stupid. Maribel and Marty discussed this and searched for models in which families had succeeded in this type of arrangement.

Although models for this are few, children sometimes switch schools for reasons other than divorce. In wealthy families that travel extensively, or Hollywood families that go on location for extended periods of time, or military families faced with frequent relocations, or academic families that go on sabbaticals or research leaves in foreign cultures, it is increasingly being viewed as enriching for the children to be exposed to a wide range of experiences. In this divorced family, this flexibility was seen as inevitably traumatizing rather than enriching until the couple went to both school boards and persuaded them otherwise. The children did fine.

Patricia and Joseph (the split-week parents) did not need to go to the school boards. They took the time to explain to their children's teachers and school principal that their children would not be staying in the same house during the week. They asked the teachers to help make the experience a positive one for their children. They suggested that the teachers incorporate different models of family into their curriculum, including binuclear families, and specifically requested, "Please don't refer to our children's living arrangements as a broken home."

In the fourth best-case family, Sally (the weekend mom) found herself always defending—even to close friends—why her sons lived with their father on weekdays instead of with her. In this society mothers are supposed to have primary care of their children; when they don't, their mothering is suspect. In fact, Sally's new consulting job demanded irregular travel and intermittent overtime. Hers and Dave's arrangement was best for their whole family, and the flexibility was a sign of responsibility rather than the opposite.

Each of these limited partnerships was planned and structured. None of these parents took their decisions lightly. They set ground rules; they listed their problems at hand, and did research on them. After quickly moving into a temporary, cooperative arrangement, they all sat back together in relative leisure—at the later stages of the emotional divorce when they were no longer in crisis—and addressed their mutual long-term problems.

These parents (and thousands like them) are adapting to meet their own and their children's practical needs. In the process, they are changing society.

Most divorcing parents don't explore their options as thoroughly as did these families, primarily because society doesn't make many options known and acceptable. These four families didn't make any headlines, unlike those that fought long public battles, or kidnapped a child.

Letty Cottin Pogrebin, in her book *Family Politics,* likens our range of socially sanctioned options of family to what she calls "the asparagus syndrome."

As a child I hated asparagus. I hated the smell of it cooking and my disgust was confirmed by one taste of the soggy, gray stalks my mother boiled to mush. Much later in life, I discovered that asparagus offers other choices: it is delicious raw, crisp as a carrot, dunked into a dip, steamed and glossed with melted butter or lemony hollandaise sauce, or served cold under a fresh vinaigrette, to mention just a few possibilities.

So it wasn't true that I hated asparagus, only that I had been given *a false choice:* overcooked asparagus or none at all. No one told me there were other options.

There are many good options in divorce—all throughout the process. In divorce, even supposing you can't achieve the best-case scenario of setting up an immediate, successful, temporary limited partnership, you will probably have a second chance, a third chance—as many chances as you and your exspouse need. And you should have the comfort of realizing that your options postdivorce, at any transition of divorce, are certainly better than the overcooked mush of a disastrous marriage, or than living daily in constant war or an atmosphere of cold enmity.

Suppose that you and your exspouse are fairly cooperative, but need help in setting up ground rules, or in distinguishing your immediate from your long-term problems. By all means, seek help. Do research. Speak to a counselor who you and your exspouse select—a therapist, a religious counselor, a wise person in your extended family. Realize that there are models available, and that, given the realities of our already existing diverse family structures—many of which are not traditional nuclear families or even families based on marriage—we must stop perpetuating mythical ideals at our own expense. Shaming families only leads to their dysfunction.

To increase our options for healthy families after divorce, we must separate marriage from family, realize what belongs in a marriage contract and what belongs in a whole-family contract. Divorce must not equal only loss; that is insane, given its current prevalence. Divorce is a legal process designed to sever marital ties. It cannot be meant to sever family ties. By truly accepting and supporting this, you and your exspouse will open the door to many possible, good forms of limited partnership. You will truly be able to discover the set of choices that minimize your family's loss and maximize its gains. The central goal of your limited partnership will be to set up a two-parent binuclear family that will continue to nurture relationships between children, parents, and extended kin. You must set up structures that are positive and as acceptable as possible given the realities of society, and that are flexible enough to meet your family members' real needs.

Defining Your Binuclear Family: Making the Implicit Explicit

But what about families that don't fit our best-case scenario? Those in which the partners are having communication problems, or in which they can't agree on the most important issues to settle first? In these families—the majority—limited partnerships will have to be talked out step by step, perhaps with the help of a knowledgeable professional, with particular attention to averting crises at common marker points. The rules, roles, and rituals that can be more implicit in best-case families will have to be discussed and even written down. But the goal will be the same: to set up temporary and permanent systems of rules that meet the needs of all members of the family—children first.

Best Interests of the Child

All divorcing parents know how important it is to make decisions based on their children's best interests. But the worst arguments can happen over what exactly these interests are. Which school should Johnnie attend—although couched in an argument over his best interests—usually boils down to a pitched battle about which parent has more authority, more power, and more control over Johnnie's life.

The phrase "best interests" means different things to different people. Experts have battled furiously for years about what this concept actually means (as we'll see in more detail in the next chapter's discussion of custody). Parents, however, are even more emotional and stubborn about the issue. Their opinions are shaped by both societal and personal values, and disagreement runs extremely deep.

Experts and researchers do agree on two very basic factors that have significant impact on children's well-being. These two factors can be said to be the foundation for a child's true best interests:

1. *Children benefit from maintaining the familial relationships in their life that were important and meaningful to them prior to*

the divorce. That usually means not only parents but also extended family, such as grandparents.

2. *Children benefit when the relationship between their parents—whether married or divorced—is generally supportive and cooperative.*

These two factors have shown up over and over in many different studies with many different populations and measures, even those in other countries. *These two factors differentiate between the children who are and are not damaged by divorce.*

It's this simple: if you and your exspouse are able to cooperate sufficiently well in allowing each other to love and nurture your children, unobstructed by loyalty conflicts, you will be doing what's in the best interests of your children. You will be allowing your children to grow, to come through your divorce with no long-term disturbances. It's not that your kids won't be upset or distressed. Of course they'll react. But once you and your exspouse can set up a working limited partnership, your family will regain a certain equilibrium and your children will most probably come through it fine.

All conflicts are not harmful ones. You and your exspouse may wish to make the following implicit rules explicit:

Keep parental disagreements between the two of you. It's when parents put children in the middle, or cause them to take sides, or threaten children with the loss by departure or disgrace of one parent, that children get hurt.

Keep disagreements nonviolent. Violence and abuse always cause harm, whether you inflict the violence on the child or on the other parent.

Manage your disagreements by setting limits on them. Normal conflict between you and your exspouse—when managed so that it doesn't take over the whole relationship or infuse the child's life—won't threaten your child's ability to make a healthy adjustment. You can limit the time ("We'll talk for an hour and then postpone further discussion until tomorrow"), the place ("We'll talk on neutral ground"), or set any other limit with which you and your exspouse both feel fairly comfortable.

Spell out what's essential. You may need to delay your argument until you and your exspouse talk out your issues with a friend or counselor. You may need to define what needs to be accomplished in key encounters with your exspouse.

Customizing Your Limited Partnership

For parents struggling to do what is in the children's best interests, the most difficult task of divorce is to disentangle themselves as spouses while continuing their parenting relationship. In marriage the boundaries between those two role relationships are usually blurred. As we saw in the last chapter, the process of letting go while still holding on is enormously complex and infused with many conflicting emotions. Even though most divorcing parents clearly know that they want to continue their relationships with their children, they don't know how to push their way through their emotional morass and emerge as a healthy family. The important question is not *whether* parents should continue to share parenting, but rather *how* they should do it. This is different in each partnership.

I have worked with difficult parents who won't speak with each other, who are embroiled in a vicious power struggle over the children. One of the most common situations goes something like this:

Client: I can't stand the sight of him. As far as I'm concerned I never want to see him again. I know the kids love him but he's not going to step foot into my house.

Me: I can understand how hurt and angry you are right now. But I also know you love your three children very much and don't want to cause them unnecessary distress. How have you worked out the parenting in these past two months since you've separated?

Client: The kids have spent every other weekend with Tom and they have dinner with him on Tuesdays. He pulls into the driveway and I send them out. You should see how edgy they are. They wait by the window and run out as soon as he comes. They don't even kiss me goodbye. When he returns them, they are always in nasty moods. I know he talks about me. He brainwashes them. He poisons their love for me. I hate him.

Me: Your oldest daughter, Jessica, is going to graduate from high school in a few months, isn't she? I assume both you and your ex are going to want to go, aren't you?

Client: Well, I guess so. We'll just sit as far away from each other as possible.

> *Me:* How about right after the graduation? You know, the time when parents usually join their child? Hug them and take pictures. That's usually a special time. How do you think you and your ex will handle that?
>
> *Client:* Hug him? Forget it. They'll be with me. Tom should attend the graduation if he wants and then just leave. He can call Jessica later.
>
> *Me:* Do you expect Tom will just go along with you on that? How do you think Jessica will feel?
>
> *Client:* I hadn't thought that all through.
>
> *Me:* Just fantasize with me a bit, here. Imagine it's seven years from now, and Jessica is getting married. I assume both you and Tom are going to want to be a part of that celebration, aren't you? Can you get some picture of how you'll both do that?
>
> *Client:* It sounds like a horror to me. We'll both be there. We won't talk to each other. I can't even imagine how we're going to manage.

When I ask divorcing parents to imagine future occasions in their family—weddings, bar mitzvahs, birthdays, even the birth of a grandchild—I precipitate their acute awareness of the fact that for the rest of their lives they will continue to be kin. And when I explain how destructive it is for children (young and old alike) to live with parents at war—even cold war—they begin to acknowledge that they need to find a better way, *together.* The anger does not magically go away, but for the first time the parents are motivated to learn how to manage it better. The motivation is their children.

The first time parents imagine a future together, they begin to form a unique idea of how they'll get from here to there. This idea is the seed for their limited partnership. The work from here on in is making that relationship explicit, and in customizing it to suit the needs of their binuclear family.

Think of the limited partnership as a contract. The contract may be oral or it may be written. It may include many provisions. But the contract will always have to include the following provisions:

1. *Partners in parenting:* A limited partnership acknowledges that you and your ex are partners in parenting—coparents. You and your ex must define the limits of this relationship.

2. *Parenting across two households:* The partnership agreement will have to cover this situation, which is unprecedented in most marriages. You and your ex will have to decide how you're going to negotiate and divide power. You will have to decide how you're going to deal with holidays, mutual obligations (for instance, your children's attendance at school or church), and illnesses. The limits you and your exspouse set will depend on the type of relationship you have, and on your willingness and ability to transcend your problems from your marriage.

3. *Practical parenting:* The partnership agreement must be a practical arrangement. When reality does not fit you or your ex's wishes—for example, when a temporary arrangement suddenly stops working—it will help if you and your ex have previously defined how you will handle such issues as sudden changes in schedule.

There are many other possible provisions that you and your ex could choose to include in your partnership agreement. The limited partnership is different for Perfect Pals—who may have an entirely implicit agreement—than it is for Angry Associates—who may wish to spell everything out on paper. You may need to outline the partnership on more than one occasion: for example, after the physical separation, you and your ex may feel that all old rules must change. You may need to make more or less effort at first than does your ex—especially if one of you left the marriage precipitously. Each limited partnership is unique. Each must meet the needs of a very individual binuclear family.

A limited partnership is multidimensional, dynamic, and flexible. It's practical; while permitting conflict the partners still must be as amicable, cooperative, and respectful as possible. Most importantly it's a contract, a vehicle in which partners follow established rules.

Children need continuity and stability in family relationships, which means that parents must form a continuing and workable arrangement. It is best if you and your ex begin to work out as much of a parenting contract as you can before you separate. Because the situation is so new to you, it's likely you'll have a process of trial and error; you may set some rules that seem fine, but later need to be altered.

Limited partnership should not be confused with custody—the

legal agreement that establishes which children live where and when, and who pays. Custody follows the partnership agreement, not the other way around. The term *custody* is what we generally grab hold of when we discuss parenting contracts because we have only legal models to work from, and we don't yet have well-defined social models. When the limited partnership is worked out first, then you and your ex will probably be able later to work out your custody decisions swiftly. I will discuss custody along with other aspects of the legal contract in the next chapter.

Recognizing the Common Ground

I was speaking with an architect friend of mine, who was living in what he called a "binuclear house"—two domains separated by, and joined by, a common courtyard. I was surprised to hear him use that term, and realized it's a good visual image of how we can construct a binuclear parenting arrangement.

In the ideal binuclear family, no matter what limited partnership agreement the parents work out, each parent's home—their own domain—will be separate and private. The common courtyard— where the two domains intersect—will exist by mutual definition. In the courtyard will be all the decisions that both parents need to make together. The courtyard may include time the parents spend together with the children, holidays, ritual celebrations, school functions, and certain responsibilities. The size and scope of the intersect will vary according to the type of relationship the parents have worked out.

The Venn diagram, used in mathematics for teaching probability and set theory, is useful in visualizing the relationship between the separate domains and their common ground. In my concept of the binuclear family, the intersection expands and contracts according to how the parents negotiate their relationship. The diagrams show how the five exspouse relationship typologies are likely to construct their binuclear families, and how much territory is in their common ground.

As you can see, even if you and your ex are Angry Associates and Fiery Foes, you still share some common ground. Take the client I spoke about earlier, who tried to visualize her daughter's wedding. She and her ex were Fiery Foes at the time. She wanted to keep their domains totally separate. So did he. But at our session she admitted that she and her ex would have to be on the same turf at the same time on a few rare occasions—situations for which she would have to

Venn Diagrams

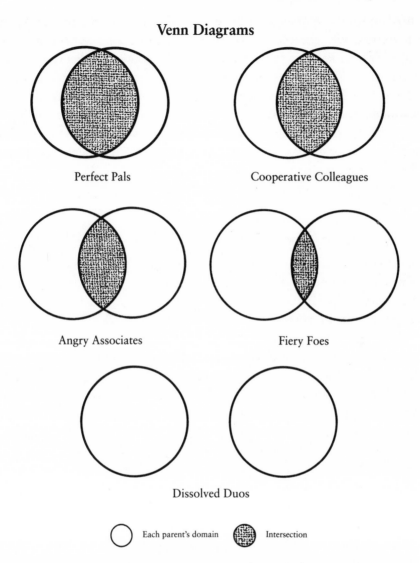

Perfect Pals

Cooperative Colleagues

Angry Associates

Fiery Foes

Dissolved Duos

Each parent's domain   Intersection

prepare. When she recognized this—that their interests would sometimes intersect—she could begin to see the need for making a mutual agreement with her ex. Their limitations of their partnership were extremely narrow. Nevertheless they did make an agreement that permitted a small, very circumscribed common ground, reserved only for rare events that both would attend, albeit painfully and without direct contact.

Perfect Pals fall into the other extreme. Their common ground is so large that it sometimes interferes with privacy. Maybe they concentrate on the children to the exclusion of themselves; maybe they're so used to working together, living together, and parenting together that any limitation (except for the one fact of divorce) seems like an intrusion. Perfect Pals may also have an almost totally implicit partnership agreement. The danger in staying Perfect Pals for too long after divorce is that any future remarriage by either partner may be devastating to the other partner.

Unless you are a Dissolved Duo, you and your ex must share *some* common ground. Making the boundaries of that common ground explicit—stating or writing down the limits—will help in constructing your own binuclear family.

Emotional Fences That Can Block the Common Ground

Up to now, this discussion of how to establish a limited partnership all sounded quite rational, functional, and positive—in the abstract. Now let's look more closely at specific problems. Even the most amicable exspouses set up emotional and practical barriers within their common ground.

It's important to remember that these blocks and barriers are present in marriage too—in good marriages. But in divorce, the fences seem higher, thicker, and more threatening. Communication is less free. Partnership talks can stall when these fences seem impossible to negotiate.

The most common barriers are value differences and issues of competition, power, and control. These complicate even the simplest matters, and when people are arguing about the long-term fate of their children, these differences can take on a life of their own.

Parents often hold different values about child rearing. One parent thinks television is instructional; the other thinks television destroys motivation, and turns alert athletes into lifeless blobs. One parent is vegetarian; the other enjoys meat. One parent is religious; the other is an atheist. One parent thinks children should be exposed to nudity; the other believes nudity is too sensual for a child to handle. One parent believes children should be allowed to stay up until they're tired; the other believes in firm bedtimes. The list goes on and on.

During marriage, the parents may have been able to resolve some of their differences. In good marriages, couples can buffer one another's views and achieve some viable compromise. But in divorce (especially when differing values contributed to the split), exspouses usually want to reassert their values (which represents individuality) rather than compromise them (which represents marriage). Conflict is bound to ensue.

Tony and Cynthia, a couple who came to me for family therapy after their divorce, had very different lifestyles and significant value differences. They'd agreed—after considerable negotiation—to share child care equally. At the time they separated, their children, Ted and Jennie, were seven and nine. Tony and Cynthia tried several different living arrangements. Starting with the children's spending half a week at each home, they later moved to a week with each parent. A year later, a job change required Tony to move; after two years the children were switching homes every two weeks.

Tony believed in strict rules and tight schedules. Cynthia was easygoing and far less structured. At Tony's house the kids went to bed at eight, had to make their beds every morning, couldn't leave the table until everyone was done, and could watch TV only after they finished their homework and chores. At Cynthia's house the kids went to bed later, had untidy rooms, could get up from the table when they were finished eating, and could watch TV after school.

Cynthia and Tony's personality differences had been a subject of considerable conflict when they were married. Sometimes they made compromises, but generally they drove each other crazy. After the divorce, the kids often nagged Tony about how much easier it was at their mom's. Tony hated constantly feeling like the bad guy and was upset by what he thought of as Cynthia's corruption of the kids.

A month after the divorce became final, Tony called Cynthia, saying they needed to meet. "Our fighting is affecting the kids." Cynthia didn't think they could work out their value differences by themselves and suggested they seek professional help. When they arrived in my office—Tony was early; Cynthia was on time—they each presented their view.

"Our kids need some consistency," asserted Tony.

"We don't need to do everything the same at both houses. I'm not your clone," said Cynthia. She spoke much faster than Tony, and much more loudly. "Our kids can manage some differences."

"They're confused by this amount of difference."

"They're learning how to adapt and be flexible by having two different parents. We've got to be honest, don't we?"

Seeing that these two caring parents had a large and well-delimited common ground, even though they were arguing, I suggested that perhaps there were some things that were important for them to agree on and others, perhaps, that were less so. We decided that the children would benefit from having consistent discipline, bedtimes, and handling of schoolwork. Cynthia agreed that at her house (in her private domain) she would monitor TV watching. She and Tony compromised about bedtimes—the kids' bedtime was eight, but if at her house it stretched to eight-thirty (and no farther), that was okay. And Tony would relax the rules occasionally at his house (his private domain) so that the children would keep the same schedule at both houses.

For the first year after the divorce, Tony and Cynthia walked a thin line between being Angry Associates and Cooperative Colleagues. As we made their contract more explicit, they became less defensive. They knew where they would compromise to do things more cooperatively, and they also knew what the areas were in which they would not try to reach agreement. In this way, they became Cooperative Colleagues, with very defined boundaries about what they could, and could not, discuss, what was negotiable and what was nonnegotiable.

Their differences regarding tidiness remained, along with some other daily patterns that were integral to the parents' personality styles. Jennie and Ted benefited from their parents' acting more like a team, but also accommodated well to the differences. "When we're at Mom's house, we don't have to make our beds, but at Dad's we do." It was no big deal.

Maribel and Marty—the long-distance couple with three children, a ten-year-old daughter and twelve-year-old twins—also had some value differences; theirs were harder to resolve. Maribel was introverted, and when the children spent the school year with her, their weekend activities centered around going to the library, museums, and art classes. They spent most of their time with adults since Maribel's friends didn't have children. But Marty was a sports enthusiast. In Marty's "on" years and vacations, he'd sign the kids up for Little League, take them to basketball games and out to movies, and play hard with them at recreational parks. Instead of art lessons, the kids took swimming and gymnastics.

Maribel and Marty, like Tony and Cynthia, had a common ground—they both were involved parents. But they had severe communication problems, and thus more severe blocks and barriers. For example, initially neither Maribel nor Marty respected the other parent's choice of leisure activities, and whenever the kids moved, neither would hesitate in yelling out exactly what he or she thought. Each parent resented the children's loss of skill in the "off" years. Insults, accusations, and call-backs (each wanted the last word) gave them quite a phone bill and little satisfaction.

The couple did not see a therapist, but they did individually consult their friends. Maribel's friends told her to stop wasting her breath, to give in to the fact that the kids would lead different lifestyles each year. Marty's friend told him to stop competing over who had the better values—to have some faith in the kids. Both parents reluctantly followed their friends' advice, and agreed to listen to the kids.

It was hard for Maribel and Marty to put aside their own biases, to listen and watch the children develop interests suitable to their own personalities, without blaming the other parent for the loss of fulfillment of their own expectations. The test came when the children switched back to Maribel's in the third year of divorce, and Betsy—who adored gymnastics—didn't want to take art lessons. Maribel agreed to the change.

What's going on here, beneath the different specifics of each situation? The two families played out virtually identical power struggles. Issues change, but the power struggle has a way of staying the same. During marriage, the parents are vested in each other's spending time with the kids—in teaching and molding the kids. After divorce, if one parent has more time with the kids, the other must have less. If one parent has more influence, the other's will wane. If one parent does mostly fun things with the kids, the other will have less fun time. The parent is more vested in taking the time, the fun, and the control, and in giving the other parent the lesser position. This lesser position threatens parents with the fear that if they do not grab more, they will also end up with less of their child's love.

For most parents, beneath the power struggle is a fear of loss. If they are not loved best, some parents fear not being loved at all. Frequently, these kinds of fears can often be traced back to early experiences, usually in the parents' own childhood. Perhaps they competed with siblings over a parent's favor, or they had a parent who withdrew love in punishment for misbehavior, or they grew up feeling unloved and unlovable. Divorce reactivates the old unresolved feelings, which then get projected onto the present situation as barriers to cooperation.

This process of regression, reactivation, and projection doesn't only plague divorced parents. Many married parents also compete for their child's affection, but for divorced ones, the threat of total loss is far greater. These fears are unfounded except in the most unusual situations. Children rarely lose love for the parent they see less frequently, who they believe is less flexible, or whose house is a bit shabby. More often they gain love, where love is given without making them pay by denigrating the other parent, or by hiding behind the very barriers that will prevent healing and moving on.

Destructive Conflict: The Highest Barriers to Cooperation

Many times parents have difficulty containing their marital anger within its proper boundaries. Their anger against their spouse spills over into their child, contaminating the parent-child interaction with devastating effects. If a mother tells a daughter over and over that her father is dumb and deceitful, she begins to think she, too, is dumb and deceitful. After all, she's like her dad, and no matter what her mom says, her dad is a part of her.

A few years ago, a father, his exwife of four years, and his teenage son were referred to me by the boy's school. The boy was skipping classes, taking drugs, and hurling angry insults at teachers, fellow students, and the principal. The parents arrived at my office separately. Both sat coldly, avoiding eye contact with each other, and instead glaring at the son. "Your jacket's ripped," said the mother. "What will the doctor think of you?" The father rolled his eyes, and muttered, "Nag, nag, nag." The son sank further into his chair.

Fiery Foes from the outset, these parents had only rare, stormy, and disrespectful contact. The boy had lived with his mother until recently when, due to a neighbor's report to Social Services, she'd been deemed an unfit and neglectful parent. Now the boy was living with his father, the father's current wife, and her two children. During a very emotional scene in my office, the boy tearfully asked his father why he didn't love him. All of the man's frustration gathered and he burst out, "Every time I look at you I see your mother." It was the first time the father had said this.

For years, the father had been verbally abusing his son, especially after long phone calls with the mother in which he'd berate her, and then hang up on her. No wonder the boy's self-esteem was extremely low; no wonder he was masking severe depression with his violent behavior at school.

The parents in this binuclear family were doing what therapists call triangulating—focusing the power struggle, which should have remained between them, onto their child. When parents are as angry as these, the child is like a low-rated transistor that suddenly has to accept bursts of high voltage. The child burns out. Triangulation can be implicit, like in this situation, or explicit: a parent, feeling angrily impotent, may actually enlist the child's help in dealing with the other parent. The parent may also try to steal the child's entire affection, and to turn the child against the other parent.

All children have times when they don't want to go to the other parent's house. Frequently it's just a temporary issue. "I'd rather go to the movies with my friend," or "Daddy doesn't pay attention to me when I'm there," or "Mom makes me eat spinach." Parents who realize that children are incredibly talented scam artists won't play into it. They answer something like, "That's something great to talk about—when you're there." The angry parent, however, may seize on this situation. "Oh, poor baby. I know how awful it must be there for you," or "What a prime jerk," or even, "Call up right now and say you prefer to be with your friend." Sometimes this works. More often, it boomerangs and the child begins to defend the other parent. Either way, the child is thrown into a painful, damaging loyalty conflict.

Loyalty conflicts always produce distress. Children hate to put one parent above the other. If they side with one parent, it means they must now side against the other. They are keenly aware that when they've hurt one parent, or pushed one parent away, they are shutting out one parent's love. That's how they interpret these triangulated situations—as being their fault and their responsibility.

Thus, a child often bears the symptoms of the parents' distress. A child's acting-out behavior can be an attempt to rescue the family, to divert attention onto himself or herself and away from the scary parental fights. This is a cry for help to parents who are so wrapped up in their own pain that they deny the child nurturance or love. The child may ultimately have to escalate his or her behavior—to scream for help—to force the parents to rise above their own problems, to now take care of him or her. In these cases the child is putting the parents' barriers and fences inside himself or herself. This internal war can lead to violent behavior, anorexia, or even suicide.

Finally the behavior may be so troubling that one or both parents call a therapist. Therapists trained in a family systems model—that looks at how all the individuals in a family interact and affect each other—will request to see the entire family even when a parent insists the problem is solely with the child. When the parents and children finally arrive, it's almost always the adults who need professional help.

When the problems in their relationship are addressed, the child's problem usually diminishes, often vanishing quite dramatically.

When children become triangulated in their parents' marital rage this can destroy them. No parent wants that. The only answer is for the child to know that both parents will cooperate in their child's best interest. This is the primary, overriding principle that parents must recognize and put before their anger.

When it comes to secondary issues—time with each parent, living arrangements, daily routines, activities, religion—there are no clear-cut answers. These depend on individual variables, such as the child's age and temperament, the parents' preferences, the parents' work schedules, and what opportunities are available. These gray areas, however—the centerfold of most interparental conflicts—distract all the participants from what really matters: establishing a cooperative partnership that permits the bonds of kinship to continue.

Looking at Options and Weighing Alternatives

Once parents have set the basic premise—that they'll continue to be a two-parent family—and have thus agreed that there is a common ground, then it's time to see what options they have. Both in living arrangements and partnership style, they have many models from which to choose. There is no one perfect solution that fits every family of divorce. It is important now to list the alternatives at hand—to make the problems and possible options for their solution as explicit as possible. There are always trade-offs and compromises, just as there are in most major decisions we make in our adult lives.

Listing the Problems and Solutions at Hand

When people cluck their tongues about the ways divorced couples restructure their families, they must also ask what choice these people had. When they do, they may find that the parents chose the best alternative, given the circumstances.

Take Belle and Jim, one of the four amicable couples with egalitarian marriages and nontraditional divorces I mentioned at the start of this chapter. They were the couple who kept the children in the family home, and took turns living there with them. Let's reexamine this temporary arrangement, and compare it with the alternatives.

Cooperative Colleagues at the time they decided to separate, Belle and Jim agreed on their common ground right away. They'd always been involved parents during their marriage and they knew they'd continue to be. They set the following ground rule: they wanted to disrupt the children's lives as little as possible. From this followed the mutual hope that the kids could remain in the same schools and day-care center and keep the same friends. They listed their problems; the most serious of these, they both agreed, was money.

Belle and Jim's first preference was to buy, or even rent, two smaller, separate houses in the same neighborhood. But they couldn't afford this. Before separating, they spent three weeks house hunting and discovered what a bargain their old house had been, and also how inadequate the selling price would be to cover the rental cost of two homes.

Neither Belle nor Jim relished the idea of sharing their home. But when they balanced the inconvenience and the relative lack of privacy against their children's stability and contentment, they judged these were acceptable trade-offs—in the short term. Neither wanted to continue this arrangement for long. They defined "a long time" differently: Belle, as the several-month period until the divorce would be finalized; Jim, as anything over a month or two. But they agreed that neither would press for a change until they could find a better solution. It worked: they have since moved into separate homes, and everyone benefited from the children's grace period. Although uncommon, and not perfectly tolerable for most parents, for some families a short-term arrangement like Belle and Jim's works.

A judge in Traverse City, Michigan, was faced with two warring parents in deadly conflict over custody of their three teenage sons and the family home. The judge made the unusual decision of awarding the house to the children, ordering the parents to alternate month-long visits. The judge said his decision was natural because each parent testified that the other was a good parent. He further stated, "Such a settlement would work only in cases in which the parents acknowledged responsibility to the children." Donald, their thirteen-year-old son, was pleased: "I couldn't believe it. I thought my ma would get us. I'm glad one of the parents wasn't left out." The mother, a thirty-seven-year-old secretary, was also pleased: "This way no one loses." And so was the father, a forty-two-year-old electrician: "They [the children] don't have to change schools or change friends."

Another unusual decision was made by Tony and Cynthia (the

therapy couple with value disagreements) when they decided to have their two children change homes every two weeks. Tony had been unemployed for almost a year before the separation. In fact, the pain around his handling of unemployment was a contributing factor in the split. Like Belle and Jim, both Tony and Cynthia were child oriented; at each crisis their first thought was, "What about the kids?" When their marriage deteriorated beyond repair, that was again their first thought. They listed their options. At this point Tony rented an apartment fairly close to Cynthia's, and the children alternated weekly between the two homes.

Finally, a very good company called Tony with a solid job offer. This was an opportunity for career advancement, a good work environment, everything of which he'd dreamed. It was a once-in-a-life-time offer—except the company was seventy-five miles away.

Tony took the job, saying that he'd somehow work everything out. But once working, he found the reality—a daily commute of three hours—impossible. This was a huge, important chunk of time that he wanted to spend with the children. He had to hire someone to get the children off to school, because his arrival time at work was 8 A.M.—which meant he left at dawn. He got home too late to have a relaxed family dinner; if the kids waited until his arrival, they were cranky and starving. Even worse, Tony wasn't available in case of emergencies, or even for the after-school activities he customarily attended. And Cynthia felt that all the responsibilities in this arrangement fell on her—which had also been a major point of contention during the marriage.

Tony and Cynthia wrestled with this problem in family therapy. They agreed they needed a new plan, but were at a loss to figure out the particulars. How could they keep both parents primary caregivers, and relegate neither to the status of visitor? Both worked; each was willing to share responsibility. One of them said, "What if one parent has the children during the week and the other takes weekends?" Neither wanted this. They disliked the idea of one parent getting all the free time, while the other got all the hard work times. They also didn't want the children to have that kind of image of them.

Finally, one parent came up with what they called "this silly idea." The other considered it and said, "Hey, that doesn't sound as silly as you would think." After unsuccessfully attempting to create other plans, and crossing off every other possibility on their list, they decided to give two weeks on, two weeks off, a try.

At first, the children also thought the idea was silly. "Do you have any better ideas?" asked the parents, and the children didn't either. The family agreed to experiment with this plan for six months. If after six months the children were unhappy, they'd try to figure out a better plan. Tony gave up his nearby apartment and found one near his job. Everyone helped with the move.

Ted—almost nine, and outgoing—liked the new situation right away. The new town was exciting. But Jennie, almost eleven, found the biweekly change of schools difficult. It was hard to make friends, and sometimes her two classes were studying different things. She confessed she was learning a lot, but even after six months, she was not comfortable. Like Tony and Cynthia, though, she rejected the alternatives as even worse.

It's not that the two-week plan was perfect. It certainly was not. But the family's willingness to experiment with unusual situations enabled them to invent, construct, follow, and ultimately grow beyond a useful and temporary solution. They set ground rules, decided what was important to each family member, listed their problems and their alternatives; they gracefully made the most of the very difficult first-year transition.

Tony and Cynthia also resolved one of the most common problems that plague the binuclear family—the conflict between work and children. With two-worker families being the norm today, and a shaky economy, with a woefully inadequate child-care system, parents must heavily compromise in order to meet economic, familial, and personal needs. Today's parents do not have the luxury of giving up one job to find another more convenient in hours or location.

Belle and Jim, and Tony and Cynthia, all maintained the stability of their relationships with their children, and the economic stability of their respective families, in the best way they could, given the limitations of their resources. They were realistic, and through listing their alternatives, came up with temporary plans in time to avert any crises, emotional or economic. In both families, the parents found better, more permanent arrangements later on.

Setting ground rules, listing problems, and weighing alternatives are very complex tasks. But they are necessary steps in forming a limited partnership during the emotional first transitions of divorce.

What needs to be considered? The children's ages and personalities, the family's economic and social resources, each parent's prior relationship with the children, and most importantly the relationship between parents. And then add the individual variables, the intangibles—your own spiritual values, your heritage, your dreams and hopes. Add these, and you can see how impossible it would be to find one set of answers to suit every binuclear family. Some arrangements will work for you and others won't. The identical arrangement could even work for you at one time and not another.

Things change; you'll need to plan for this as well. Your needs, and those of your ex and your children, will change dramatically over the years, as will your resources and your entire system of relationships. You may want to explore a one-year plan; a plan that will stay put until the divorce is finalized; a plan for the years the children live at home. List the variables; set your family's goals.

Clarifying Boundaries

We've already seen how couples need to set new boundaries when they separate. The boundaries must be fine-tuned at each transition in the divorce process. Boundaries—the rules defining who participates and how—are central to how a family functions. When families separate into two households, little can be taken for granted. To reduce the stress and ward off crises, everyone needs to know precisely who's responsible for what and how they're going to do it. These rules tell the children and their parents how the family is going to work. From the daily routines to the big celebrations, all occasions will need clear guidelines. In the binuclear family, you'll need to clarify boundaries on several levels: between the two domains, between the two parents, and between each parent and child.

How permeable are the boundaries between domains? Can one parent have access to the other's house? When Mommy picks up the children at Daddy's house, can they take her to their room to show her their new turtle? When Daddy arrives at Mommy's, can he come in and chat for a while? Can he go to the refrigerator and get a cold drink? Can he sit down and watch a favorite TV show with the children?

What about the boundaries in the relationship between the two parents? Will the parents freely call one another? Will they play together with the children? Will they have regularly scheduled meetings? How about an occasional dinner? Will they attend parent-teacher conferences together?

How separate will their relationships be with the children? How much say does each want the other to have over how time is spent with the children? Who gives the birthday party? Who takes the children to the doctor? Who calls the teacher to talk about a problem in school? These daily responsibilities must be discussed, and control delimited.

It's not that couples don't argue over sharing these responsibilities when they're married. But these arguments are more likely to turn into civil wars among the divorced, who have anger waiting to flare anywhere it can.

These are just a few of the many questions parents need to ask during the process of clarifying boundaries. They may have already covered some of the issues when they set the common ground and listed their problems and options. But now it is time to be as specific and explicit as possible. For most couples it is helpful to write the answers to these questions in a limited partnership agreement as soon as they can during the separation transition.

What if you can't stand talking or even writing to each other? The more couples disagree, the more critical it is to detail their rules in a formal written contract. This may spark quite a bit of temporary unpleasantness, but it will generally maximize the long-term possibilities for a successful postdivorce relationship.

Angry Associates and Fiery Foes will especially benefit from mutually writing a highly specific and explicit limited partnership agreement. However, they'll need professional help: lawyers, mediators, or a family therapist. The more complete and explicit a discussion they can bring to the table, the less they'll have to fight about in front of the lawyers.

When parents are Angry Associates or Fiery Foes, most of their conflicts arise over boundaries. Either the boundaries keep arbitrarily shifting, causing uncertainty and frequent power struggles, or they're too rigidly defined, not allowing for necessary interdependency. In the first case, children bear the brunt of the ambiguity, tiptoeing around, not knowing what's going to spark a blowout between their parents. In the second case, children live compartmentalized lives. Often forced into making choices between parents, they develop painful, damaging conflicts of love and loyalty.

Cooperative Colleagues will also benefit from writing down their agreement, although they won't have to be quite as specific or detailed. Many couples will only want to set down the general principles that will guide their more specific day-to-day discussions. For example, they may put in writing that holidays will be shared equally, whereas

Fiery Foes might have to set down which holidays belong to whom each year. Many Cooperative Colleagues will find it helpful to arrange weekly or monthly meetings, in which they'll plan upcoming occasions, and list the new problems and solutions at hand. Other couples will be able to spontaneously discuss these issues as they arise.

Perfect Pals are usually quite comfortable with informal, even relatively implicit agreements. Ongoing discussions and compromises are common.

In clarifying boundaries, the rule of thumb is: the more open, trusting, and cooperative you and your exspouse are, the less you'll need formal, detailed written agreements; the less cooperative you and your exspouse are, the more you'll need to specify even the tiniest detail of future interaction. Even then, you'll have arguments whenever someone's needs change. No written contract, no matter how complete, can ever include all possible contingencies that come up in the daily life of any family, no matter how ordered.

Boundaries regulate the power and control in the relationship. When parents are Cooperative Colleagues, it is easier for the family to cope with more flexible rules, to have permeable boundaries. However, when there are unresolved conflicts, it is easy to get into serious power struggles, for example, when one partner sets rigid boundaries about issues not mutually agreed upon.

Most couples aren't aware of many of the areas that are implicitly in need of clarification. I was working with a Cooperative Colleague couple recently who had been separated for several months. They had hashed out a complex living arrangement for their three-year-old son: this plan seemed to be working fairly well. One Sunday afternoon when the father returned the son at the scheduled time, the boy gleefully told his mother about going to church that morning and receiving communion. This came as a total shock to the mother, who was Jewish. She hit the roof. She railed at her soon-to-be exhusband, "You have no right!" It turns out that the father had not attended church during the marriage so the issue had never come up. On this particular Sunday, in order to please his parents, the father accompanied them to church, "and, of course," he explained, "I brought my son!"

The boundaries had never been established about which issues deserved a phone call and which issues were solely the decision of the parent during solo time with their son. This particular situation opened up unresolved value differences about religion, which expanded to the child's current day-care center—nondenominational but housed in a synagogue. From that evolved a series of additional conflicts about values. The explicit argument was whether a child needed to have one religion or could be exposed to both. Not so hidden was the issue of power. Who had the right values? Whose values would win? If they decided on exposing the child to both religions, could they do so in a value-free way? Or would each parent try subtly to persuade the child to join his or her own faith?

This kind of unraveling of a partnership agreement is not uncommon and can get explosive. Openness is critical. When parents don't have the skill necessary to come to a mutual decision, it's time to seek the help of a therapist or mediator. Learning good problem-solving methods can save many divorced parents from spiraling into major battles. It is often the case that someone with an objective eye who is knowledgeable about relationships can help the couple resolve specific conflicts. At the same time the couple can be taught skills for handling future differences.

The presence of children means that each domain can't be totally self-sufficient. Yet, certain walls must be nonpermeable to the other partner—brick and stone. Parents may decide that what they do when the children are with them is not open for mutual discussion, that their ex is not welcome beyond the living room in their home, that they never wish to see each other alone. Other boundaries will be semipermeable—window glass and garden space. Parents may decide to mutually handle school-related issues and conferences, to celebrate birthdays together, to interview doctors together. The common ground may include values, family rituals, mutual time. The more semipermeable the boundaries, the more flexible the common ground the parents will share.

Most of my examples thus far are about parents who are striving for equal parenting. Although they often don't divide the child's time equally, they have a stake in the principle of equal rights and shared responsibilities.

The majority of divorced parents, however, have more traditional arrangements. These arrangements give rise to some very common problems in boundaries and power as wives and husbands struggle in their new exspouse roles.

Limited Partnerships in Less Egalitarian Situations

In more traditional marriages, the mother bears primary responsibility for the children. The practical considerations in child rearing lead exspouses of these marriages into the most common postdivorce relationship. In this pattern, the mother keeps the children during the week, and the father has them every other weekend, plus one evening during the week. It is the natural progression from the parental roles the couples adopted when they were married: it recapitulates the pattern established in the marriage.

Almost 25 percent of the families in my study had some variation of this traditional arrangement. In 90 percent of these families, the mother had the primary home and she carried the lion's share of responsibility all through the transitions of divorce as she had in marriage. There were some minor variations: some children spent every other weekend with their father and stayed overnight; others saw their father every Saturday *or* Sunday but rarely stayed overnight. Still others, who lived far away, saw their father only on holidays and for a couple of weeks during the summer. Most parents alternated holidays. In the summer fathers and mothers each took care of the children for some specified amount of time.

The Most Common Struggles

The children in these more traditional, less egalitarian families clearly lived with their mothers and visited their fathers. The only people who were satisfied with this partnership arrangement were a minority of the mothers. Most parents deeply disliked this partnership arrangement. Fathers expressed pain, anger, and remorse about their limited role in their children's lives. Mothers felt flooded with responsibility and angry that their exhusbands were not carrying a fair share.

Power and control conflicts are almost inevitable in these more traditionally based partnerships. Commonly, the primary parent (usually the mother), the one who tells the kids what to do each day, wants more say about the kids than the exspouse. The other parent (usually the father) feels like a visitor in his children's lives, always dependent on the goodwill of his exwife. As the parent with less direct influence, he feels powerless—controlled by his exwife who he feels is setting all the rules. Usually the father, who's likely to earn more money, tries to use money to equalize the power imbalance. And then pandemonium breaks loose.

Many of these more traditional families end up as Angry Associates or Fiery Foes simply because they cannot explicitly resolve the power issues. The exspouses drive each other crazy with guerrilla tactics. Fathers may temporarily withhold spousal or child support. They may refuse to pay for things they didn't mandate: "You want Mara to go to private school? Then you pay for it!" They may take a sick child to a second doctor for consultation because they didn't choose the first. Each exspouse then complains about the other's manipulative attempts to wrest control. Although these scenes do not need to play themselves out in this manner, they usually do. Control struggles seem to be inherent in arrangements in which one partner controls the purse strings and the other the children.

When you've come from this type of marriage, you must be very aware of these issues. In my study, some Cooperative Colleague and Angry Associate parents did manage to reduce the effects of their power struggle. These are the limits they set:

Both parents explicitly agreed that the children must not get caught in the middle of their struggle.

Both parents acknowledged their differences in power.

Both parents agreed they would not attempt to control each other. They made a firm contract: neither money nor the children would be withdrawn from the other partner, even during struggles for control. In other words, they put their mutual commitment to the family first.

These limits have to be set whether you and your ex have always been cooperative, or whether you are trying to go from an angry relationship to a cooperative one.

Betty and Sam, a couple I worked with recently, found themselves embroiled in a war when Betty wanted to send Stacey, their twelve-year-old, to a private school. All their dormant power issues erupted. "She needs the smaller classes and individual attention!" Betty said indignantly. "Don't you want her to go where it's best for her?"

"It's horribly extravagant," answered Sam. "It's easy for you to spend my money, isn't it?" Their parenting agreement stated that Sam had to pay for school, but they hadn't worked out the details. "Besides, she's doing fine in public school."

"You don't know her as well as I do," asserted Betty. Sam hit the roof.

After two weeks of pitched battle, which was threatening to end in a lawsuit, I suggested to Betty and Sam that they make this a third-party decision by consulting Stacey's teacher. They had a conference in which the teacher sat them down and told them what she'd previously hinted to Betty—that Stacey needed more individual attention. Sam and Betty looked at Stacey's work; the justice of the teacher's comment was obvious. The teacher highly recommended two small private schools in the area; following the conference, the parents visited the schools together. The mutual decision to send Stacey to private school came relatively quickly.

Consulting a knowledgeable third party worked well for Betty and Sam because it instantly defused the struggle over power. The issue now became Stacey's welfare. Once they'd spoken to the teacher, both parents could make a cooperative decision to do what was in Stacey's best interests.

Unlike Betty and Sam, most of the Angry Associates and Fiery Foes in my study stayed mired in their warfare. They couldn't step back from the conflict, not for a second. Talking the issues through, or bringing them to a third party, they saw as threats to their pride. These parents felt bad about the stress they were creating for their children, but they also felt it was their exspouse's problem and not theirs. Fathers blamed their exwives for pushing them out of the family. Mothers blamed their exhusbands for not caring. Trying to sort out how this all got started invariably revealed a complex battle strategy on both sides, with escalating attacks and counterattacks. There were always maneuvers aimed at sapping the enemy's will—maneuvers so subtle that even the players had become unaware.

Tanya and Bernie, an Angry Associate pair from my study, are a case in point. Their issue—Tanya wanted their twelve-year-old son Teddy to go to tennis camp—was very similar to Betty and Sam's fight over Stacey. But the resolution was quite different.

Tanya told Teddy to go ask his father to give him, for his birthday, the huge price of a stay at tennis camp. She left a message on Bernie's phone machine that this was the only present Teddy wanted. Bernie called back incensed. When Teddy answered the phone, his dad shouted at him: "She put you up to this. It's blackmail." Teddy—caught in the middle—said, "Dad, it's my own decision." Bernie hung up the phone and sent him a bike.

Teddy had wanted a bike, and wanted peace even more, so he sent his father an enthusiastic thank-you note. But Tanya was furious. The issue of tennis camp remained unresolved. A month before camp started, Teddy still didn't know if he was going; his tension by now was affecting his schoolwork. So Tanya sent in the deposit and told the camp to bill Bernie for the rest. Bernie, furious, paid half and sent the rest of the bill to Tanya.

On the first day of camp, the other kids and parents witnessed an ugly scene. The director would not allow Teddy in until Tanya paid the balance. Teddy cried and begged his mom either to pay or let him go home. The campers gave Teddy a nickname: Crybaby. Camp was not fun for Teddy.

Gender Perceptions

In his first interview, Bernie tearfully explained how hard it was to stay involved. "Every time I call, Ted's too busy to talk. He's reading, he's showering, he's watching TV." Other fathers in my study said the same thing. "Why does she set up so many barriers? I've called back three times just to say hello!" Fathers spoke about their pain when their children didn't acknowledge a holiday or birthday. One father—who'd made enormous sacrifices for his children—broke down and sobbed. "My kids didn't even call to wish me Happy Father's Day. It's like they want to wipe me out of their existence. She could have reminded them. She could have helped them buy a card."

What did the mothers say about the fathers? "He always calls just before bedtime. It's hard enough getting the kids calmed down, and it never fails—just as I have them ready for bed, he calls and disrupts everything. I keep telling him to call earlier but he says he's in meetings until 7 P.M., working to pay the support check." Other mothers say that denying the father is the children's choice. "He manages to call when the kids are in the middle of their favorite TV show, or playing with a friend. I say, 'Your dad's on the phone,' and they grump and groan. What am I going to do—force them to talk with him?"

Delia Ephron, in *Funny Sauce,* her book of short pieces about binuclear families, depicts this typical scene in a poem she calls "Phone Calls."

> "Hi, Daddy, it's Josh."
> "Hi. What's happening?"
> "Mom bought me a new pair of sneakers."
> "Hey, that's great. What color?"
> "I don't want to! I don't want to! I'm talking to my dad! . . .
> Dad, Mom says I have to clean up my room now. Hold on."

"Hold on? I can't hold on while you clean up your room.
That's ridiculous. . . .

"Josh? Are you there? Josh, pick up the phone. Josh?"

"Hi, it's me. Can I speak to Josh?"

"He's eating dinner right now."

"Okay, I'll call back later."

"Hi. Can I speak to Josh now?"

"He's going to sleep."

"Just put him on for a second, okay?"

"This is not a good time."

"I just want to say good night to my son."

"If he talks to you, he'll get all excited."

"So what?"

"So then I'm stuck with a hyped-up kid who can't fall asleep."

"Just tell him I called."

The media and concerned citizens moan and groan about the declining involvement of many divorced fathers over time. Usually they focus on the lack of regular financial support—"deadbeat dads" and "absentee fathers." "These dads are irresponsible," goes the argument, "and they need to be coerced." Certainly in some cases, this is true. But it is also true, as many fathers noted, that the process of withdrawal from their children's lives was painful and came about only after considerable distress, and then only as a last and desperate choice.

From these fathers came the excruciating litany: "She's withheld my visitation." "She's dangled me on the phone for hours." "She's picked fights with me in front of the children." "She left me out of Christmas." "When our baby walked for the first time, my wife didn't even tell me."

These fathers said that after years of struggling against the odds to make their relationship with their children work, they finally—for their own health—gave up. "It was just too painful. I had a serious heart attack. I decided, better a healthy dad who's able to pay the bills, than a dad who died at the ripe old age of forty-seven. She probably wouldn't even have let the kids attend my funeral." "I decided not to bother. My kids hate me now, anyway." In the most extreme cases, fathers document what psychiatrist and author Richard Gardner calls a "parentectomy"—a negative brainwashing of the children by one parent against another.

Mothers in my study, on the other hand, claimed that the fathers were totally at fault. "The kids were all packed and waiting. He didn't show up." "Jim didn't bring our daughter, Robin, home at three as we'd arranged. I'm sitting there biting my nails and it's four, five, six. At seven-thirty he waltzes in without even apologizing. Meanwhile I'm sitting there all that time worrying that they're dead."

"My husband Jonathan—he's a jerk—just lets our son Brian play in the street! He's just five years old! And Jonathan's bringing home girlfriend after girlfriend. Brian's out there alone. A car could hit him while Jonathan's concentrating on having his fun."

These mothers tell of exspouses who were not only unreliable parents, but who sent their support checks late, made only partial payments, or didn't pay their court-ordered support at all. These mothers felt they did everything possible to keep their exspouses involved, and it was only after they'd tried everything that they finally gave up.

This vicious cycle of blaming and fault-finding, common to Angry Associates and Fiery Foes, has devastating effects on children. It doesn't really matter who's to blame. Even these families can form healthy limited partnerships. But the parents must get help and make some enormous changes.

Sam and Betty, who argued over daughter Stacey's schooling earlier in the chapter, did two good things: they consulted a third party about the issue, and they did research. Sam stuck to his guns and stayed involved, even though doing so temporarily involved a loss of pride.

Bernie and Tanya, who fought about Teddy's tennis camp, could have been saved from war by consulting a third party. Bernie's idea of paying half could have been the beginning of a compromise. Tanya's idea of sending Teddy to camp over Bernie's objections could also have been the beginning of putting Teddy first. Instead, she tried to manipulate the situation through Teddy, which only escalated Bernie's anger. If they'd consulted a third party together, these parents could have seen the vicious cycle that had entirely swept them up. They could have listed mutual problems at hand, and come up with mutual solutions.

How Gender Affects Perception in These Relationships

So how involved are fathers after divorce—really? It depends on whom you ask. There are clear gender differences. Mothers say their exhusbands are less involved—see their children less and take less responsibility—than their exhusbands say they are. Fathers report that they visit consistently and frequently. They also say they're more personally involved. This was a consistent finding in both the Binuclear Family Study and the 1981 Cross-National Study (see Introduction), as well as in other studies conducted in the United States. Many of the large surveys are based on mothers' reports only, and may underestimate the actual time fathers spend with their children, at least according to what fathers themselves report.

Interpreting these differences is difficult. Are mothers underreporting, or are fathers overreporting? Certainly, in most families, mothers and fathers use different yardsticks to measure parenting responsibilities. When a custodial mother compares her exhusband's responsibility to her own, it is bound to be dramatically less. For many fathers, however, having total responsibility for their children's care even two Saturdays a month may be more than they did during the entire marriage.

What Helps Fathers Stay Involved?

A second important question is: What helps fathers to remain involved with their children after divorce? In the Binuclear Family Study, our first interview data (one year after the legal divorce) clearly showed that the kind of relationship mothers and fathers had with each other impacted the father's relationship with his children. When the relationship between the parents was unsupportive and conflictual, fathers were less involved, whereas a cooperative relationship facilitated continued involvement. However, our third interview data (five years postdivorce) showed that whether fathers continued to be involved with their children was no longer correlated with how they related to their former wives. During the time between the second and third interviews (three and five years postdivorce), there was little change in how involved fathers were. This was true for fathers who saw their children often, as well as for fathers who saw them infrequently. In other words, fathers' involvement with their children gets established in the first year or two after the divorce, then stabilizes thereafter.

What this finding underscores is the importance of the first years after divorce for setting the tone of the interparental relationships. Ground rules must be set early in the divorce process. How conflicts are resolved will impact the father's relationship with his child, a crucial factor in a child's adjustment to the divorce.

Based on the findings from the study, a picture of the "most involved father" might look like this: He is a joint custody parent who is satisfied with the custody decision. He is likely to be single, as is his former spouse, and has more than the average years of education. He keeps frequent contact with the exwife, and they are supportive of each other's relationship to their child. Although the relationship is not free of conflict, neither parent allows the conflict to interfere with parenting. The father feels satisfied with his relationship to his child and to his exwife, and he feels like a contributing parent rather than like a visitor in the child's life.

Also revealed in the study was that child support and a father's emotional involvement are related. Fathers who stay in touch are more likely to continue to pay what they've promised. The issue then is, given that unequal divorced parenting arrangements are common and particularly fraught with power issues, how can fathers remain involved with children?

How Can These Partners Establish Limited Partnerships That Encourage Maximal Parenting?

First, there has to be some degree of cooperation and communication between parents, no matter how odious this contact is for them. The distaste each feels can be minimized if the limited partnership includes the following rules:

The child comes first.

The child has a right to two parents. No parent will be totally kept away from the child by the other parent, except in clear cases of abuse in which contact has been limited by the court. No parent will denigrate the other parent to the child, or triangulate exspousal conflict through the child.

Interaction will be minimal and centered around the child.

Boundaries will be clearly specified.

The common ground will be limited to what is absolutely agreed to be necessary by both parties.

These rules won't make for a good divorce, but they will certainly improve a disastrous one.

A couple, recently referred to me by their lawyers, arrived in my office unable to exchange a civil word with one another. Married for eleven years, parents of two sons, each blamed the other for the escalating holocaust of the past year. They had a temporary joint-custody agreement. The boys spent the weekdays with their mom, the weekends with their dad.

The mother complained: "He doesn't know the first thing about discipline. He lets them run wild. He insists upon taking them to movies they are too young to see. They spend hours at the video arcade, then go to McDonald's. His girlfriend comes over, and he puts on a video for them and forgets about them." She added tearfully, "I'm really scared they'll hurt themselves—and he won't even know it."

The father's response was, "She's overreacting. She never gives me any credit. She's controlling, overprotective, and rigid. When I come to pick up the boys, she gives me a list a mile long about the things I should do with them. I don't mind taking them for haircuts, or to play soccer, but I don't need to be told what they need to eat, what time they need to be in bed, what they like and don't like. I think I know my boys well enough to make these decisions myself. She doesn't need to call five times a day to check up on them."

During this first session it was clear to me that these parents were too caught up in their own angry power struggle to see what was best for their sons. My initial attempts to discuss child-rearing values so that they could establish some mutual ground only ended up fueling the old marital battles. When I met with their sons—ages eight and ten—the picture became even clearer. Each parent bad-mouthed the other; each parent grilled the boys about what they did and said when they were with the other parent; each parent presented himself or herself to the boys as the better parent.

It took half a dozen meetings with the parents, both individually and together, to come up with ground rules and with a mutually agreed-upon list of parenting decisions, such as bedtimes, appropriate play activities, and how much TV time. I then compiled the list for them, finding suitable compromises, interjecting my own views on age-appropriate issues. Once we committed the final list to paper, I asked them each to sign the parenting agreement. They had to agree not to further discuss the agreement—not to interact very much at all with one another.

The plan was a rigid one: in addition to the rules about parenting, exact times were specified for picking up and returning the boys, for each parent to call, for the boys to call the other parent. We hadn't found the ideal solution by a long shot, but by reducing negotiations, they could better control their conflict. By clarifying the boundaries and clearly defining the separate domains, by keeping the common ground very minimal, we reduced the children's exposure to their parents' cross fire.

Angry Associate and Fiery Foe couples can benefit by setting up nonnegotiable rules with a third party. The agreement will allow each of these parents to move on. Although rigid rules have one big downside—they don't respond to change—setting up and keeping a rigid partnership agreement is far healthier for these families than is using the children as conduits for their parents' rage. Although this form of "parallel" parenting is clearly not as desirable as a cooperative coparenting partnership, at least the children will have some relief from the parents' constant battles.

Some Special Considerations

What about the children? Can the parents' partnership agreement help them to adjust?

A critical situation in any binuclear family is the time when children have to move from one parent's house to the other's. No matter how often—or how seldom—the children make this transition, it is a difficult time for both children and adults. Children must shift gears when they say goodbye to one parent, one home, one way of life; and they must reintegrate themselves into the other parent's life. The partnership agreement can help parents to ease the children's crossings—but only a little. Most of the work is emotional, and it has to be done at each and every crossing.

Easing the Crossings

No matter how cooperative parents are, children have to make adjustments as they cross from one parent—and one home—to the other. Some children do this rather smoothly, whereas others have a hard time.

These transitions are hard on the parents too. Each crossing stimulates feelings of loss. When Janie leaves her dad's house to go back to her mom's, she's already preparing herself to miss Dad. Not only will she miss Dad but she'll also miss the things that he'll do without her when she's gone. He may go to the movies, or watch special TV programs, or buy special foods that she likes. Dad initially mourns the loss of Janie. Even though he may feel relieved to be free from child care, he'll miss their routines and their special times. He'll also miss being a part of her daily life during the time she's at her mom's.

It's not unusual for children to be angry or clingy or distant for a few hours, or even a day, before they adjust. Janet and Sybil, Patricia and Joseph's children (one of the four families with whom I began this chapter), reacted very differently. On the days they changed homes, Janet, the younger child, regressed. She sucked her thumb more, became whiny, clung to her mother. Sybil acted very differently. She'd start to let go even before she left. She'd be more independent and somewhat ornery.

Parents often unknowingly transmit their feelings of insecurity to the children, adding to the stress. Perhaps they're feeling jealous, or competitive, or angry with the other parent. Maybe Dad is regretful that he didn't spend more time with the children during their stay.

Parents can ease the crossings. Standard routines help. How about including the other parent in discussions about family and daily life? Rituals help too. Tony and Cynthia (the two-week-with, two-week-without parents) each had a special way that they spent the night prior to the children's switching homes. Tony liked to stay home with the kids, make their favorite spaghetti dinner, and watch their favorite Friday night TV programs with them. Cynthia usually took them out for dinner and a movie. On Saturday morning, the parent with the children drove them to the other parent's house. Because Tony and Cynthia had a cooperative relationship, they all had brunch together. In this way the children eased into the crossing and the parent whom they left didn't feel immediately empty. Cynthia knew she'd feel acute pain on Saturdays, so she always visited friends when she returned home from Tony's house.

Patricia and Joseph (the split-week parents) tried to ease the transitions for Janet and Sybil by using their color-coded calendars. The children kept track of the days on the calendar. They checked off things they'd done that week and, with their parents' help, listed activities that they were planning to do when they returned. That helped them have a feeling of continuity. They also noted special things they did at the other parent's house as a way to include both parents. Because Janet was having difficulty letting go, they established a nice ritual in which she'd say goodbye to each of her special toys, telling them that she'd be back in a few days. Each time she chose two of her toys—which changed according to her mood—to take with her to the other parent's house.

Children need reassurance. They are very sensitive; if they think a parent is going to be upset and lonely when they leave, departure will be all the more difficult for them. This is true for any family—not just for a family of divorce.

cathy®   **by Cathy Guisewite**

CATHY Copyright Cathy Guisewite. Reprinted with permission of Universal Press Syndicate. All rights reserved.

Recently I worked with a family in which the seven-year-old son refused to sleep at his father's house. When I saw the whole family together in session the boy silently sat holding his mother's hand. When either I or the parents directed a question toward the boy, he shrugged, said "I don't know," and turned to his older brother—who quickly jumped in to rescue him. So I saw the child alone. He spent most of the session crying and finally blurted out, "She'll kill herself if I leave her alone." I asked him how he knew that. "She cries a lot at night. I sometimes hear her and cuddle up next to her. Sometimes, I even make her laugh. She says she doesn't know what she would do without me."

Children can handle the transitions only as well as the parents can. When a child shows real difficulty when it's time to move, parents need to look at their own behavior, at the subtle messages they may be giving. It's important not to overdramatize the leavings. Making them a normal part of your family life will help the children do so too.

Parents need to recognize how their children individually cope with the changes. If your children need to be distant for a few hours, give them space. If your daughter is angry when she arrives, give her the opportunity to express it, and depending on her age, help her to understand what she's feeling. If your son is clingy when he leaves, hug him, and talk about some of the things you'll do together when he returns.

Limited Partnerships in Families with Older Children

We've spoken a great deal about creating limited partnerships when there are young or adolescent children. But what about the divorces of parents with older children? How do the children of such divorces generally fare? Do older and adult children create any special considerations for the parents in setting up and maintaining the limited partnership?

In 1985, several of my students and I examined how young adult children (ages nineteen to twenty-four) reacted to recent (less than two years) parental divorces—midlife divorces that had occurred after long marriages. In particular, I wanted to know whether the children's reactions might differ depending on the type of exspouse relationship their parents had.

Although at the time there had been some studies on adult children's reactions, these had focused on divorces that occurred when the children were considerably younger. It was clear from the void in the literature that society generally assumed that once children reached age eighteen, they weren't seriously threatened by their parents' divorce.

What we found surprised us. The thirty young adults we interviewed had a wide range of responses to their parents' divorce. Some felt relieved. Others felt abandoned. Still others felt overwhelmed and depressed. Some had good relationships with both parents; others were angry with one parent; still others were angry with both parents. Some experienced little disruption in their lives, whereas others had to drop out of school because of financial loss. Still others told us they took time off to help a very distressed parent recover from the divorce.

Although we didn't interview the parents themselves in this study, we asked the young adults to categorize their parents' relationship in one of the five typologies. This was easier for them to do than we'd anticipated. With only three or four sentences briefly describing the type, the participants quickly and knowingly classified their parents. Then we analyzed the interviews, looking for differences based on the designated category.

Interestingly, the groups split in about the same percentages as we found in the Binuclear Family Study. About 40 percent said their parents were Cooperative Colleagues; fewer than 10 percent said Perfect Pals; the remaining 50 percent divided equally between Angry Associates and Fiery Foes. In a similar concurrence, 65 percent said their mother had made the decision to divorce.

One major issue emerged as particularly distressing: 55 percent noted that their parents' divorces were related to extramarital affairs. Of these, almost three-quarters said their parents were either Angry Associates or Fiery Foes, and they also noted it was their fathers who'd had the affairs. In most of these situations, the young adult children remained angry with their fathers and more emotionally close with their mothers.

Although the sample was too small to draw any definitive conclusions, it was surprising to find out how much these young adults perceived. The ones that felt relief, even if they categorized their parents as Angry Associates or Fiery Foes, were those who described their parents' marriages as "bitter, angry, always fighting, cold and empty."

The divorcing parents of young adults might wish to pay special attention to holiday arrangements. Every participant in the young adult study told us that some of their biggest losses were felt around the holidays. "I feel like a mobile Santa Claus now. I'm at Mom's in the morning, Grandma's in the afternoon, and Dad's for dinner." Another participant said, "We always used to take a big ski trip together. Now it's so darn quiet and somber. Dad's off with his girlfriend, and the rest of us are mourning with Mom."

Another special consideration is that older children are likely to feel their parents' loyalty conflicts even more than do younger children. They are going through a stage of life in which they're making the first hesitant stabs at forming their own future families—dating, falling in love, even getting engaged, marrying, or having children of their own. While they may feel important when one parent or the other draws them into a triangulated argument, this will be very damaging for the young adult. Parents of older children must consider what general messages they are sending about marriage, family, and home.

Although those whose parents had more amicable relationships didn't feel torn between parents, most of the adult children in my study still talked about the acute losses they felt in family, the instability, the reduction in financial resources. When constructing the limited partnership—if they can do this without triangulating their problems through the children—parents of young adults may wish to ask the children for their ideas. They must set clear limits, and children and parents must all understand that the final partnership agreement is the parents' responsibility, not the children's. But by asking for and including some of their children's ideas in a cooperative limited partnership, the parents may reassure their children that they will gain from the divorce, as well as learn how to cope with their loss.

The Limited Partnership Over Time: Changing the Contract

Almost as soon as you've set down your partnership agreement, and at many points along the line, your circumstances and those of your exspouse are bound to change. Children grow up, parents change jobs and residences, exspouses repartner and remarry. Your partnership agreement must change, too, to suit the new needs of your family.

The cooperative relationship is what makes the good divorce, not any one agreement, not any one condition. It's not equal time, or equal money, or any other rigid criterion that will help you to know when to change your agreement and how to change it. It's sticking to the same process you've already learned. If the partners could negotiate and resolve earlier differences, they'll have learned useful strategies for adapting their limited partnership. If not, here's another opportunity to learn those skills.

Remember the steps in constructing a partnership agreement? First came agreeing on the common ground and setting the ground rules. Then came listing the problems and possible solutions—making the implicit wishes of both partners into explicit compromises. It's rare that the common ground will have to be entirely renegotiated. More commonly, you'll have to list the new problems and come up with a new set of possible solutions.

There's a whole range of limited partnership possibilities, tailored to individual situations. In some of these relationships it works to share a holiday; in others it doesn't. When the child is ill, maybe you'll be able to depend on your ex; maybe you won't. The more able you and your ex are to cooperate, the more flexible your contract can be, and the easier it will be to work out the logistics.

Angry Associates and Fiery Foes are rarely able to adapt well to changes—even such minor changes as the child getting sick when it's time to return to the other parent. Since they've had to specify even the tiniest detail in their parenting agreement, any change will seem far more complex and threatening than it would to Cooperative Colleagues, who merely set out general principles.

In Angry Associate and Fiery Foe families, it will usually work best for the exspouses to parent separately rather than jointly. They will probably carefully alternate or divide holidays. If both parents want to attend parent-teacher conferences, they'll probably contact the teacher separately so that they can make arrangements directly— not through the other parent. When a child's illness requires a change in visiting plans, it will probably be better to postpone the visit rather than have one parent show up at the other's home.

Major adaptations, of course, cannot be done entirely separately. The parents will have to painfully rewrite the rules. Suppose one parent in an Angry Associate family wishes to move to another state; an entirely new agreement may have to be drafted.

Cooperative Colleague families are far more flexible about change. The four families I introduced in the beginning of the chapter are a case in point. Over the years, they maintained good relationships with their children; the parents continued to be good limited partners in an equal, mature relationship.

Adapting to Change

Over time, the kinds of partnerships these four families developed influenced the living arrangements, and in turn the living arrangements changed the partnerships. Changes in living arrangements were prompted by developmental transformation in the family. The changes were never easy. They required shifts in the family's equilibrium, which then created new conflicts. Negotiating adaptations—as in structuring the initial limited partnership—required compromise, trade-offs, losses and disappointments, as well as gains and welcome changes.

Sally and Dave (the weekend mom and weekday dad) separated when their sons were ten and twelve. At first, the boys spent weekdays with Dave and weekends with Sally. But Sally and Dave's younger son, Craig, missed seeing each parent more frequently. The partners renegotiated: in the next phase they split each week between the two households. When they reevaluated this new arrangement six months later, both partners agreed it felt too fragmented. They then decided to try alternate weeks.

Then Sally got a long-awaited promotion. She had to travel frequently, which would take her away from home several nights during the week. She hired someone to care for the boys in her absence.

In response to Sally's new schedule, Dave proposed that they return to their original plan of several years earlier: The boys lived with him during the week and with Sally on weekends. Sally revisited her earlier fears. She felt threatened. Would the boys, now thirteen and fifteen, become more attached to Dave than to her? Would Dave become the primary parent? What would her friends and family think?

Dave and Sally talked over these fears. They agreed that when Sally was in town she could have a spontaneous evening with the boys; whenever she was available, they'd include her in their school activities. Dave requested that he have a weekend day with one or both boys when special occasions arose. The limited partners now negotiated a time frame. This plan would not be permanent. If Sally's work schedule changed, they would review the plan.

Sally felt less guilty about her travel now because even though the boys were with Dave, they'd remained extremely close with her. Dave enjoyed having most weekends free. The boys liked the stability of their school week. On weekends, although they spent a lot of time with their friends, they also had more opportunity to be with Sally. They also liked the independence of being able to bike between both their homes. Their parents encouraged this freedom, and developed a system so that they knew where each child was at all times.

Sally and Dave could flexibly negotiate changes because they had a cooperative relationship. They certainly had disagreements, and they didn't spend time together as friends, but they were able comfortably to have an occasional dinner together. They had a basic trust and respect for each other when it came to their sons.

Patricia and Joseph (the split-week family) did not adapt to change as easily. This couple had separated when their children, Janet and Sybil, were three and six. At first, Patricia and Joseph had been Angry Associates. Each fought to be the primary parent. In those initial stages Patricia and Joseph were unable to negotiate directly with one another. With a lawyer they'd reached a temporary separation agreement: the children lived with Patricia during the week and spent Friday through Sunday noon with Joseph, as well as one weeknight for dinner.

Feeling left out of his children's daily life, Joseph asked Patricia to consider another arrangement, one that allowed him more time. Patricia refused. They continued this tug of war for a while, until they found themselves exhaustedly agreeing to seek help. After several sessions with a family mediator, Patricia realized that Joseph sincerely wanted to be with their daughters more. It wasn't a power play, nor did he want to take anything away from her. He just wanted to be more active in his young daughters' lives. Though Patricia resented that he wanted to be with them more now than when they were married, Joseph could respond that he regretted his former distance. Talking about unresolved feelings about their married parenting relationship helped to diffuse the present anger. Patricia and Joseph were then able to decide on a different arrangement—flexibly sharing the week.

Some fathers spend more time with their children after divorce than they did when they were married. Some report that the divorce made them realize their kids' importance to them; others note that having an independent relationship with the children is now less tense and more enjoyable; still others say that spending one whole day with the kids is more than they did when they were married.

Other fathers decrease time spent with their children over the years. This may be due to one or the other parent's remarriage, or a residential move by one parent, or by a child's choice. Older children sometimes choose to spend less time with a nonresidential parent because it interferes with their increased peer activities.

Limited Partnerships Mean Expanded Opportunities

A good divorce does not require that parents share child-care responsibilities equally. It means that they share them clearly. Whatever living arrangements and division of responsibilities parents decide upon, they cooperate within those limits.

Relationships between men and women, and parents and children, are in a great state of flux right now. Gender issues, the virtues—and failings—of the traditional family, even the idea of equality, are all in question. But although the discussions and debates have increased, little change is showing up as yet in the data.

There's always a lag between the time social science research empirically documents family changes and the time families actually begin to make subtle changes. The four families described in this chapter may be pioneers today, but tomorrow they will be seen as just regular folks. By then all of these partnerships and contracts and strange new models will have become much less strange to your family and to all families, as more and more exspouses strive to be equally involved and responsible parents.

Your family is the laboratory for society. When you set the common ground with your exspouse, you tell society—better than any theoretician—what two exspouses can expect from each other. When you agree on your ground rules, you tell society the rules for a real partnership, instead of desperately and vainly wishing that you had an ideal partnership.

When you and your exspouse decide to put your children first, and to make your fight with each other second, you are supporting families and not destroying them. When you and your exspouse list your problems and come up with possible and realistic solutions, you—like the four families in this chapter—are gracefully making the most of your situation, and maximizing your entire family's chances of structuring a successful life postdivorce.

Even when your discussions break down, when you and your exspouse must seek out a third party and research your point of view, you are showing a family in growth rather than a family in dissolution.

I firmly believe that your legal divorce—the part that is likely to be settled by lawyers—should come after your limited partnership agreement, not before. Once established, the kind of limited partnership that works best for both the children and the parents will lay the foundation to make the legal divorce support that vision—not the other way around. By setting up and following family rules for negotiation and compromise, you and your exspouse spend less money on lawyers, while demanding and receiving your emotional and financial due. Your children and you can only benefit from this process.

6

The Formal Divorce
MAKING IT LEGAL

GOING FROM MARRIAGE to divorce is like hiking up an unmarked trail in earthquake country. Toiling along, you come to a fork in the road. You're alone, there are no trail markers, and you have neither a map nor a compass. Suddenly you feel the earth rumble beneath you. All your fears of the big earthquake surface. You don't know which path to choose. They all seem treacherous. It's getting dark, and you blindly make a choice. The new path winds up and down, back and forth. You anguish over whether you're going to make it. You wish you'd thought ahead. And then the big one hits.

The physical separation is "the big one" in divorce. When you and your spouse part, your life crumbles. The legal divorce that follows can feel like a long series of aftershocks, those smaller earth rumblings that continue to shake you to the core.

Since the first moment of the first transition, you've been navigating a wilderness of potential crisis. And each fork in the road has not merely been a passive marker point. It's also been an active *choice point*—an opportunity to map, control, and even change your own best route to your own and your family's long-term survival.

One of the most important sets of choice points is the *legal divorce*. This is a group of actions and documents in which you and your ex encode the compromises of your limited partnership into a variety of legally binding agreements—*custody, spousal support, community property,* and *child support.* In this chapter, we will discuss all of these.

On the surface, the legal divorce may seem fairly cut and dry. Be-

165

neath, though, it's as emotional as anything you've ever faced. Everything tangible becomes loaded with emotional significance grounded in the pain of separation. Your choices may seem rife with the possibility of escalating anger, long-term pain, psychological damage for your children, and new handicaps at a time when you most wish you could start from scratch. But if you handle the choice points of the legal divorce wisely, you can minimize the negative impacts on you, your ex, your children, your friends, and your extended families. You can let go and move on.

What Goes into the Legal Agreements?

As a married couple, you and your partner made many intimate negotiations. Once resolved through constructive argument, the creation of a new habit, or postponement, these may have been practically forgotten. Decisions on such issues as child care, investments, your home, your pension plan, and your children's schooling became incorporated. You probably never gave a second thought to what all these decisions—even the ones you avoided—might mean if you ever divorced. It may be a major shock to learn that they all factor into the legal package.

Who was more responsible for the children during marriage? Your ex and you will disagree, perhaps, in your answers; both answers will probably factor into your custody arrangement. Who earned more? Did one of you lessen your income by dropping out of the labor market to take care of children? Did one partner send the other through school on the promise of future income? This type of question will figure into your spousal support package. The summer cottage that one of you wanted and both of you got will become part of the community property settlement; the standard of living both of you established for your family will become the common denominator of the child support award.

Each legal package sets up a complex choice point—a series of small markers and decisions that adds up to a large set of binding conditions with which you'll have to live. The overwhelming weight of so many shocks all at once is traumatic. The legal divorce is, after all, a totally new, unwelcome, and extraordinarily complicated experience for most people. The jargon alone may drive you up the wall. The constant, mysterious, threatening demands may tempt you to throw up your hands and get a lawyer to take over.

Don't. Consult with a lawyer if you feel the need to, but do not give him or her decision-making power over your important and far-reaching family issues.

Taking Charge

One of the major problems with today's approach to divorce is that what is essentially a family situation—a problem of kinship, emotional bonds, and intimate habits—ends up being settled by legal means. In fact, one of the big goals of this book is to return control of the divorce to the family. It's true that marriage is a legal contract, among other things, and that to break that contract requires a legal procedure. But why does breaking the contract take so much more time, money, and emotion than did making the original contract?

One answer is that it's because our marital contracts are unwritten, ambiguous, and undefined, growing over years into a patchwork of implicit agreements. Marriage is a contract based on romantic attachment, and unlike entering a business partnership, the rules for ending the contract are not spelled out in advance. It's only when we want to break that contract that we realize even unwritten agreements are in fact real contracts with legal implications. The spouses must divide the spoils of marriage; the kingdoms must be dismantled. The divorce contract is explicit and it usually comes fairly early in the process.

Another answer is that the legal system has a stake in keeping the business of divorce in its own hands. Today, divorce is big business.

Although divorce, like marriage, requires a legal document, the legal process should not define the nature of the divorce any more than the legal marriage defines the nature of the marriage. How children will continue to be provided for and nurtured is a parental decision, not a decision to be made by the state. How the mutually accumulated property—endowed with memories, good and bad—is divided should be decided by the expartners, not turned over to legal experts. Because divorce is not yet normalized in our society, with no clear rules, rituals, and positive role models, we face a highly ambiguous process. We turn to lawyers to provide an external formula that will resolve the ambiguity and bring retribution for the hurt and pain.

Reducing Anxiety

It's understandable that after the physical separation you might want someone to rescue you. You may feel powerless, incompetent to manage daily life, angry, lonely, and scared. Even if you think you've handled the first three transitions well, you're still likely mourning your marriage, and painfully aware of the giant decisions ahead. Well-meaning friends and family are probably warning you to protect your interests, to get what you can, to sock it to your ex to balance all your suffering, all your worry. But a lawyer cannot rescue you from these unwelcome circumstances.

In life we face many situations that profoundly shake us. It's normal at first to feel out of control, to reflexively seek security. But during these times we tend to get tunnel vision. We narrow our perception and focus on one magic answer—not what we'd select if we had our full, conscious range of vision. After the shakeup of physical separation, we may think our magic answer is the lawyer. It isn't. The answer is to widen our perception again and to once again set ground rules and list all our options, because we are now facing yet another transition. Lawyers can be helpful at this time by providing basic information and a road map through the legal system.

A way to effectively deal with the legal divorce—a way to deal with any such complicated set of choice points—is to break the process down into smaller, more manageable pieces. Listing your ideas about custody, for example, is not as overwhelming as trying to list everything at once about the entire upcoming legal agreement. Listing what you want to happen today, a week from now, a month from now, is not as overwhelming as trying to list goals for your entire life postdivorce. Once you understand the smaller elements, and handle each one separately, the whole process may begin to seem like a life-affirming challenge rather than a life-threatening one.

You need to find your own answers to the following questions:

When should I see a lawyer?

What's my primary goal for now—is it to educate myself about my rights, to protect myself from my exspouse, to get immediate financial support, to get revenge? Are my long-term goals the same, or different?

What do I want to accomplish with the lawyer? What are the areas in which my exspouse and I have mutual interests and compatibility? And what can be left outside the litigation, and dealt with simply by myself and my exspouse as part of our limited partnership agreement?

Timing Is Key

What if it's just after the physical separation and it seems you have to make a zillion overwhelming decisions all at once? What if you're obsessing: "Who gets the car, the house? The money? Who gets the kids?" What if your ex demands that you try to solve everything all at once?

Don't rush into legal divorce. In the last chapter we saw many couples who were able to set up temporary practical agreements that tided them over until they could think rationally about more permanent limited partnerships. For some couples, their divorce process ends at the physical separation—they find themselves trying marriage again.

Try not to move forward into legal matters in the midst of your greatest emotional upheaval. You were married for a while. You may have decided you needed to physically separate to reduce the stress, but that doesn't mean that two seconds from now you have to be legally divorced.

After the physical separation your feelings change daily, even hourly. Give yourself time to think. Get used to the idea of living separately. Figure out what that means in your lives.

When should you first visit a lawyer? When is it crucial? This depends on your personal timetable. Some people go very early in the process, even before they've clued their spouse into their decision. Some go before they're ready.

Others aren't sure. They want to know what their rights are, what is legally theirs. They may have heard horror stories of spouses clearing out joint savings accounts, closing charge accounts, hiding assets. At this stage, most are looking for advice and information. It's okay to do this early on, if you realize that what you need is to educate yourself.

Some people see a lawyer when they find out that their partner has already seen one. At this stage, the purpose is usually one of protection. This is also appropriate as long as you make sure not to be reactive. Get the information you need. Understand your rights. Consider the information carefully before making any decisions.

Frequently people arrive at the lawyer's door in the middle of a crisis. "He moved all his clothes out last night. How do I stop him from coming back and clearing out everything else?" "I got divorce papers dropped on me yesterday. What do I do?" "My wife left with the kids yesterday, saying she wanted me to be gone when she got back. Why do I have to be the one to move?" Again, the rule of thumb here is to get information from a lawyer to better understand your options without having the lawyer take over. Take the time to think it over.

One major exception is if you or your children have been threatened with violence. Then you'll need to take immediate legal action, like getting a restraining order. Protect yourself. But unless you are facing imminent physical danger, it is best to cool down before you react. Other situations, such as possible abduction of children or the draining of bank accounts by one partner, also require immediate legal intervention.

There's no one right time to begin a legal divorce. In general, though, you're better off if you've already done your limited partnership agreement—if you've already navigated as much as you can of the emotional divorce. If you are Cooperative Colleagues or Perfect Pals you've probably already made some of the hard decisions. Maybe you've considered how you're going to share child-rearing responsibilities. Maybe you've even decided on the house—whether you'll keep it or sell it. Maybe you've sat down and divided up the furniture and mementos. Maybe you've even cried together about the pain. Completing as many of these tasks as you can before you start the legal divorce will grant you considerable savings in time, money, and energy.

If you're Angry Associates or Fiery Foes and you rush into the legal divorce on the heels of fury, you'll probably use your lawyer to get even, further escalating the costs to you, both economic and emotional.

I'm not suggesting that you engage in legal game-playing—in prolonging the legal divorce with escalating power plays and stalling techniques. That would only make matters worse. What I do suggest is that you postpone your initial entry. Work through some of the very difficult emotions and tasks of separating. I locate the legal divorce as the fourth transition because, ideally, it should be only a rubber stamp for decisions already made in the earlier transitions.

What Will Have to Be Settled Via Lawyers?

I've already urged you to define the legal divorce as narrowly as you can—to work through as many issues as you can in the limited partnership agreement. But there are three issues that will certainly have to be incorporated in the legal agreement: *custody, property,* and *child and spousal support.*

Custody

First, let's examine *custody*, which is the legal term for who will be responsible for the children, financially, emotionally, and physically. Even if in marriage your actual efforts were drastically unequal, legally, married spouses are defined as equal custodians. In divorce spouses must legally decide how, in the future, they'll share their responsibility: with *joint legal custody, sole legal custody,* or *divided legal custody.*

The four egalitarian couples we followed in Chapter 5 stayed egalitarian in divorce and chose the option of *joint legal custody.* As a concept, joint custody is quite vague; many arrangements are possible within this category. The Cooperative Colleague and Perfect Pals in my study came up with a dizzying array of options, which very much depended on what their living situation had been prior to divorce.

The four egalitarian couples arranged *physical custody*—a separate decision dealing with actual physical care of children—differently. Only one chose alternating *physical custody*—the couple who took turns keeping the children in alternating years. This is not a common arrangement.

Most often, the egalitarian couples in my study chose *joint legal custody* with *joint physical custody*—they shared legal *and* physical responsibility for the children. They divided the child care by week or month; they shared living arrangements and responsibility fairly equally.

Sole physical custody—in which the children live primarily with one parent—was an option that most egalitarian couples rejected. But it was the most common arrangement in traditional families, who usually specified *joint legal custody* with physical custody assigned to the mother. In these cases, the mother kept the primary home; the father kept a secondary home and a significant share of financial responsibility. Both parents were legally considered equally responsible for their children's welfare, though their duties were different.

What if you and your exspouse don't choose joint legal custody? There are two other options: *sole legal custody* and *divided legal custody*.

Sole custody means that one partner is the primary parent and the other gets visiting rights. Some courts now refer to this as primary physical custody, with visitation referred to as secondary physical custody. Many sole custody situations seem, on the outside, to be the same as joint custody arrangements specifying sole physical custody. But they are not. They are different in principle; whether a parent's responsibility for a child is joint, primary, or secondary works out to quite a different relationship, in each case, over the period of the child's lifetime.

Divided custody sometimes occurs in families with two or more children. In this situation each parent gets sole custody of one or more children. For example, if there are two sons, the older son is the responsibility of one parent and the younger son is the responsibility of the other parent.

Whatever your exspouse type, you may choose any of these options. Any of these options can produce a good divorce. It's likely if you are a Perfect Pal or Cooperative Colleague couple that you will choose joint custody with one of the variations of physical custody.

Angry Associates and Fiery Foes can end up with a variety of custody arrangements as well. They may, however, be so embittered that they can't agree the other's care would amount to anything good for their child. This may spark a legal battle over custody. Here a child becomes the pawn of the parents' resentment. What has happened to the child's best interests? The process becomes protracted and even more painful, confusing, and damaging than usual, as the child is yanked from one parent to another.

Take Lita and Robert, a Fiery Foe study couple in their thirties. Their son Jonah was six; for four years he'd been bounced around like a tennis ball. At the time of their separation, both parents had lawyers and were readying themselves for a full-blown custody battle. Their temporary agreement assigned physical custody of Jonah to Lita; the schedule allowed Robert to see him on Wednesdays and Saturdays from noon until Sunday at 6:00 P.M. During one of these scheduled visits, Robert left town with Jonah and disappeared for three weeks. Located at his brother's house in an adjoining state, he was ordered to bring Jonah back to his mother.

The fight escalated and six months later it ended up being litigated in court. Joint legal and physical custody was awarded by the judge. Lita and Robert divided up the week equally. But their anger was still flaring and each week Jonah witnessed a major battle between his parents. Within three months he was having sleep disturbances, was wetting his bed, having nightmares, and vomiting daily. Lita went back to court to request sole custody. The plan was modified and Jonah spent weekdays with his mother and weekends with his father. Robert continued to fight for joint custody. At the time of our last interview this battle was still going on. Robert and Lita had not established any workable limited partnership agreement and they continued their power struggles over custody in the legal arena.

Thus working out custody is just like working out all the other issues in your limited partnership agreement. The legal custody decision should simply formalize whatever plan will best work for your child. Anything less, and you've opted out of your responsibility as a parent.

The second major issue you'll settle with lawyers is the division of *property*, tangible and intangible. *Tangible* items include savings accounts, the family home, cars, art, furniture, season tickets, china, linens, photo albums, and anything else you and your spouse accumulated over your years together. *Intangible* property includes pension rights, and more recently, the value of professional degrees, such as medical and law degrees. If you put your husband or wife through graduate or professional school, you can ask that you be repaid for that investment. You can also ask that you receive some benefit from potential earnings in the future. Whether you actually get any compensation depends on each individual situation, the state you reside in, and the norms of your local court.

Division of Property

Again, it will help if you begin to work out who will get what as soon as you can in the limited partnership agreement. There are as many ways to divide property as there are divorcing couples. Items can be sold, proceeds divided, parties can be bought out of assets, and courts can make different provisions for different assets. The value of material possessions is often subjective; what means most to one of you may be worth less to the other.

Property does not have to be divided fifty-fifty. Whatever arrange-

"Some people say you can't put a price on a wife's twenty-seven years of loyalty and devotion. They're wrong."

Drawing by Leo Cullum; © 1993 *The New Yorker* Magazine, Inc.

ment works for your family should be accepted by the attorneys. Winning in this situation does not necessarily mean getting a larger physical share of material goods: it means setting a secure kinship structure for your binuclear family as a whole, over time.

Support

The third major issue to settle with the help of lawyers is *support:* How much money should go to children *(child support)* and exspouses *(spousal support)*. The legal assumption is that as spouses, you and your ex had the same standard of living and equally shared the benefits of joint income. It's fair that you should start divorce with a standard of living similar to that of your exspouse. When there's a large difference in how much money you and your exspouse earn—actually and potentially—*spousal support* (once called *alimony*) is meant to equalize the standard of living—or at least to prevent vastly unequal standards of living.

The legal assumption in child support, however, is based on the needs of the child. Several factors are taken into account in a child-support discussion: how much it costs to raise a child (there's no universal agreement on this, though today many states have come up with guidelines); the family's prior standard of living; the income of both parents. For example, say in the married family the children went to private schools, took piano lessons, and attended tennis camp. Lawyers and courts would assume that the children were accustomed to this high standard of living. Private schools, piano lessons, and tennis camp would become part of the child-support calculations during the divorce.

What often complicates these issues is that they may have been points of contention during the marriage. Joanne and Bruce, a study couple, are a typical example. Joanne had come from a family that almost worshiped education; her parents had sacrificed so she and her brother could go to private schools. But Bruce was adamant his children should follow his own path—through public school. "Children need to learn about the real world. They need a school that includes children from all walks of life, not just rich, spoiled kids. Don't shelter kids; it ruins them. And what do you think our taxes are for anyway?" Joanne and Bruce had fought this battle many times during their sixteen-year marriage, but Joanne had always won. During the legal divorce the battle surfaced again and escalated to litigation. The judge decided in favor of Joanne, based on the children's accustomed standard of living during the marriage. Bruce was ordered to pay child support that included private school education for all three children.

The goal of the legal process should be to settle these major issues—custody, property, and support—in a way that benefits and does not damage the family or any of its members. The interests of any children, of course, must come first. Children must be assured, and this must be encoded into the legal agreement, that they will be financially supported to the best ability of both their parents. They must feel as protected and secure as possible, particularly in the knowledge that they will continue to have two parents.

How hard will it be to negotiate custody, property, and support? The difficulty and complexity of the legal discussion will generally match how long the marriage lasted and what were its assets. But even in the simplest, briefest marriages, custody, property, and support are sufficiently challenging on their own. Any topic outside these issues—to the extent it's humanly possible—should be kept outside the legal discussion. Any topic within these issues—and there are many legal and human factors to each—should be researched, thought through, and decided as methodically as possible.

The first matter to decide is your choice of lawyers and other professionals. Who will help you to simplify your divorce and to maximize your situation? Your choice is crucial. In choosing a lawyer wisely, you'll exert quite a bit of control over the final outcome of your legal divorce.

Professional Negotiators: Your Options

There are now a number of different ways in which to settle your legal divorce: from adversarial through friendly; from lawyers through mediators. Historically, first and foremost has been the adversarial process via lawyers. Because we hear so many horror stories about messy and drawn-out battles over custody, property, and spousal support, we begin to think that litigated divorces are the norm. But in reality, they represent only a very small minority of the approximately 1.2 million divorces every year.

The theory behind the adversarial process is that when partners divorce, most of their interests suddenly become nonmutual. As spouses the two individuals may have been viewed as partners, but now they are often seen as enemies and they see themselves that way as well. Instead of mutual interests they now have personal interests, which need to be protected by counsel, to which they are legally entitled.

In some cases, the positives of the adversarial approach may outweigh the negatives. Say in your marriage one spouse earned more, had more access to the financial records of the marriage, and now has greater earning potential for the future. Or perhaps that spouse is self-employed or independently wealthy. The less economically powerful spouse is entitled to a fair share of the assets (in community property states, 50 percent) and to some future security. When the spouses disagree on how much money there is, or when one spouse denies the other access to financial data, then the weaker spouse does indeed need an advocate to protect his or her interests. Clearly, if this is your situation, you *might* prefer the adversarial legal approach.

But suppose you and your spouse are Perfect Pals or Cooperative Colleagues. If you have goodwill for each other and if you keep all the financial data mutually accessible, you may have better alternatives than to duke out all your issues via adversarial lawyers. You could each hire a lawyer—one who is collaborative and doesn't rush into the courtroom—and insist that you are part of every decision, every step of the way.

If you and your exspouse trust each other, you may even be able to use the same lawyer and resolve court matters fairly quickly. Though the lawyer may only formally represent one exspouse in court, the law doesn't mandate that both be represented. If your mutual interests outweigh your personal interests, using one lawyer might be a good and economical alternative.

Sometimes a lawyer isn't even necessary. Remember, the legal divorce includes the issues of custody, property, and support. When there's no property to divide, no custody to settle, and nobody's requested spousal support, the exspouses can sometimes entirely bypass lawyers and complete the entire legal divorce *pro se*—on their own.

The last and potentially best alternative is mediation. Mediation is a process of settling the disputed issues with the help of a third party. The mediator can be a lawyer, a therapist, or a lawyer-therapist team. Most importantly, it is a self-empowering process that encourages the participants to take responsibility for making decisions.

Frequently, two options are combined. Both spouses can elect to have individual lawyers who negotiate issues about property and support, and they may decide to work with a mediator to resolve the limited partnership and custody issues. In this way, they have partitioned the issues, using one form to resolve one set of issues, and another to resolve a different set of issues. It is not unusual for couples to choose one option in the beginning, such as deciding to use the same lawyer, hit a snag in their decision-making process, and later decide it is better to have two separate attorneys. Sometimes the situation works in reverse: a couple starts out in an adversarial process, becomes aware that the process is escalating the situation, both emotionally and financially, and they back off to either a one-lawyer negotiating model or a mediator.

Currently, the most common method of resolving the legal divorce is still the adversarial approach. However, within that approach, there is a wide range of choices. Some will lead to negotiations that are respectful and amicable; others will lead to long, drawn-out negotiations that are filled with acrimony; still others will lead to painful custody evaluations and prolonged litigation.

Choosing a Lawyer

When deciding on a lawyer, research carefully. Ask for suggestions. Use the community to check out lawyer reputations. Ask your therapist (if you're seeing one) for some recommendations. Then interview one or more lawyers to see who most suits you and your situation. You might consider bringing a friend with you, someone to help you judge the wisdom and chemistry the lawyer has with you, to witness what went on, and to help with both remembering the discussion and adding questions you might not think of at the moment.

Some lawyers are more open and knowledgeable about family dynamics than others; they will try to de-escalate clients' battles and help them to negotiate differences. There are many professionals around who have witnessed too many destructive fallouts from divorce wars, who themselves may even have been through divorce, and who are committed to keeping the proceedings civilized. Some of these lawyers will even refer you to a therapist to work out some of the emotional issues before jumping into legal negotiations.

Good lawyers can smell out a potentially escalating issue in their first visit with a client. I know some who say they can identify the booby traps in the first few minutes.

Others enjoy the battle. They see their purpose as helping their clients get all they can. The difference between win-lose lawyers such as these, and win-win lawyers, such as the above, will be immense—particularly to your children.

The American Way of Divorce

Although divorce also requires a legal decree in European countries, nowhere is it such big business as in the United States. The American way of divorce is war by proxy. Steeped in the stereotypical model of Fiery Foes, each spouse hires a gladiator to do battle for them—a litigator. Those battle-hardened warriors treat spouses as angry enemies who need protection from the tricks and maneuvers of their expartners.

Our model is a highly dysfunctional one for most divorcing spouses. It destroys the potential for cooperation so essential for a good divorce. Although I would like to see the adversarial process replaced by a more cooperative, spousal decision-making model, I don't blame the lawyers themselves, or even the legal profession. They are only responding to our social norms.

"Concerning your former husband, the law allows two options: nailing him to the wall or letting him twist slowly in the wind."

Drawing by Maslin; © 1993 *The New Yorker* Magazine, Inc.

Many lawyers are just as dissatisfied with the process as I am. They say they frequently advise their clients not to pursue aggressively with adversarial tactics, but it is the client who insists. When I ask lawyers why they continue to represent that client, they answer that if they don't, the client will find another lawyer to do what he or she wants.

The legal profession as a whole will not take the lead in stopping this vicious cycle; they are not about to give up the lucrative specialty called family law. The American way of divorce can only be stopped by spouses themselves, as they become aware of more cooperative models. When adversarial lawyers become a glut on an uninterested market they will eventually need to discard the traditional model. They'll either leave the specialty of family law, or redefine it with more family-enhancing models of dispute resolution.

Emotionally and financially, divorce does not have to be this costly, if both you and your exspouse decide to stay in charge. It's your divorce, it's your family, and it's your future.

Courting Disaster

Here's a typical Fiery Foe couple who came in to see me for their first mediation session. They are very steeped in the American ethics of individuality and equality. They have hired two of the most reputable lawyers in the city. After initial progress, negotiations had stalled. The lawyers referred them to me for mediation.

The husband begins angrily. "Sally and her shyster lawyer are trying to milk me for all I've got."

"I just want what's fair," retorts Sally. "Byron wants me to live on nothing."

"You hear that? I've supported her for twenty years!"

"You call that support?" She rolls her eyes, and he explodes.

It's thirty seconds into the session, and not only haven't they exchanged one single direct word, but they're ready to walk out. After I intervene and we discuss matters a bit, it becomes clear that since they consulted their lawyers (each advised them not to speak about the settlement issues to each other), Sally and Byron became more mutually suspicious.

Within the emotional divorce, issues of fairness, getting one's due, making up for inequities, and anxiety about how to live on less in the future have already created tension between the spouses. Adversarial lawyers step into that breach; they may widen it by suggesting defensive or aggressive tactics. The anger between Sally and Byron had in only a short time mushroomed and hardened; it had already cost them and their children more than they ever thought was possible. In general, the more heated the battle, the longer it takes, and the more the litigants will have to pay.

Though adversarial lawyers were not the best choice for Sally and Byron, they are the best choice for some couples in certain situations. Take Ruth and Ben, for example—a couple in their forties with three children. At one of my speeches, Ruth was one of several audience members who stood up and told horror stories. Ruth's husband Ben was an alcoholic. One day he withdrew all the money from their joint account and fled, leaving Ruth with the three kids and no money. A lawyer eventually found Ben and obtained spousal support.

Shelley and Steve, a study couple in their twenties, demonstrate another common situation. Shelley had a lucrative specialty store; Steve (after helping to set Shelley up in business) was attending graduate school. For about six months Shelley had salted away most of her income in private accounts. When they separated, she denied Steve access to her records. Steve eventually hired a lawyer, who gained full disclosures of Shelley's assets and negotiated an equitable settlement.

In cases where one spouse has physically abused another, the injured party should always hire a lawyer to protect family members who may be subject to future abuse.

In cases in which no one has been abused and no one has absconded from responsibility, couples might want to consider mediation to settle their legal divorce.

The Team Approach

The principle of divorce mediation is extremely simple: instead of being adversaries, exspouses are viewed as a team working together. Guided by a professional mediator, they themselves define the best interests of their continuing family.

What's great about the mediational approach—aside from its effectiveness in dealing with the immediate issues at hand—is that it teaches couples a cooperative process. They'll be able to use what they learn to cope with the new issues that will, in the future, inevitably arise. Take a family of divorce in their early thirties, with two small children. Say they litigate. Would their experience help them to settle, in three years, which school their children should attend? Or to decide, in twenty-five years, who throws their eldest child's wedding party? Litigation wouldn't help them. Mediation would.

In evaluating which alternative to choose—mediators or traditional lawyers—there are several important issues to consider. Power is the first of these issues. Because neither of the spouses in mediated settlement will have a personal advocate, mediation tends to work when the power has been clearly defined.

Take Ron and Christine, a couple whose divorce I mediated last year. Ron entirely controlled the finances, and was used to making all the decisions about where the children went to school, which lessons they attended, and so on. He'd also been the one to leave the marriage. We began mediation from an entirely unequal power base. I advised Christine to consult a lawyer after our first meeting in order to clarify her legal rights. We postponed our second meeting until she had done so. By the time we met again, Christine had learned a great deal of pertinent information; this greatly strengthened her position. The mediation now proceeded from a far more equal base of power.

Bill and Charlene, on the other hand, started mediation from fairly equal positions of power. Their problem was their handling of conflict. Bill had a very short fuse and extreme intolerance of differences of opinion. But Charlene loved to argue. She'd attempt to prolong conflict and wear Bill down. In mediating their divorce, I recognized that Charlene could hold her position better and longer, and I supported Bill until he was confident he had equal say and equal power. The settlement of issues could then proceed.

A third issue in choosing mediation or litigation is what type of divorce process is mandatory in your part of the country. There are two types of mediators: public mediators, who are part of their state's family court system, and private mediators, who work on their own. In only three states—California, Maine, and Iowa (pilot program)—are all divorcing couples obligated to mediate their differences through a public mediator provided by the family court services. The number of these mandatory mediation sessions differs, and the scope of issues handled is the same as that in a litigated divorce. In these states, it's only when mediation fails that the divorcing couple proceeds to litigation. Thus mediation is defined in certain states as one stage in the divorce process. In other states, it isn't.

Mediation is not perfect. Because it's so new—California legislated mandatory mediation in 1981—it's not yet a well-monitored specialty, which means almost anyone can hang out a shingle. Also, our knowledge of the long-term outcomes of the mediation process is still quite limited. If the idea of private mediation appeals to you and your exspouse, you must find an expert, qualified professional.

Like any type of professional, mediators each have their own special skills and special knowledge. Some are generalists: they mediate all the issues in divorce. Some will just handle one particular subset of divorce issues.

Say you and your ex have been able to resolve the property and support issues, but you're stuck on custody. If you choose to have your divorce mediated, it's likely that you'll want a custody specialist. This specialist will likely be someone from a mental health profession who has knowledge of child development and family dynamics as well as considerable expertise about divorce.

But suppose you and your ex have been able to resolve custody; economic issues, though, are driving you up the wall. You'll benefit most from consulting a property and support specialist. This mediator will more likely have started as a lawyer; his or her expertise will be strongest in issues of long-range financial planning.

Suppose that although you and your ex are fairly cooperative, you have no idea how to have productive discussions with each other about long-term plans. In these cases I would recommend a generalist—someone who has knowledge of family law, is well trained in conflict-resolution strategies, and understands the family dynamics in divorce.

I recommend that you list your knottiest issues in the divorce, and then assemble a list of possibilities from sources you trust—from other divorcing couples, from your therapist or counselor if you have one, even from your lawyer. Choosing a mediator requires investigation. In some cases you (either alone, or you and your exspouse) may wish to interview several about credentials and approach before making a final decision.

I believe that as it stands, mediation is a good option under most conditions. It's true that the profession needs refining: we need more research on mediation, and we need to improve the standards. I am in favor of a team approach because it provides the expertise of two disciplines. A combination of a lawyer and a therapist (ideally a male/female team) will probably maximize the ingredients—skills, knowledge, gender understandings—with which a divorcing couple needs to season their own particular stew of issues.

Emotional Issues: Displaced Anger and Power Struggles

Like all the other transitions of divorce, the legal divorce tends to re-stimulate fights unresolved from the earlier stages. Dividing property, arguing custody, and trying to prove one's need for support, even under the auspices of the best-chosen mediator or lawyer, will sometimes tug you straight back into the past. A discussion of outstanding mutual bills can spark screaming battles about how spendthrift one partner was. The seemingly simple question of who gets the living room furniture can become a war about heirlooms and family. Chats about your children's whereabouts on Saturday mornings can swiftly metamorphose into all-out gender wars, a costly way to spend your hours with the lawyer or mediator.

What are the dynamics of these struggles? How can you avoid or limit crises during the legal divorce?

Choice Points: Will We Get Revenge or Will We Move On?

The legal divorce forces an item-by-item accounting of the marriage balance sheet in a much more detailed way than most couples have needed previously. We've already discussed the emotional divorce in Chapters 4 and 5—the emotional taking stock of the assets and liabilities of the relationship. Now, the legal divorce requires spouses to attach dollar signs to each item. This process escalates the anger, both about the original losses and about the fundamental difference in value exspouses now place on each item.

Though the specifics will differ in each divorce, the choice points tend to be similar. How you address each point and how you use the services of the professionals you've hired—whether mediators, lawyers, therapists, or some combination—are critical factors in your legal divorce. They can affect how long the legal divorce will take, and how intense the fights will get.

The legal process can add fuel to the already raging fires. Suppose during the accounting one expartner cannot make a decision. The other expartner often does something precipitously, or on the advice of his or her attorney, as a way of getting the other person to act. The other person then retaliates, upping the ante. The anger ignites and eventually rages out of control; in divorce these brush fires can last for years. Sometimes a partner decides to put out the fire, and even pulls back. But it may be too late to prevent irreversible damage.

Lawyers often get used in these situations as a way for exspouses to disclaim responsibility for acts of retribution. It's easier to look your exspouse in the eye and blame your lawyer than to face up to what you've decided. "My lawyer advised me not to let you see Timmy until you've paid child support." "Well, my lawyer told me to change the locks and not let you get the furniture." "I didn't just grab everything from the safety deposit box—the lawyer told me to." "Well, my lawyer told me to make a big budget." After you spring the surprise, you can then sanctimoniously proclaim, "I'm not the one who hurt you"; "I'm not the one who got so angry"; "I'm not the one who's keeping you from seeing Timmy." The result is another bitter escalation of the war.

What's the alternative? Reclaim responsibility. Take charge. Your lawyer, mediator, and therapist are your employees—you are not theirs.

Be very careful about what problems you bring to lawyers. Their purpose is to thoroughly advocate your position, to negotiate, and if that fails, to litigate what you've defined as your biggest issues. Unless you're rich, revenge obtained through a lawyer will hit you as hard as it will hit your ex.

At each of these choice points—before you pick up the phone to call your lawyer—take a deep breath. Perhaps you should pick up the phone and call a friend, a therapist, or a counselor instead. Decide if it's in your children's best interest at this choice point to get revenge, or whether your entire family would be better served by your publicly listing the problems dispassionately, addressing them mutually as best as you can, and then moving on.

Displaced Blame: "No Fault" and Fault-Finding

No-fault legislation heralded in a new era of divorce. No longer must you publicly prove that your spouse is a culprit, or that he or she was cruel and inhuman to you. No longer must you publicly trump up a case of adultery, so common in the 1950s and 1960s. Today, all that's needed (in the public legal divorce) is for one spouse to claim irreconcilable differences from the other. There's no need to give examples or justify it in any way.

No-fault divorce. That sounds so simple. As in marriage, in which all you have to do is get a blood test and license, you may expect in a no-fault divorce to obtain an appropriate document, arrange the care of the children, divide the possessions, and wait the specified time. Sometimes it is that simple: when there's nothing to be divided, or when the spouses have decided everything between themselves. As we've seen, lawyers aren't even necessary, if the spouses have decided to file documents *pro se* (by themselves). After a waiting period of about six months, depending on the state, their divorce is officially stamped and they're free to remarry.

So if it's so easy, why doesn't divorce happen this way? It's because the legal term *no-fault* has absolutely nothing to do with a couple's emotional reality. As anyone who's been within a mile of a typical divorcing couple knows, people need to blame someone for the breakup of their marriage. They need to find a cause for their pain. It's much easier to blame the exspouse than to look within for answers, particularly in the early stages. The lesson? Displacing the blame onto your exspouse will not resolve your pain.

One of the interesting findings in my study is how, over time, blame shifts back and forth between exspouses. Sometimes, when anger finally begins to diminish, so does the blame. It's a rare couple in which both partners were exactly equal in breaking up the marriage, but it's an even rarer couple in which one partner was solely at fault—even in those seemingly crystal-clear cases in which one partner had an affair and the other stayed faithful. Looking deeper, with the different perspective that comes over time, the betrayed partner comes to see how he or she contributed to the problems, which usually began months or even years before the affair. Like Manuel and Maria in Chapter 4, a couple may have mutually ignored the seeds of the divorce since the marriage began.

The legal divorce has its own timetable, which is not the same as that of the emotional divorce. Because the legal divorce feels cleaner than the fuzzy, more open-ended emotional divorce, families sometimes attempt to settle mutual, private issues via legal means. If you find yourself or your exspouse acting impulsively and ragefully through lawyers, if you find yourselves rushing a legal decision or procrastinating—even against professional advice—you may wish to reexamine your limited partnership agreement.

Many of my subjects in the Binuclear Family Study expressed deep regret at their third interview about how they'd behaved around the time of their separation and legal divorce. One woman whose husband left her because he was in love with her best friend noted three years later, "I wish I hadn't moved all his furniture out when he was at the office. I wish I hadn't been so spiteful, putting insulting signs on his stuff and all. I was so mad, though, I just couldn't help myself." A man whose wife left him because she'd fallen out of love said at our third interview, five years postdivorce, "I can't believe what I did to her those first six months. It's like a bad dream, how I terrorized her. Following her, jumping from the bushes when she was opening her car. Icepicking her tires. Calling in the middle of the night, screaming curses. And do you know the worst? I'd bring the kids back three hours late, just so she'd worry. I'm not proud of these things. I have no idea what came over me."

Another man, who felt abandoned by his wife, kidnapped the children in revenge. Five years later, he deeply regretted it. "I was so desperate. She was leaving me and she'd threatened me with maybe never seeing them again. Even though I knew she didn't mean it, I freaked. It was like she'd taken my whole life away. So I grabbed the kids out of school and ran to my brother's, in Oregon. The kids were so quiet and scared. It was awful, and they still feel angry."

These stories are all too common. The daily news is filled with tales of spousal kidnapping, spousal assault, even spousal murder. The villain of each of these stories is a spouse seeking revenge for the emotional pain of divorce. The victim—and hero of these stories—mostly becomes the attacked expartner.

In Terry McMillan's bestselling novel, *Waiting to Exhale,* one of the characters, incensed at her husband's affair, drags all his stuff out into the yard and holds a garage sale. The sale is more like an orgy—everything, even his pricey car and his state-of-the-art skiing gear, she sells for one dollar per item. Later, when the reality hits and she needs money, she kicks herself for giving away items on which she could have made some profit. For the heroine of this book as well as the hero or heroine of your own story, the revenge impulse may be momentarily energizing, but it does not end up helping anything or anyone—least of all you.

We saw how normal it is to feel angry during the emotional divorce, and how divorcing couples use this anger to cover up their underlying feelings of sadness and loss. That doesn't make the anger any less real—it just means that when you're angry and want to strike back, you must examine your impulse, not act on it.

It's important to express your anger in a nonpunitive way. It's also important to realize how sad you are. This won't necessarily make you more vulnerable to your exspouse; your successful handling of your emotions puts you in a more powerful position.

If you and your ex can manage productive conflicts that don't escalate out of control, if you two can listen to each other and resolve your issues in the context of mutually agreed-on ground rules, then by all means express your anger—along with your regret, love, pain, and even your humor. If, however, you can't fight constructively—if, perhaps, you haven't been able to agree on your limited partnership—then express your anger to your friends, to your therapist, or to your support group. But don't act out with your ex. Don't impulsively bring it to your lawyer. And don't take your anger out on your children. The sound and the fury signify that you've got your work cut out for you.

20-20 Hindsight on the Legal Divorce

What's the consensus about the legal divorce one or more years after it's been completed?

With 20-20 hindsight it's easier to see choice points; it's easier to see where you should have stood your ground and where you should have yielded.

By their third interview, over 50 percent of the participants in the Binuclear Family Study were unhappy with their lawyers. They complained that the lawyers had charged too much ($100 to $400 per hour), had made things worse than they needed to be, and had drawn out the battles and the anguish. There had to be a better way, said these exspouses—a way in which they could have taken control in earlier stages; a way in which now they could still take control. Let's see how the way couples addressed certain choice points affected the long-term outcome of their divorces.

"It's not fair," fumed Anna, a mother of two, at her first interview. "I can't believe I didn't see this coming. Ten years out of the labor market and now I have to start all over again. While his salary's been going up, up, up, I've been taking care of the kids, helping him, inviting the officers of his company to dinner. I'm out looking for temp work and I have no retirement policy and no benefits." Five years later, Anna was still looking for a good job—she had been awarded the home and primary custody of the children. And she was still worrying about retirement. "Tim's already retired," she bitterly noted.

Another woman we interviewed, Jenine, was still fuming at her husband's infidelities a year after the divorce was finalized. She was planning on returning to court to request an increase in child support and had hired a new lawyer for the postdivorce litigation. When I asked what she wanted from her divorce, she said, "To make my husband pay for all the pain he caused me. He doesn't know what he's in for," she said. "He thinks he can just go his merry way, doing whatever he pleases. Well, now he's got a tiger by the tail." Three years later, Jenine and her husband, Bruce, had used up most of their savings in litigation.

"I always knew Bernice was vindictive," said Jack, three years postdivorce. "She seems so agreeable on the outside, but boy, when it finally came down to the wire, she went after me for every cent." Said Bernice in a separate interview, "Jack was always secretive about what he called *his* money. I knew he was stashing it away and I wanted my fair share. My lawyer really had to dig to get the true financial picture."

With 20-20 hindsight, it's easy to say what some of these couples might have done differently. In the legal divorce, Anna might have pressed harder to bring both Tim's retirement and hers onto the bargaining table. Perhaps she might have been able to win the price of going back to school and increasing her employability. Jenine and Bruce, however, needed to do far more work in the emotional divorce before beginning legal proceedings. Jenine may have satisfied herself that she was powerful for a few months, but she ended up draining the family's assets.

Jack and Bernice are a more subtle case. Perhaps if they'd each made their feelings known and had established a better-defined limited partnership they could have felt happier with the final result. Perhaps not. Divorce, like any set of developmental transitions, may leave many unanswered questions.

How about the other half of the participants? They were satisfied with their legal divorce. These couples had several traits in common. Most did not pursue an adversarial battle. Some couples used a lawyer, or even two lawyers, for advice. (At the time mediation was not yet a common option.) Often the lawyer merely incorporated the decisions the couple had made themselves and drew up the necessary paperwork. Still others had worked out their differences with the help of a third party—a therapist, mediator, or negotiating attorney—and frequently someone who'd been their family attorney for other issues. Most of these couples were Cooperative Colleagues and Perfect Pals. Although there were conflicts, their anger did not override their desire to settle issues with civility, creating as little distress as possible for themselves and for their children.

Charles and Sally, after a nine-year marriage, were one such couple. "My parents had been through a hellish divorce when I was a kid, and I was determined not to hurt my kids," said Charles when we interviewed him three years postdivorce. His exspouse Sally and he tried out a number of parenting plans, spent much time with their attorney and accountant, and divided up the assets before seeking a custody decision. "I was worried when Sally said she wanted to see a separate attorney, but it turns out she only wanted a second opinion on some of the financial stuff that had long-term implications. Her lawyer suggested some changes and when she conceded on a couple of other things, I agreed."

Why were Sally and Charles so fortunate? They took control of their legal divorce, and they recognized they still had a mutual interest in doing so. As much as possible, they kept their emotional (private) issues out of the legal (public) arena.

Separating the Emotional and Legal Divorce: Gender Issues

Sometime during the legal divorce you'll be tempted to give away your power to your lawyer. Don't do this. Beware of the lawyer who says, "Don't worry. I'll take care of it all for you." You mustn't expect your lawyer to take over tasks that properly belong to your emotional divorce—dismantling your marriage; restructuring your family relationships. Your lawyer is your consultant, your counselor, your hired hand—not your rescuer.

Why do people allow their lawyers such power? The motivations differ depending on gender. Women tend to disempower themselves through a lack of experience; men are used to delegating responsibility in their professional lives.

If you're female and if you haven't previously dealt with lawyers, you're likely to feel unsure of how to protect your rights. Your husband is likely to have earned more and to have garnered the lion's share of economic power in the relationship. You must now empower yourself with knowledge. Learn all you can about your legal rights, your family finances, and each factor in your legal divorce, whether these have been implicitly hidden from you as part of a gender issue, or explicitly hidden as happens in some ugly cases. Turning decisions over to your lawyer further disempowers you. By learning about the issues and stakes at each choice point and by then making your own decisions, you'll gain power for future negotiations.

If you're male and you're tempted to delegate your divorce to a lawyer, you must realize that how you end a business partnership is miles away from how you end a spousal partnership, especially when children are involved. If you are concerned about the welfare of your children, if you want to be a responsible and involved father, then you must continue to relate to your children's mother. When you remove yourself from direct responsibility at this critical juncture, relinquishing decisions to a lawyer, you remove yourself from acquiring the tools you'll need in order to maintain your family ties after divorce.

I am not advocating going without consultants. Quite the contrary. Find the best consultants, and use them wisely. Consult on all legal decisions, on the children's developmental needs, on what kind of living arrangements work best at which ages. Consult with experts on the pros and cons of any choice for which you feel insufficiently prepared, either legally or emotionally. You have a whole range from which to choose: teachers, lawyers, mediators, therapists, child development specialists, divorce experts, family court staff, support groups, and books. All can offer you valuable, timely information and empower you to securely, safely navigate each choice point.

You need to know the costs and benefits, both economic and psychological, of whatever path you select. When in doubt, don't choose suddenly or arbitrarily. Trust your conscience, wait a moment, and seek a second opinion. Make an informed, considered decision, over a period of time.

Even many years after the legal papers are signed, new issues are likely to arise that necessitate making new decisions. The more that exspouses have been responsible for making their own family decisions during the process, the more likely they will be able to continue to do so in the years to come.

Three Golden Rules: Compromise, Flexibility, Acknowledgment

One of the inescapable realities of divorce is that we don't ever purely get our way. After the legal divorce you'll have less of everything—savings, spendable income, furniture, time with the children. It's simple arithmetic: when things are divided, whether into halves or by some other equation, each person ends up with less. The money that used to support one household now needs to support two; there's no way, unless there's a lot of surplus, that it can stretch as far. Dual-income families usually feel the loss just as greatly as do one-income families. Most dual-income families need both incomes to sustain them; dividing their net worth in half produces only half of the resources each had in the past.

Accepting the necessity of compromise is one of the hardest tasks of the physical *separation* and legal *divorce* transitions. It isn't until now that the realities hit. Suddenly you realize the enormity of the losses. In the separation you said goodbye to your partner, your future dreams, your romantic illusions, your role as part of a couple in a very coupled society. Now in the legal divorce you may find that you have to suffer even greater material losses—a lower standard of living, less cash, worse housing, as well as the loss of luxuries you used to take for granted.

Accepting compromise is your best hope, however. If at this choice point you accept this fact of life, you can then move ahead to make the next important decisions of how much you will compromise and on which issues. Again, there are no easy answers.

Now you must negotiate, negotiate, and negotiate. About 90 percent of divorces today are negotiated settlements. Today, it's only the rare divorce that gets litigated, that goes to trial and gets decided by an arbitrator or a judge. Most are settled by the exspouses, either by themselves or via lawyers or a mediator.

Whether mediated or not, your negotiations occur in the context of what a court of law would decide if indeed you went to trial. This concept of negotiating in the shadow of the law provides some guidelines for what are usual and customary decisions. But the law is not all that clear and fixed. Instead, there is a range of accepted solutions that provide natural boundaries for your discussion on the legal divorce.

Take child support. Most states now have guidelines for how much money it takes to raise a child. Where you fall within the spectrum will depend on individual needs. The child who needs special medical attention, the one already enrolled in private school, the one doing special costly activities—these may win support above and beyond the baseline.

Each partner's lawyer usually interprets the guidelines into the best possible outcome for his or her client. So, lawyer A may tell his or her client that the child support can be increased above the usual award because of certain extenuating circumstances. Lawyer B advises the other spouse that the extenuating circumstances are insufficient to warrant the increase and that, in fact, the child's inheritance warrants a decrease.

Given the individual differences, the wide range of precedents, and the differential spins adversarial lawyers put on the data, it's easy to see how difficult negotiations can become. When they're excruciating, don't get caught in a need to win at any cost. Winning at any cost usually ends up making you both losers. You will become the villain. So remember the three golden rules; and when you can't, cool down, take a break, and talk to a friend.

Getting Stuck

Generally, during the legal divorce, spouses tend to hone in on one major issue—one major battlefront. Usually it's not the real issue, but it's the one with which each can most hurt the other. When couples get stuck on one issue, this indicates that one or both are still mired in the emotions of an earlier transition.

Often the major stuck point is custody. Under the guise of seeing to their children's best interests, divorcing parents lock horns and play out their anger, often battering their entire family over who gets more time with the children. Even mediators can get caught. But the escalating hostilities are often based on trivial differences. A couple recently referred to me by their lawyers managed to escalate a single discussion over whether the father would bring the children back on Wednesday night or drop them at school on Thursday morning into a full-blown custody battle in ten minutes.

In custody battles, spouses may deliberately blacken each other's reputation, or systematically destroy a once-loved partner in legal degradation ceremonies that strip everyone of dignity. They may minutely detail every failing and every indiscretion—the affair of years ago, the period of unemployment, the drunkenness at an office party. But as we have seen, the blame and anger are cover-ups for sadness. They do not accomplish their goal. And when the dust settles, children are left wounded. They will feel responsible for choosing one parent over another, or hurting one parent, or causing the bitter warfare. Fortunately, only about 10 percent of custody cases actually reach the courtrooms in heated litigation. But in these cases, parents return time and again to the courtroom, often over a period of years, raging at one another in a public arena, reopening everyone's wounds. It is those Fiery Foe divorces that create the most irreparable long-term damage for families and children. They also jam up the already overburdened court calendars.

Sometimes the stuck point is the property settlement. The movie *War of the Roses* was a biting satire depicting the rageful escalation of a divorcing couple who both refused to leave the house. By the end the house was wrecked and so were the spouses.

Several couples in the Binuclear Family Study spent as long as six months living together—without speaking—because both exspouses refused to leave. Some even continued to share the same bed, managing not to touch or speak. One woman, married for nineteen years, said: "We had this invisible line which neither dared to cross. I woke up every morning feeling achy and stiff because I was so tense all night. We each slept on the outer edge of the bed. I can't believe we slept like that—for three whole months. Neither one of us would give up the master bedroom." Other couples staged get-even battles, hoping to make the other so uncomfortable that he or she would capitulate and move out.

In the custody battle the stress that a hostile territorial situation produces is often manifested by the children. In one family, while the parents viciously fought over who would "keep their three children," the teenage daughter got pregnant. In another family, a six-year-old became school-phobic while his parents battled over where he'd spend Christmas. In still another, a ten-year-old started wetting her bed; her parents couldn't settle whether or not she could spend overnights with her father. Adults also show the effects of the stress, tending to interiorize the exterior conflict. Increased drinking, dependency on tranquilizing medication, and depression are common problems for parents stuck in escalated divorce fights. Sometimes they even get physically ill.

What happens when battles over stuck places get settled? Outside—except in the most extreme cases—the family seems to settle down. Whether they've dealt with the stuck place through negotiation, mediation, or litigation, they seem to move on. But, within the family, the battle over a stuck place can last for years, especially if the parents need to keep their anger alive. Years after the initial legal divorce is over, this anger can erupt into legal aftershocks. The court dockets are overloaded with Fiery Foes and Angry Associates who revive such battles after they'd been settled to everyone's seeming satisfaction. That is because after the initial settlement, both spouses felt like losers. Now, years later, they're still stuck, even though each may have realized that no one can win this fight.

Take the very common situation of Sue and Steve. The children live with Sue for most of the time, spending some weekend time with Steve. The legal divorce specified that Steve would pick up the children at her house at 6 P.M. on Friday and bring them back twenty-four hours later. It's 6:15 on Friday night and Steve hasn't arrived. This used to happen in their marriage. Says Sue, "I'm always on time or early, and he's always late. What does he think—I have nothing better to do?" It was an issue that they'd never resolved. After they'd separated Sue had expressed relief to her friends. "Finally I can live my life—on my own time."

By 6:25 this Friday, when Steve arrives, apologizing for being stuck in killer traffic, Sue says in a tight voice, "It's not my fault you can never think to leave early." As the children and he rush out, she snaps, "You better be here promptly at six tomorrow." But he arrives at 6:15. After several episodes like this, with Steve sometimes on time and sometimes late, Sue decides not to be controlled by Steve. So, the next time he's scheduled to arrive at six, Sue tapes a note to the door: "Kids and I stepped out. Back by seven—Sorry!" Steve fumes as he waits.

Several more games of "who's in control" get played. Steve sends the child support check a few days late. Enraged, Sue calls him. The next month, Steve sends the check two weeks late. She calls him on Thursday to tell him that she and the children have plans for Friday night and he should pick them up on Saturday instead. He calls his lawyer, saying Sue is not adhering to the court order about visitation. She calls her lawyer, saying Steve is not adhering to the child support order. The lawyers write letters to each other. World War III is on its way.

This power struggle can be played out in a dozen different ways. The stuckness comes from neither person realizing that a fight is not the way to work out issues unresolved from marriage.

When Jill was angry at Jack for seeming to have it all—a new girlfriend, a new car, freedom—she made it difficult for him to see their mutual children. Soon Jill got a live-in boyfriend. Angrily, Jack began to send support checks late, or to send only half the amount. Finally, he didn't send them at all. The more you insist on winning a battle over a stuck place, the more bogged down and drained you will become. These battles are all-consuming. They leave you little energy for work or kids.

If you go through legal divorce letting anger prevail over reason, panting to win, to get even, to get your fair share, you will end up with a bad divorce. You will prolong the process, it will cost you more money, you will fuel your anger, and you will make your children miserable. Weigh your urge to win carefully. Will "winning" be worth the extra hour a week of time with the children you could have had? Will it be worth its cost in child support, or spousal support? There are always trade-offs. There is no fair share. Nothing can make up for the pain.

The Unresolved Custody Controversy

Whatever the level of mutual rationality, when parents enter the arena of legal custody they are often unaware of how politicized the entire social issue of custody has become. It is a discussion steeped in personal values, colored by professional discipline, and anchored in gender politics. You will have to have an idea of where any expert you choose—lawyer, mediator, therapist—and any expert your exspouse chooses fall along the custody debate continuum. Evaluating the experts and the discussion in this way will help you in timing your arguments with your exspouse and choosing your battleground wisely.

In a recent article in the *Los Angeles Times,* the spokesperson for the Coalition for Family Equity, Dorothy Jonas, asserts, "It comes out to a simple crapshoot, a matter of which judge you get." The "it" to which she refers is the legal custody decision.

What may surprise you is that who has better odds of getting custody is decided more by social context than it is by children's needs. Before the 1800s, when children were considered the property of their fathers, fathers got custody. During the 1800s, as we saw in Chapter 2, as domestic life became the women's domain, the court presumption shifted to the mother. The legal system evolved the "tender years" doctrine, which basically says that babies need their mommies. Although the tender years doctrine at first included only children up to age six or seven, the mother became the generally favored parent even in battles involving older children: until quite recently fully 90 percent of custody awards went to mothers. In the 1960s, to get custody, a father had to prove his wife grossly incompetent, mentally deficient, abusive, alcoholic, or drug dependent.

Enter the late 1970s, a time of increased social consciousness of equal rights. The legal statutes reacted. Now custody could no longer be awarded on the basis of gender. Within the short span of fifteen years, joint custody—which first began as a grass-roots movement— went from an alternate arrangement that parents could request to being the most prevalent form. In 1980, only three states had joint custody statutes; forty-eight states did in 1992. In nineteen states, joint custody or shared parenting is the presumption or preference; in twenty-four states it is an option that can be requested by parents; in five states it can be given at the option of the judge. Unlike the father-custody presumption of two centuries before, and the mother-custody one of the 1950s, joint custody laws are not simple. They are much vaguer, far more complex, and much more open to individual interpretation. Parents now have to find experts who can argue for them, and each expert states in his or her opinion which parenting plan is likely to meet the child's best interests.

What really does meet the child's best interests? If gender now can't be the determining factor, what is? That depends on whom you ask. The father who wants to quit full-time work now that he's divorcing, who wants to stay home half-time with his children and has found custody experts to support him, has one answer. Ask his exwife and her experts, and you'll get quite another.

The custody debate rages at all levels of politics. The fathers who are part of the Joint Custody Association, or the Children's Rights Council, are fathers' rights advocates. They'll reply that men who share physical custody 50-50 have the best record of child-support compliance, and will conclude that joint legal and physical custody should be a presumption of the courts. But ask another group, the National Organization for Women (NOW), and they'll argue that the courts should presume that mothers are the preferred custodial parent. Today, they say, joint custody doesn't work because women continue to carry the primary child-care responsibilities; joint custody serves only the interests of men who want to reduce child support and have control but little or no responsibility for child care. Ask any judge, lawyer, mediator, or therapist, and they each will have their particular bias on this emotionally loaded subject. And the mix of experts in your case may determine who gets custody.

Debate Number One is about stability. What will make your children the most secure? Some experts assert that when children can live with one parent in one home most of the time—i.e., have a primary residence—that is stability. Others—and I am one of these—say that no, stability means continuing healthy relationships with both parents.

Debate Number Two is about conflict. Can two conflictual, even feuding, parents work together in a child's best interests? Can a court mandate coparental cooperation?

Debate Number Three is about who gets custody in those cases in which the parents cannot work together. When the animosity between exspouses is so lethal that the child may suffer long-term damage, what happens when both parents demand custody? If one parent is not proven incompetent, who will get custody? How can a judge decide?

The subtext for each of these debates is Debate Number Four—gender.

Is Equality Fair?

A few years ago, major feminist groups, such as NOW, supported joint custody as an issue of equal rights. But recently, they have come out against it. Currently, these women and men are questioning whether joint custody is fair to women. Having had some years in the field to see what are the actual ramifications of so-called 50-50 decisions, these people see some disturbing results, particularly economic ones. Although actual numbers are not yet available, they assert that many women receive less child support in joint custody decisions than in sole custody yet they continue to carry the same responsibilities. Along this same line, in the past the family home usually remained the property of the custodial parent. Now, with joint custody, this is no longer *pro forma*. Often the family home is sold, or ends up with the parent who can tolerate the expense—often the father.

The issues of custody are linked with money issues, even though the courts have tried to keep these issues separate. In sole custody, the noncustodial parent usually pays the custodial parent child support. In joint custody, because parental responsibility is supposed to be more evenly divided, less money may actually change hands. Each parent may be responsible for expenses incurred when the children are with him or her; major expenses may be shared or each parent may pay directly for specific items. For example, you may end up paying for the orthodontist while your exspouse may shoulder the nursery school payment. The custody decision has everything to do with how you and your exspouse divide your assets.

Given that women have not yet achieved economic parity with men, it is likely to be damaging to them to be treated equally in custody decisions. How can we claim to make decisions based on equality when both partners don't come to the table with the same amount of chips? How can we take away women's major leverage—their power over their children's lives—without any return? Thus joint custody is so faulty, goes the argument, that custody presumption should return to the historical primary caretaker—the mother.

In this argument, even mediation is bad because it stifles the legitimate anger of women. The present legal system is bad because it's patriarchal, and continues to compound the already extant unfairness to women. Mediation becomes a form of coercion, emphasizing means over ends, harmony over justice, and efficiency over due process.

A counterargument emphasizes fathers' rights. Joint custody is as good a solution as we're likely to get, say the fathers' rights groups that now exist in every state. They argue that mothers are still given priority in the courts. Fathers lose their children all too frequently. And fathers are asked to pay unfairly large amounts of child support.

Which argument is supported by the evidence? Both—and neither. The research on joint custody is just not yet sufficiently developed to solidify one position or the other. Joint custody, as a grass-roots movement, only began in 1978. We are still at the stage of experimentation; the results of this major social movement are not yet in. It is impossible to conduct major controlled studies—such as assigning children of the same age, gender, temperament, intellect, and class to equal groups with designated custody arrangements—to see which ones fare better. We are thus left with following large groups of children over time who live in different custody arrangements, and seeing how they do. Even then, we will still not be certain that they would have fared better, the same, or worse in a different custody arrangement.

I am doubtful that we will ever have the kind of definitive evidence that parents and policymakers want, about which kind of custody arrangement is in the best interests of all children. As I discussed in Chapter 5, I am convinced that when parents are cooperative and sincerely care about their children's best interests, they will devise a limited partnership to benefit those children. It won't always look neat and tidy, and sometimes it will even look unusual, but it will be flexible enough to meet the changing developmental needs of children and their parents. In these situations, parents will often need to put their own needs second. I have spoken with mothers, for example, who wanted their children to live with them full-time, but who have compromised because they know how important it is for children to continue their close relationship with their father. And I've also spoken with fathers who wanted their children to spend more time with them, but realized that their children needed to have one consistent home during the school week.

When the solution for living arrangements comes from two motivated parents who have a cooperative relationship, this usually meets the best interests of their children. However, when warring parents remain stuck in their rage, and joint custody is negotiated or awarded by the court as a compromise between two litigating parents, children are likely to continue to carry the burden of their parents' conflicts.

I also believe that, even though we still have many problems with joint custody, we'd be shortsighted to return to the old system of sole mother custody. We must not trade off family relationships for issues of gender politics. If we really want more equality between men and women, we face seriously redesigning our family structures. Giving mothers sole responsibility for children—whether in marriage or divorce—will not further equality. Such custody arrangements disadvantage women in the workplace, which handicaps them economically. One of our goals for enhancing families is to involve fathers more in family responsibilities. By assuming that fathers will share responsibility after divorce for children—physically, emotionally, and economically—we will be moving toward that goal. Unfortunately, we are now in a difficult transition. The equal sharing of family responsibilities by both fathers and mothers is not yet a reality. But we are slowly moving in that direction, and soon, I hope, it will be.

Does Joint Custody Mean Equal Responsibility?

I've wrestled with this issue for many years, and conducted in 1978 the first study of joint custody that was not based on a very small convenience sample. Forty-one joint custody parents—whose names I got from the court dockets—were interviewed one year and three years postdivorce.

What I found in this study, conducted in San Diego County, was that joint custody certainly did not, in practice, mean equal parenting. Many joint custody arrangements looked much the same as did sole custody arrangements: the mothers still carried primary responsibility for the children, no matter what the courts had decreed. Other arrangements, however, were creative and functional. In these arrangements, the parenting was indeed shared equally; however, more men than women expressed satisfaction with the results.

Since twenty-six of the ninety-eight couples in the Binuclear Family Study had also had joint custody arrangements, I was able to compare findings from the two studies, and to look at differences in legal custody arrangements. In the Binuclear Family Study, joint custody fathers were much more satisfied with their arrangements than were noncustodial fathers. There were no significant differences in satisfaction, however, between sole and joint custodial mothers.

Both fathers and mothers can claim that they've been treated unfairly. Absentee fathers, those in default of child support checks, can claim that they've been forced away, that they stopped seeing their children because of the pain of being a nonparent. Mothers can claim that these fathers were never involved. Both fathers and mothers can state with reason that traditionally the other side has had the better deal. Each can claim, "I've done all the work while my partner has had an easier time of it."

So what will the unresolved custody controversy mean to you, as you and your exspouse work out your legal divorce?

None of the traditional claims—as emotionally compelling as they are—is the argument that will be most valuable to you in settling the issues of custody, property, and support. The most valuable argument is what's in the best interest of your particular family's children.

Custody is a legal term, fraught with the negative connotations of ownership. Children simply are not possessions. Although I am very concerned about the economic inequities that women suffer in many divorce decisions, and although you perhaps share the same concern, I still generally recommend joint custody over sole or divided custody. As fraught as it is with debate and old emotion, joint custody is still the most open, fair option we have. I think that parents should start divorce proceedings with the same assumption—that they'll both continue to have equal rights to the children.

The fact that many fathers (most studies indicate about half) only partially comply or do not comply at all with the terms of the child support order is a very distressing situation for both mothers and their children. There are no easy answers to this problem. My study, the Maccoby and Mnookin study, and several others indicate that there is a strong relationship between compliance and contact between fathers and their children. I believe strongly that if fathers stay involved emotionally with their children, they will also be economically responsible.

Divorce cannot right the inequities of society. Women today earn seventy cents for every dollar men earn; women today are responsible for most of the household and child-care tasks. We can't make mothers richer by giving them sole custody. Trying to do so will only perpetuate the regressive families in which mothers are overburdened and fathers underinvolved—a dysfunctional system both for children and for parents. Over the long run, such a position will only continue to undermine women. For how can women compete in the marketplace if—married or divorced—they are overwhelmed by primary responsibility for mutual children?

Given that each partner usually has less after divorce than before, we can't make equal what never was equal in the marriage. A good legal divorce will realistically separate the marital partners into two distinct economic units, so that assets, income, and child-rearing responsibilities are fairly distributed, and economic and practical sacrifices are equally shared.

In loading the joint custody debate with gender issues, we do a disservice to families and to children. We cannot allow our legitimate concern about these important issues to overshadow our aim of providing children with good families after divorce. We cannot continue to enlist lawyers and experts in the hugely expensive bad deal of exacerbating our pain and our children's pain. Let's start with a better proposition: to argue over gender inequities elsewhere, and to resolve our legal issues as quickly and thoroughly as we can.

There Is No Timetable

Finally, you should realize that there is no one timetable for settling the legal divorce. Some couples will quickly resolve these issues; others will worry and negotiate for years. For some couples the transitions of divorce will come relatively smoothly and chronologically. For others, the transitions are sloppy and they overlap. For still others, one or more of the processes of divorce may be repeated again and again. You may begin discussing your limited partnership, for example, right after the decision, only to break off during your legal divorce; then after a period of months or even years you may renegotiate your partnership.

The answers to every question raised by the legal divorce are unique for every family. I've seen couple after couple work out these issues, painfully, one by one. There is no easy shortcut: there is only the very real pain and puzzlement of choosing a path along an unmarked trail.

In the legal divorce—as in the emotional divorce—we must never forget our goal: to get through the country as quickly and as healthily as possible. We cannot get lost in our bitterness or even in our gender debate, and lose sight of the entire landscape, which—as bleak and threatening as it may seem—has its developmental lessons to teach us. We must, instead, find our path and help our children to find theirs.

In the middle of earthquake country, we realize that the time and place for arguing, yelling about our fear and disappointment and rage, probably is not here and now. Instead, we look for our landmarks and our possible oases, and move on. In the legal divorce we must do the same. Only by keeping to the narrow path of our useful issues—custody, property, child and spousal support—can we successfully navigate the hazards of this lonely path, and come out whole and safe at the other end.

7

When the Family Expands
The Aftermath of Divorce

WHEN HER FIRST-GRADE teacher asks Janie to describe her family, Janie stands. She starts to talk quickly—Janie has a lot of ground to cover.

"Well, there's Mommy and David, who I live with during the week. And then there's Daddy and Barbara—I go live with them on Saturday and Sunday, except when there's a dance recital—then I stay at Grandma's, cause she loves ballet. My younger brother Timmy lives with Mommy and David all the time, because my daddy isn't his daddy—his *real* daddy is David. Then there's my older brother, Jeffrey, who comes and plays on Christmas and other times when I'm at my Daddy's. Jeffrey's mom lives in Seattle and Mommy and David don't like her. I have a baby sister, too. Nina lives with Daddy and she's just starting to walk, and when I go there on weekends I teach her stuff. She can say 'Hi, Jay-Jay.' I taught her that.

"My sister Teresa and I play a lot. She's almost the same exact age as me. She lives at Daddy and Barbara's all the time, except sometimes when I go there on Saturdays she's gone to stay with her real daddy. Teresa calls my daddy 'Steve' but sometimes she calls him 'Dad,' and her real father she calls 'Daddy.'

"I've got a really big brother who's in college—Greg. He comes home for some holidays when he doesn't go to Seattle to see his mom. He mostly goes out with his friends when I'm at Barbara and Daddy's, but a couple of times he took me to the movies, and one time he drove me all the way to his college."

Counting on her fingers, Janie proudly states, "That's three brothers and two sisters, two *real* parents, two *other* parents, four grandmas, and three grandpas! We have the biggest family in the world! And I like them all. Well, almost all of them."

These days, many people feel like they're part of "the biggest family in the world." The reason can be summed up in one word—*remarriage*. Today, a vast majority of those who divorce—about 85 percent of men and 75 percent of women—remarry within three years. Add the percentage of those in committed relationships who have chosen not to formalize their union with legal contracts, and the number swells to approximately 90 percent.

The number of remarriages and resulting stepfamilies has kept pace with the swell in the number of divorces over the past two decades. Families like Janie's are now a common phenomenon.

Clearly, couples who divorce are not permanently disillusioned with the entire institution of marriage—only marriage to the person from whom they have been divorced. When you recouple, not only will you have to abruptly, personally, shift gears, but your binuclear family will expand in complex and confusing ways.

When you recouple or remarry, your new mate will bring along a whole new branch of extended family. Each member of your original family will have to readjust. Every child and every adult will be faced with both structural changes and relationship changes within the family. You and your exspouse will need to adapt the original limited partnership; you'll need to reconfigure the rules that guide the interactions between the adults, and between parents, children, and stepchildren. You'll change roles to accommodate to the new family members. And you will establish and follow new rituals that help mark the changes.

This chapter addresses the fifth transition of divorce—the *aftermath*—which, as you may remember I said in Chapter 3, will last for the rest of your life. The aftermath is a bit different from the other transitions. It's the stage of your divorce that looks to the future more than it does to the past. The aftermath of divorce brings new hope, new possibilities—and new problems.

When Is the Old Life Over? When Has the New Life Begun?

There is no hard and fast rule to say when the fourth transition—the legal divorce—ends, and the fifth—the aftermath—begins. The timing varies, according to you and your exspouse's personalities, couple typology, and stage of life; sometimes the transitions overlap. But—like the other transitions—the aftermath is defined by its own characteristic marker points.

For childless couples, the major choice point may come at the moment when one moves on to another love, at whatever transition this happened in the divorce. Childless couples have to deal with fewer lingering remnants of their marriage—no custody or child support issues; simpler issues of property settlement and spousal support—and thus, they tend to have generated less anger during the legal divorce transition. By the time of the aftermath, a relatively large proportion of these couples have both moved on to other relationships and many may have reestablished genuine friendships with each other. For other childless couples, the first marriage has by the time of the aftermath sunk into the far distant past. Some men and women in this category have sought out new mates with children, thus producing "instant" families. The aftermath stage of these divorces will be spent entirely with the new family.

For couples with children the timing of the aftermath transition is strongly affected not only by their own developmental stage but also the age of the children. Clearly, a couple in their fifties with adult children has navigated a very different path through their divorce than has a couple in their twenties with infant children. The aftermath transition will be very different for these couples, even given identical levels of cooperation. And once the exspouses remarry—bringing some of the most sweeping choice points of the aftermath—the couples' situations will diverge even more.

So how do you know when you've reached the aftermath transition? In the aftermath, you may not have finished every bit of negotiation on your legal divorce; you have, however, gotten through most of it and your path is clear, at least for the immediate future. Jim and Margaret, for example—a Fiery Foe couple from my study—were still waging a custody battle over their ten-year-old son Thom when, four years after divorce, Margaret remarried. Thom was distant from, but respected, Margaret's new husband. Though he adored his father, Jim, he found himself much more comfortable in Margaret's new home than in Jim's. Though the custody fight was not yet over, both exspouses could see how it would end. Their aftermath transition began the week both independently decided they needed to move on. Within two months they'd willingly sat down together for the first time and mutually reached a decision about Thom—he would stay with Margaret during the school week through sixth grade, when they would renegotiate.

You'll know you've reached the aftermath stage when the problems from your old marriage are no longer absorbing all your energy. You've dealt with the physical and emotional problems of separation. You and your ex have reached some consensus—even if it's a hostile, armed truce—on a limited partnership, and on how to apportion care of your mutual children. Either your ex or you—or both—may have begun a new relationship; you may even have a new child. But the most common and most characteristic marker of the aftermath transition is the choice point when you suddenly must reject or absorb a whole new group of strangers into your binuclear family.

Suddenly you're standing, sticking a hand out for a shake, facing your ex and your ex's new mate. Both of you are checking each other out, saying, "Nice to meet you," while your exspouse shifts from foot to foot. You don't have the vaguest idea of what to call each other. You don't know whether to move forward, or to run for your life. You have definitely reached the fifth transition.

Complex Kinships: Who's in the Family

One thread that runs through this book is that language matters. The deficits that we have in our language of divorce and the scarcity of good role models make it harder for divorced families to move through the inevitable choice points and crises and to emerge as healthy binuclear families. When families expand through remarriage, the flaws in language and role models become even more pronounced. Let's look at some of the confusions that permeate the aftermath, in the light of our language problem.

The Family Structure—From the Child's Point of View

Our first problem is point of view. Kinship terms are relative: they spin out from one central person. We speak of someone's mother, not someone who is only a mother: someone's mother is inevitably someone else's child. Though this sounds obvious, a few of the most baffling problems of divorce can quickly and easily be reframed by speaking of your binuclear family from one person's specific point of view, and that person is not yourself.

The simplest, most useful way to diagram a family of remarriage is from your child's point of view. The child is the person who has most at stake in the binuclear family. The child is the family's strongest reason for staying together.

What does a binuclear family look like from a child's point of view? Let's look at Janie's family, with whom we started this chapter. The first thing we see is, it's huge. It includes many adults in addition to Janie's biological mother and father: grandparents, aunts, uncles, cousins, and intimate friends of the family, some of whom are related to her mother and some to her father. The second thing we see is that Janie is clear about her relationships with every family member, even though she might not have a role name for each individual. She mentions parents first, then stepparents—new spouses of biological parents. She calls her stepparents by their first names. The third thing we see is Janie's specificity about her sibling relationships. She differentiates brothers and sisters by age, by degree of biological relationship, by propinquity (how frequently she sees them), by geographical proximity, and by personality.

If the new stepparent has a child from a previous marriage, the child gains a new stepsibling. If the parent and stepparent have a baby, the child then gains a new halfsibling. Plus the child has stepgrandparents, stepcousins, stepaunts, and stepuncles. All these people—some blood-related, some not—now form the child's binuclear family.

The diagram below shows the complicated kinship network of any binuclear family. The rectangles show all the possible permutations of new kin that are created by remarriages, even when the parents' new spouses were themselves divorced. At the bottom of the diagram there's a list of the relationships that result, which are as yet unnamed.

You may want to diagram your own binuclear family through the point of view of your child. It's relatively easy to do, and may give you a great deal of insight into your aftermath transition, especially when you look at the people you don't want to include, who are particularly important to your child, and the people who you know affect your life but for whom you don't have role names and with whom you've had problems in figuring out a useful relationship. The lack of naming of these relationships causes a great deal of confusion, both when we try to refer to these people by their roles in the child's life and in our emotional relationships.

Of course, your binuclear family diagram will keep changing over the years. A real family is always changing through death, birth, and

The Child's Binuclear Family System

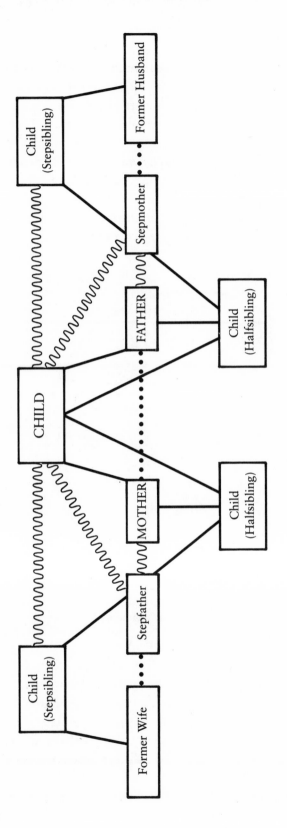

Key:

• • • • • Marital relationship terminated

——— Blood Kin relationships

∿∿∿∿∿ Kin relationships created by divorce and remarriage

Relationship Without Identifying Terms:

Mother–Stepmother
Father–Stepfather
Stepmother–Stepfather
Stepfather's child–Stepmother's child
Halfsiblings from mother's marriage–Halfsiblings from father's marriage

remarriage. What determines how close family members will be? Geographical distance and personal choice are important, and so is recognizing that everyone on the diagram is part of the child's kinship network. The most crucial factor is often how important that family member is to your child.

Unlike nuclear families in which we have nomenclature for extended family, such as great aunts, third cousins, and sisters-in-law, binuclear families have many relationships that either don't have any commonly acceptable kinship terms or have only pejorative terms. This general confusion is portrayed in the cartoon below.

THE FAMILY CIRCUS®   **By Bil Keane**

10-8
Copyright 1980
The Register and Tribune
Syndicate, Inc.

**"Greg's mother is divorced from his real daddy,
and she has a step-husband now."**

Reprinted with special permission of King Features Syndicate.

Columnist Ellen Goodman tells the story of how a ten-year-old describes her binuclear family, who's sharing a beach house for the summer. "First of all there is her father—visitation rights awarded him the month of August. Second of all there is her father's second wife and two children by her first marriage. All that seems perfectly clear. A stepmother and two stepbrothers.

"Then there are the others, she slowly explains. There is her stepmother's sister for example. The girl isn't entirely sure whether this makes the woman a stepaunt, or whether her baby is a stepcousin. Beyond that, the real puzzle is whether her stepaunt's husband's children by his first marriage have any sort of official relationship to her at all. . . . Nevertheless, she concludes, 'We are in the same family.' With that she closes the subject and focuses instead on her peanut butter and jelly."

Cohabiting Partners Add Even More Confusion

The kinship chart does not include one important and extremely common set of relationships. What if one of the child's parents has a live-in lover? Though cohabitation is now extremely popular, there's no socially acceptable term to describe it.

When preparing for our second round of interviews in the Binuclear Family Study, we wanted to interview all the adults who had significant relationships with the mutual children of the exspouses. We therefore asked to speak with all the participants' new partners—married or not.

The first problem was to define *cohabitor* for the study. After a thorough search of the literature, I was astonished to see that there was no agreement about this among sociologists—much less in the rest of society. Are cohabitors only those people who live together all the time? What about those couples who live together only on weekends? What about those whose living arrangements differ markedly from traditional households—for example, a nonmarried couple who takes turns living at each of two houses? We found some people who said they were cohabiting, even though they maintained separate households, because they spent most of their time together in a committed, monogamous relationship. Others shared a home seven days a week. In the study, we ended up including as cohabitors any partners who spent twelve or more nights a month with the biological parent participant.

The next confusion was how to address the cohabitor—by what role name. We were stuck. The Census Bureau calls cohabiting partners *spouse equivalents*. We adopted that term, and sometimes used the role description *stepparent equivalents*. But what could a child call these very important adults? If before Janie's mother remarried, Janie and her mother's live-in friend Milton were walking down the street, how would she introduce Milton to her friends? "Hi, Jennifer, this is Milton—my stepparent equivalent." *Boyfriend, partner, live-in lover*—none of these terms denotes a relationship to the child, or is appropriate for a child to use. Prejudicial expressions are common in the United States: *living in sin, illegitimate children.* This cumbersome, unappealing, judgmental, or adult language makes it difficult for parents and parent figures to speak with children about very complex practical and emotional matters. It's difficult enough to communicate with children about the repartnering and remarriage processes without adding the embarrassment of inappropriate language.

For a variety of reasons, some divorced people choose not to remarry. They speak about how bad a time they had during the legal divorce; how the legal formalities of marriage have lost their meaning; of their reluctance to intermingle their assets and have them governed by marital property laws. In Sweden, cohabitation is more socially accepted. There, similar laws govern cohabitation and marriage; Sweden's remarriage rate has recently declined as its cohabitation rate has risen.

How Binuclear Families Change in the Aftermath of Divorce

Today, the kinships described previously are no longer rare. Most binuclear families contain at least one stepfamily; many contain two. One in three Americans is now a stepparent, a stepchild, a stepsibling, or some other member of a stepfamily. If the current trends continue, we can expect that by the year 2000, nearly half the population will be part of a stepfamily.

The Binuclear Family Study echoed these trends. Three years postdivorce, when we interviewed participants for the second time, eighty-seven families of the original ninety-eight had expanded through cohabitation or remarriage, sometimes both. In almost half these families, both exspouses had recoupled: 59 percent of the women and 77 percent of the men had found new partners.

Who were the new partners? Many were divorced parents themselves; in these cases the study participant had become a stepparent. In ten of the families, a new child had been born to a study participant and to his or her new partner.

Later in the aftermath transition—by the time of the third interview, five years postdivorce—there were some additional remarriages and a few new children. But there were also some breakups of second marriages, and even some redivorces—a 7 percent decline in the number of marriages. Now 51 percent of the women were recoupled, and 71 percent of the men.

FAMILY STRUCTURE AT
THREE AND FIVE YEARS POSTDIVORCE

*(Numbers are N's Except
Where Percentages Are Indicated)*

	3 years (N = 96)*	5 years (N = 95)*
Neither parent recoupled	11 (11%)	17 (18%)
Mother recoupled, father single	11 (11%)	11 (12%)
Neither partner nor recoupled pair has children	2	2
Only partner (CP-CPFS) has children	7	2
Only recoupled pair (R-CP) has children	2	2
Both partner (CP-CPFS) and recoupled pair (R-CP) have children	0	1
Father recoupled, mother single	28% (29%)	30 (32%)
Neither partner nor recoupled pair has children	6	8
Only partner (CP-CPFS) has children	17	15
Only recoupled pair (R-CP) has children	4	5
Both partner (CP-CPFS) and recoupled pair (R-CP) have children	1	2
Both parents recoupled	46 (48%)	37 (39%)
No new kids	6	3
Only Mom's partner has children	15	10
Only Dad's partner has children	5	3
Both partners only have children	6	5
Only one recoupled pair has children	4	5
Both recoupled pairs only have children	0	0
One partner + one recoupled pair have children	6	8
One recoupled pair + both partners have children	3	1
Both recoupled pairs + one partner have children	0	1
Both partners + both recoupled pairs have children	1	1

Missing cases were filled in from information from spouse who was interviewed, if available. Percentages may not total 100 due to rounding.

What's striking about the table is the sheer number of variations. There are simple binuclear families that have only grown by one adult, plus that new partner's relatives—families in which the number of children has remained unchanged. There are a few highly complex binuclear families that have grown by two adults, each bringing children from a prior marriage. There is even one enormously complicated binuclear family. In this family, five years postdivorce, both exspouses remarried partners who each brought children from a prior marriage; then each of the recoupled pairs had a child or children of their own. What does this say about the aftermath of divorce? That any amount of new complexity is possible and even expectable, and therefore you must use the plainest possible language with your children.

When we chart the binuclear family from the child's point of view, who's in and who's out suddenly seems so clear. What we have to address now is how we react to our subsequent feelings of threat, intrusion, indifference, or even rage.

From the Inside Out: Accepting and Integrating New Kin

When my older daughter graduated from the University of Wisconsin, where I was teaching at the time, my ex, his wife, and their two children came out to spend the graduation weekend. Although my ex and his wife, and my second husband and I, had by then celebrated a couple of occasions together, this was the first time he'd said he and his new wife would bring the children. I wanted to create a truly pleasant weekend for my daughter, so I invited my ex and his family to come over for dinner on the evening they arrived.

While I nervously prepared a simple dinner, wondering what my ex would think of my new house and my new life, I tried to relax. My daughter picked them up at the airport and checked them into their motel. They all arrived just as I put the flowers on the table.

My daughter came in first, holding her five-year-old brother's hand. "Justin," she said, "this is *my* mommy." Nothing had quite prepared me for this. He looked so much like my daughter had looked at the same age. Of course I'd seen pictures, heard cute stories, but to see him in the flesh! That was profoundly unsettling. He looked like my kid. But who was this child to me?

I felt kind of like I did with my nieces, who I saw every couple of years. Maybe I was like an aunt. Should I hug him? Pick him up? Was that too intimate? The moment was passing. Finally I mumbled, "It's great to meet you," and went on to greet my next few challenges, hoping that Justin and I could get beyond this stranger stage real soon.

A day and a half later—by the time my daughter's graduation rolled around—we had. As the eight of us joined the huge crowd walking into the ceremonies at the football stadium, this little hand grabbed mine. It was Justin. When he looked up and saw who the hand belonged to, though, he quickly looked around for his mother. Sarah, walking right behind us, smiled and said, "Oops, wrong mom." He kept my hand and grabbed hers too. We were a strange threesome. First wife, second wife, and child: not all blood-related, but kin, nevertheless. When we took our seats in the huge stadium, looking around at the sea of faces, I wondered how many people in that crowd had family albums similar to ours.

Kinship Feelings Grow with Time, Necessity, and Occasion

Over the years, then, you can expect your exspouse, or you, or both of you to recouple, each bringing a slew of new relatives into your binuclear family. Your family album begins to fill with pictures of strangers: a new parent figure, perhaps some new children, new babies. At home your child speaks about new grandparents, aunts, uncles, and cousins who you are not particularly inclined to welcome. They're all "steps," of course, which doesn't make them "family" in the same way that you, your kids, and even your ex have become. But the longer they stay around, and the more they become part of your child's life, the more these new relatives will truly feel like family. The problem is that they're your children's family. How, then, are these strangers and you related? This question is puzzling to many.

Dear Abby:

My husband was married before and has a twelve-year-old daughter who lives with her mother in a distant state. I'll call my stepdaughter "Carla."

My husband can afford to fly Carla here only twice a year. My husband and I also have a daughter who will soon be three. The problem is that we would like to have a family portrait taken and can't decide whether Carla should be in it or not.

I do not dislike Carla, but we see her so seldom, it's hard for me to consider her part of the immediate family. . . . Should we have the portrait taken with just my husband and me and our baby, and hide it when Carla visits? Or should we wait several months for her next visit to have the family portrait taken?

Abby, how important would it be for your readers who are stepchildren (grown or otherwise) to have been included in their absent parent's new portrait?

Maybe it wouldn't mean anything to Carla. Am I making a big deal out of nothing?

> Signed,
> Unsure Stepmom

Dear Unsure:

Please do not have a picture taken that you will have to hide when your stepdaughter visits. Better to include her in the family portrait whether it will mean anything to her or not than to exclude her and risk hurting her.

We now have a large number of parents who live with children who are not their blood kin, and who also have biological children who reside somewhere else. Does how often we see someone determine whether they are bona fide members of our family, or does blood define kinship, or does emotional connection define it? Whether you were the leaver or the left in the old marriage, whether it's you who've remarried or your ex, the ripple effect of a remarriage will alter every relationship in your family system.

Jealousy Rears Its Ugly Head

You didn't expect to feel upset, but you do. Who is this interloper who's grabbed *your* house, *your* kids, who's living off the fat of the land provided by *your* support money! It's not the fact that your ex is walking around starry-eyed about someone else, you complain—but why do *you* have to welcome that person with open arms?

Or perhaps you're the one who's starry-eyed about some new partner. Say that you and your ex have had an amicable but fairly distant relationship; you figure the new person won't upset your ex too much—that wouldn't be rational. Anyway, you and your new partner have been dating for six months and the kids and your ex have been fine about it, so moving in with your new partner is no big deal.

Surprise! Your ex calls—in an absolute fury—the morning after the kids spend their first weekend with you. "Why didn't you *tell* me you two were living together! Have you thought about the consequences of having my kids climb into bed with both of you? Do you know how upset the kids are that you've moved into that person's house? They hate you for it!" You're stunned. Where is all this coming from?

Timing and Territory

Commonly, one exspouse recouples before the other. The other perhaps is not ready to have a new set of choices thrust upon him or her. The uncoupled exspouse has to shift to make room; so do the children. This is incredibly stressful because it is not at all under the control of the uncoupled exspouse.

Even in a nuclear family, the addition of a new family member brings a great deal of stress. When a new sibling is born, for example, older children may feel threatened and displaced, perhaps terrified of losing their place in their parents' heart. In a binuclear family, the stress is greater. The territories are often both more precarious and more defended; the common ground—which was, after all, achieved through a great deal of painful negotiation—is newly threatened. The timing, as we've said, is off for one of the exspouses. And then there's the most stressful part of all—the frequency of the demand for change.

One of the big differences between nuclear and binuclear families is the sheer amount of people who join the family picture. More new people, more often, means more stress, more demands, more frequent necessity for adaptation, and more chances to fail as well as to succeed. The threat of loss is always present for every member of a binuclear family each time a new person arrives on the scene.

Gender Differences

As in divorce, gender differences also emerge in remarriage, and throughout the aftermath transition. In general, men recouple more quickly than do women. Because they usually have less responsibility for child care, they may be freer than their exwives to join the singles world. They tend to date more, to have better opportunities. Finally, they also tend to marry women who are younger than their exwives.

Each of these factors is potentially maddening to an exwife, and can cause a great deal of insecurity.

Why do men have a wider range of opportunities? Because our prescriptive norm in society—our prejudice—is still that a woman should marry "upward"—find a man who is older and wiser, and has more education and income than she does. Thus (if she and her potential mates buy into the norm) as a woman gets older and wiser, more educated and successful, her pool of available men becomes smaller and smaller. This diminished pool is most striking for African-American women. A double standard still exists: a forty-five-year-old man can date a thirty-year-old woman without anyone looking twice; in the reverse situation a woman might be judged critically. The same double standard also exists relative to educational level and professional status.

Remarriage

Remarriage of an ex raises all sorts of anxieties, and some of these are gender-related as well. After their bad deal on the dating scene, women more often face a difficult transition when their exhusbands remarry. Look at the numbers: it's likely he'll remarry more quickly (almost 50 percent of male exspouses remarry within a year after their divorce), to a younger woman (the average second wife is four years younger than is the first wife at the time of the exhusband's remarriage). It's likely that the limited partnership—no matter how amicable and stable—will deteriorate during the man's remarriage. The amount of deterioration and its duration will depend on the civility and amicability of the exspouses. Cooperative Colleagues are likely to have a brief storm and then soon restabilize.

In the Binuclear Family Study, we found that more women were jealous of their exhusband's new wife than were men of their exwife's new husband. Women tended to worry about the losses their exhusband's new marriage would bring. What will they lose? What will their children lose? Does their exhusband's new wife have children of her own? Will these children become more important to him than the mutual children? Also, will he become less flexible than he was before about child care? About financial support? Will they have to compete with the new wife for time, affection, and money? Women were afraid that their exhusbands would write off their old family in favor of the new. They also were more likely to be jealous and competitive toward the new wife. They wondered if she was prettier, younger, smarter.

The men focused on their children. They expressed such worries as: Will her new husband become more important than I am to the children? Will the kids like their mother's new husband so much that they'll forget me? Will they call him "Dad"? The men didn't express much personal jealousy or competition about their exwives' new mates.

The gender difference on remarriage issues extends throughout the whole family—into the extended family. Because women are usually the primary parents, and the kin-keepers of the family, they're more likely to continue a relationship with their ex in-laws postdivorce. In a study of women fifty and older, I found that maternal grandmothers continue to see their grandchildren more often after divorce than do paternal grandmothers. The parents in the Binuclear Family Study reported the same thing. Whether paternal grandparents continued to have a lot of contact with their grandchildren depended on two factors: how involved their sons stayed with their children, and whether their daughter-in-law was still involved with them.

Some in-laws are unable to accept two affiliations and may shift their loyalty from the first spouse of their child or sibling to the second spouse. When this happens, the remarriage is a greater loss for the first spouse—severing that person from half their extended family. Thus, during the aftermath of divorce, exspouses may want to take special care to reestablish family relations on both sides. The in-laws can help. Wise paternal grandparents will realize that their best link to grandchildren may be the children's mother—their ex daughter-in-law.

Thus, timing, territory, and gender differences are all crucial in determining how difficult it will be for a particular binuclear family to negotiate the transitions of remarriage. But one other factor also figures in: who remarries.

When Your Ex Remarries

You've told everyone how relieved you'll be the day your ex remarries. If you were the one who initiated the divorce, you may have added generously that you won't even feel a tiny bit jealous. When the marker point hits, though, you're shocked by a sudden storm of feelings.

Fear, anger, and jealousy—as well as relief—are the most common emotions when one's ex remarries. If you feel abandoned, if your self-esteem plummets, you are not alone. The exspouse's remarriage can temporarily reactivate the ambivalence of the early transitions of divorce by stimulating unresolved feelings.

If you've had any lingering fantasies about reconciling with your exspouse, they will end now, sharply, painfully, and abruptly. These feelings will be exacerbated by tinges of romantic feelings for your exspouse—echoes from your early courtship days, and instant review and reassessment of the reasons why you divorced.

If you're single and didn't want to divorce in the first place, your exspouse's remarriage is a very particular choice point. This occasion has, for you, the potential of creating a crisis that can closely resemble what you went through during the physical separation. Even if you were the one who left the marriage, your exspouse's remarriage is likely to stimulate old anguish, resentment, and even love.

Karen and Roger—a study couple—had been divorced for almost two years when Roger announced he was planning to remarry. Karen had left the marriage; Roger, the wounded party, had long taken the line that she'd deserted him. Although they'd spent the first eight months of separation as Angry Associates, by the end of their legal divorce they'd become Cooperative Colleagues. Said Karen at her first interview: "Roger found someone right away. Then there was a whole long line of attractive women for the next two years. I always knew he'd remarry one day and kept telling myself how comfortable I was with the situation. Anyway, the second he said he was going to marry Carole, I hung up. He seemed so happy. What did she have that I didn't? I felt old and ugly and was working for a slave-driver, and she was eight years younger and owned her own business. They'd be happy together and they'd win over the kids. I hated Carole, and I hated myself for being so irrational, so jealous, so first-wife-ish.

"The truth is, she's a really nice person, which makes it worse. What if I made a mistake in leaving Roger? If she loves him—this nice person—maybe he's better than I gave him credit for. I feel so ashamed, but I keep wishing they'd have a disaster. If his marriage fails, then I'll know I was right to leave him."

Like Karen, many exspouses are shocked by the depth of their initial reactions. But Karen's distress was short-lived—as are the initial painful feelings of most Cooperative Colleague exspouses going through this marker point. After a few months during which she'd snap at Roger, in which she made some snide remarks about Carole that she instantly regretted, Karen refocused on her own life and defocused on Roger's. After a few months they were cordial once more.

How you react to your ex's remarriage depends on a variety of factors: how soon it happens after you divorced; whether you're the leaver or the left; how satisfied you are with your own situation; whether or not you've recoupled; your children's reactions; your relationship typology—all are critical. How you found out about the remarriage and when (if your ex was involved with the new mate before you separated, it's harder) also affect both your own adjustment and the incipient change in your relationship with your ex.

If you feel good about your life, if you love your work, if you've found a new partner, your ex's new spouse will probably not seem like much of a rival. You may be unsettled for a bit, but your discomfort is apt to dissipate quickly. If you were the leaver and are still feeling guilty, you may also feel relieved. But if you're going through a bad time, if you feel deprived, if it all happened too quickly, if your ex has established an enviable life, perhaps with new children, you're likely to feel quite angry.

This happened in the case of another study couple—Robert and Paula. When she remarried, he was devastated. "I still can't believe it," said Robert in his first interview. "One day after the final decree, they go and get married. It was cruel. She swears she wasn't sleeping with him all along. What a load of crap. I can't even look at her without wanting to grab her and shake the truth right out of her. She wants to be friends now. Ha. I can't wait to tell the kids what their mother is really like!"

Robert and Paula are a good lesson in how to become Fiery Foes. Quick remarriage to someone the leaver knew before the divorce is one way. What matters is not whether it's true or false that Paula slept with her new mate, Peter, before she and Robert divorced; it's what Robert believes that's important. As we saw in Chapter 4, when there is an affair, followed by a deception (whether actual or perceived), the ex-partner's anger can escalate out of control. If the exspouses don't resolve the issue, and then one of them quickly remarries, the anger will become so pervasive and the "wronged" partner will feel so abused that he or she may feel an overwhelming urge to retaliate. Unfortunately, the children will get caught in the middle.

How could this situation be defused? If Paula could be honest with Robert during this time of remarriage, and even more, if she could apologize for hurting him and allow him time to process both the pain and her apology, that might help. If Paula could have been honest all along, that would have helped still more. A point I made strongly in Chapter 4 is worth repeating here: accepting responsibility for your own feelings and actions is crucial to having a good divorce.

As we saw in Chapter 4, most of us do some things during the divorce process that we later regret. We instinctively lie, get defensive, hide in fear, or even retaliate. When we recognize what we've done, we can then accept our own human weakness and apologize to our ex. Only then is mutual forgiveness possible. If Paula could empathize with Robert, apologize, and wait for a while, this crisis could sink back into its components: fact finding, choice making, and acceptance.

When You Remarry

If there's one thing we know for sure, it's that second marriages are not the same as first marriages. Especially if you are a parent, the choice points are different. They are also different when you remarry from when your exspouse remarries. You carry a whole lot more baggage into a second marriage than a first. There are the children—not only yours but your new spouse's as well. Then there are the exspouses. And the extended family of the new partner as well as the old: new in-laws, perhaps a few ex in-laws too. All these *extra* people jam into your marital bed, even when you and your partner are alone.

You don't have the same freedoms this time around. Remember when you fell in love for the first time—the luxury of thinking about the two of you? This time you have the children and the children's other parent to consider, and it's likely that they're not going to be particularly happy about your remarriage. These people, as much as you care about their welfare, place very real restrictions on your marriage plans. Don't be surprised if sometimes you find yourself angry: it's normal.

As we saw in the previous section, the first exspouse to remarry can expect a big reaction from the other exspouse. To navigate this marker point more easily, plan on giving attention to your ex, no matter how angry you may be. Your children's other parent deserves to be told about your plans to remarry—told directly, and told soon. This will help you as well as your ex. If you procrastinate, if your ex finds out about your plans secondhand from the children, or worse yet, from mutual friends or family members, the subsequent bad feelings may poison your future interactions. If you're Angry Associates or Fiery Foes, and don't want to call or see your exspouse, then write a short note about your plans. Expect changes on every level in your binuclear family—in your relationship with your exspouse, in your exspouse's relationship with mutual children, in your own relationship with mutual children.

When Melinda and Bill—a study remarriage couple in their late thirties—happily announced their wedding plans, they were shocked at their children's reactions. Melinda's daughter was fourteen and her son was eleven; Bill's sons were in college. Said Melinda, "My kids had known Bill for two years and they adored him. But when I told them we were getting married, and moving out of our tiny apartment into his house, they flew into a rage. My daughter screamed, 'You're ruining my life!' My son ignored me and switched on the television. All I could think of was, how could they be so selfish?

"Bill's kids were even worse. They didn't even congratulate us. No, all they wanted to know was, how he could give their rooms to my children, and how they were going to deal with my kids being around all the time when they were home on vacation, which happens about three weeks a year. They also wanted to know if Bill could take them skiing that Christmas as usual, and if he was leaving them the same amount in his will. And—as if that wasn't enough—when I told my ex, he said, 'Great. Now I won't have to pay so much child support.' I just didn't get it. After all the pain I've been through, you'd think they would be a little bit happy for me."

These children's reactions are not unusual. Children often resent having to change the pattern of their lives for your remarriage. After all, you're the one who's in love—not them. Your new partner, to them, may seem like an intruder, someone who's horning in on your love for them. Your new partner's children threaten their territory and their time with you; they may feel that your remarriage represents losing what they need and gaining nothing. What you can do at this marker point is actually quite substantial. If you acknowledge their feelings and reassure them of your love, you'll step down the emotional temperature. Also, if you give them adequate time to adjust, if you make only necessary changes, as slowly as possible, you won't be creating a sudden crisis they can't handle. Perhaps you and your new partner might try living together first on the weekends only; perhaps you can take this transition in easier stages than "We've met and we're getting married."

What about the home? Many couples prefer to move into an entirely new environment, rather than choose one partner's home over the other's. In that way, all the participants are starting fresh. Nobody's territory is being invaded; nobody's room has been seized by an unwelcome stranger. In this way, two sets of children can begin to see their new blended-family home as "our house," rather than as "my house" or "your house."

Check your expectations against reality. You can't expect to be an instant family. You can't reasonably expect that your kids will instantly love your new partner, that your partner's kids will go ga-ga over you, that your two sets of children will even tolerate each other, much less love each other. Emily and John Visher, founders of the Stepfamily Association of America and authors of several informative books on the subject, warn:

> Caring relationships take time to evolve. The expectation of "instant love" between stepparents and stepchildren can lead to many disappointments and difficulties. If the stepfamily relationships are allowed to develop as seems comfortable to the individuals involved, then caring between step-relatives has the opportunity to develop.

Renegotiating the Limited Partnership: Minimizing Conflict

The remarriage of an exspouse can awaken old issues. It also presents, to both spouses, the opportunity to request changes in the limited partnership agreement. These requests can be unilateral or bilateral. Most often, one exspouse wants to renegotiate child-care responsibilities or child support obligations.

If you're the one who's remarried, you can minimize conflict by requesting change only as absolutely necessary. Try not to change your agreed-on schedules with the children—at least not right away. Give your exspouse time to adjust to your remarriage. If your exspouse remarried and is pressing you to instantly renegotiate, you can say that you need time to adjust, to see how things will develop, before agreeing to any changes.

It's quite understandable that a remarriage might bring a renegotiation of schedules, especially when the new partner has children from a former marriage. Maybe the adults are trying to negotiate an occasional weekend alone together; maybe they're trying to negotiate a family Thanksgiving for the first time. Unless the original exspouses have been Cooperative Colleagues for quite a while, it's unlikely that the remarriage of one will bring instant flexibility to the other. Although many divorce agreements include clauses on schedule changes and child support revisions in the case of remarriage by one or both exspouses, nobody realizes how the other exspouse will feel about these revisions until the new situation actually presents itself.

Child support agreements are always open to revision when there's a change in circumstances; remarriage definitely fits the bill. You'll feel differently about the negotiation depending on who's remarrying and who's paying. If you're doing both, you may feel that because you now have a new family, you're justified in wanting to reduce payments to the old; perhaps, too, your new partner resents the outlay (especially if she is receiving less support from her own ex). The reality in these cases is that a remarriage is not generally viewed by the court as a change sufficient to reduce child support, regardless of your own change in circumstances. To even present this issue to your ex would likely create serious conflict without much resulting benefit.

If you're the one receiving child support, your ex may believe that since now you share a home and a second income, it would be reasonable to reduce child support. Most noncustodial fathers believe they're paying too much child support anyway: Why support their wife's new partner too? In these cases, you might try sitting down with your ex and going over how the money he contributes is spent on the children—and only the children. The exhusband may prefer to foot specific bills: summer camp, school, the orthodontist, piano lessons; this will eliminate any nagging suspicion that he's the one who'll pay for the new bedroom set you and your new husband just bought on credit.

Another very common problem is that one exspouse's new mate lives far away. Say that you're the custodial parent, living in New Jersey, and that you've met and fallen in love with someone who lives in Massachusetts. After exploring all the possible options, you decide that the only feasible solution is for you to move to Massachusetts. But this will necessitate a change in the amount of time your ex will spend with the children. You tell your ex about the dilemma and the response is, "No way I'm going to be a long-distance parent." Simultaneously, your mutual kids are complaining because they'll have to change schools and leave their friends. What do you do?

Unfortunately, there's no one right answer. Try to put yourself in your ex's shoes. How would you feel if the situation were reversed—if your ex were the primary parent who suddenly announced an imminent remarriage and move to California? Though any solution will bring pain, you'll minimize the conflict by understanding your ex's position. If you can together redefine the problem as a dilemma shared by the whole family—you, your ex, your children, and even your new mates—then it's likely that you'll all be happier with the result. Go back to Chapters 5 and 6. Set the new ground rules and list the new problems and all the possible solutions, no matter how silly they seem. If you're flexible enough, you'll find the answer—an imperfect answer that you'll all try to make work.

If the remarriage doesn't require a major overhaul because of a geographical move or some other huge change in circumstance, be conservative with your limited partnership. Try to stick with the agreed-upon terms. Reassure your ex that he or she will not be replaced by the new partner in your mutual children's affections, or in the amount of time they get to spend together. Reassure your ex that your remarriage will not negatively affect the financial arrangements. Take the lead in offering reassurance, even when your ex hasn't expressed anxiety. Likelier than not, the anxiety is there.

And, of course, reassure the children. Whether it's you who's remarrying or your exspouse, the children must know that they'll still be as important to both parents as they were before the remarriage. With any remarriage, the children's hopes that their parents might reconcile are destroyed: deal with their anger and realize what a difficult time they're going through. Ask them about the changes, and expect at least some outbursts against the new person entering their life, who's caused so much upheaval—who's maybe even forcing them to move. Take the time to weave the threads of life back together, one by one.

First Wives, Second Wives

Many first wives feel angry with second wives, at least early on in their relationship. The anger generally takes one of three common forms.

"She stole my husband." Whether or not the first wife's perception is true, she's directed her anger at her exhusband onto the second wife. The anger is said to be *displaced*. Displacing anger and blame for the failed marriage onto the "other woman," the first wife can salvage her own ego and exonerate her exhusband of any wrongdoing.

"They're both monsters." In *fused anger,* the first wife's fury is directed at both the ex and his new spouse. Fused anger often occurs when the exhusband finds a new, and often younger, wife immediately after the divorce.

"If you get more, I'll get less, so watch me grab it all." When there's competition between the first wife and the second, either over children or over territory, the anger is *direct*. The first wife is angry at the second, rather than being angry at the ex or about the actual divorce. She picks fights about money or about the children, believing that there's not enough to go around.

If you're a first wife and you find yourself reacting reflexively angry with your exhusband's second wife, you should step back, take a deep breath, and try to better define what you want to get from the situation. In today's family dynamics, you and your husband's new wife are likely to be the kin-keepers, the people who will hold together your child's binuclear family. Choose your battles wisely: the second wife is just as threatened by you as you are by her. If your exhusband or your children get caught up in the battle, you could have a crisis on your hands. You will strongly benefit from redefining roles and rules before such a crisis happens.

I've concentrated on the relationship between mothers and step-mothers because the Binuclear Family Study showed that relationship to be more difficult than that between fathers and stepfathers. Female parents appear to be more involved with each other—both positively and negatively—than are male parents.

The lack of strong feelings and direct emotional expression parallels general characteristics of male behavior in our society. Men, in general, are less articulate about their emotions.

First Husbands, Second Husbands

Although the men participants didn't express nearly as much feeling about one another as the women did, when questioned, some did talk about feeling threatened by the presence of another father figure in their children's lives, especially if it interfered with their relationship with their exwives. One man told of how he was being cut off from his ex by her new spouse. "Every time I call, he answers. When I ask to speak with Joline, he tells me she doesn't want to talk with me. I get so enraged I end up having a shouting match with him and wind up slamming down the phone."

One of my clients recently expressed his distress when his daughter invited him—and her stepfather—to her father-daughter Girl Scout dinner. "I felt hurt that she wanted to include him too. This should be our special night. But I could see that she didn't want to have to choose between us. It was actually not a bad evening. She liked having us both there and he's pretty easy to be with."

Nonresidential fathers—especially long-distance dads—feel the loss of their daily presence in their children's lives. When his exwife remarries and a new man becomes a daily fixture in his child's life, the father may feel his loss even more acutely. If the child's new stepparent takes on an active role in the child's life, the father may feel more competitive or may feel that because he doesn't see his child often he doesn't stand much of a chance.

Confused Roles, No Rules

When my father died, the funeral was held in New Jersey, very close to where my ex and his family live. It was a cold, rainy day. The pallbearers—my father's five granddaughters—accompanied his casket to the grave. My younger daughter was shivering, wearing only a lightweight jacket. As the pallbearers started their procession across the cemetery grounds, a woman took off her raincoat and lovingly spread it over my daughter's shoulders.

My aunt, standing next to me, said, "Who's that?" I replied evenly, "That's Sarah. You know, Allen's wife." My aunt looked at me disapprovingly. "Really, now. What's she doing here? She didn't even know your father!"

Later, I found myself not quite knowing how to introduce Sarah to members of my father's extended family, many of whom I hadn't seen for over twenty years. "This is Sarah. Remember my exhusband Allen? She's his wife." Or worse, "This is Sarah—my daughters' step-mother." Introductions done, everyone nodded politely, but I could see confusion clouding their faces. How could this be? The first wife and the second wife, looking quite close and comfortable with one another? Something strange about the whole thing.

Sarah's reason for attending the funeral made a whole lot of sense to me. My daughters had been very close with my father, and were deeply saddened by his death. Sarah knew that and came to offer her support. When I noted that and thanked her for coming, she let me know she also attended because of respect for me. Although it's over fifteen years since then, I still appreciate her consideration. It wasn't easy for her to walk into alien territory alone, her only connection being my daughters and me.

Sometimes, in a death or crisis, we drop our considerations of pride for a moment and reveal what's beneath: respect for each other and for our children. All of us, first wives and second wives, are in the same boat. Sometimes we can let down our guard and simply be human.

Barring a transcendent situation, it's helpful, if you're the first wife, to approach the second wife with mutual concerns. In dealing with these concerns in a dignified manner, you can subtly negotiate what each of your roles will be within the binuclear family that now includes both of you. In the same way as you dealt with the limited partnership—by setting ground rules, by mutually listing problems and solutions—not only can you enjoy the benefits of rapprochement but you may well learn that you have a new friend. Later in this chapter, we'll see a binuclear family that has formed itself around two strong women.

A Fuzzy Kinship

Sarah and I have a fuzzy kinship. We share secrets; we've shared beds with the same man; we've shared the same mother-in-law; we've heard about each other through the children. And we now have over twenty-five years of history. Clearly, we're family.

But what are we? People have named this relationship: wife-in-law, co-wife, coparent, my child's stepparent. None of these names seems to stick.

A binuclear family may include all sorts of fuzzy kinships. What are ex in-laws, for example, with whom you're still close? Says Marjorie, one of my clients: "His mom and I still have brunch together, with the kids, every month." The ex mother-in-law of a colleague of mine sends her birthday cards and invites her over for dinner, as well as spending time with her grandson. To say these relationships are "ex" anything seems paltry, given their richness. They are fuzzy relationships, and they are fine.

And so we return to the problem of language, with which we began this chapter and this book. "So tell me, Ted, what's your relationship with your exwife's cohabitor? And with her cohabitor's children? Hmmm. They live with your children, don't they? Then yes, they're your children's stepsiblings. No, not legally. But it sounds like they all see each other as family."

Not only is this interview technique cumbersome, but nobody can keep track of who you're talking about. I used to jot genealogy notes to myself such as, FSCPFS—former spouse's current partner's former spouse. Today, I use family diagrams and fill in the blanks with people's names. Then I refer to them by name rather than by kinship relationship. They are all fuzzy kin—from the inside (the child's eye view) out. Anyone the child hugs belongs on this chart—plus some others.

From the Outside In: Joining an Established Binuclear Family

We've spoken a great deal about bringing new kin into the binuclear family, from the point of view of those who constructed the family. What about people who join the family through remarriage? How are they affected by the existing relationships, and what can they do both to ease their transition and to make themselves not quite so dependent on the aftermath of someone else's divorce? What's the stepparent's point of view?

Second Wives, First Wives

First wives, as we've seen, often start their relationship with second wives in anger. Either displaced, fused, or direct, anger it is, and it isn't a pleasant, welcoming environment.

While the first wife may feel that you reflect adversely on her, you may feel that you live under her looming shadow. You hear about her all the time from your husband; you may even be sitting on some of her furniture and reading her books. Do you have to take her anger as well?

There are many things you can do both to alleviate a bit of the anger and to protect yourself from being damaged by it. The anger is there, but it doesn't have to land on you.

Very often, a second wife will bring this anger on herself by interfering in the relationship between her husband and his ex. Randi and Steve are a case in point. Steve had divorced Elaine at the time of his first interview and was married to Randi by the third interview five years later. When we interviewed Randi, she was hopping mad. "Steve's so passive," she complained. "He needs my help to protect his rights." But Randi's interference in matters pertaining to the first family—she'd called his accountant and lawyer to report what she called "Elaine's dishonesty"—only led to trouble for the entire binuclear family.

When you marry a man who has an exwife and children, you're entering a complex situation. This situation is not likely to become simple—certainly not through any misapplication of your efforts. Such interference can be practically irresistible and is usually disastrous for the second marriage; it's not surprising that the divorce rate for second marriages is even higher than that for first marriages. Here are three rules that will help your marriage to survive, and will decrease your own discomfort:

> *First, stay out of any conflicts between your husband and his ex.* Friction already exists; if you jump in you'll hurt yourself. Even though you may only want to show unity with your husband, you can only make things worse. Especially stay away from court proceedings involving child support, custody, and visitation—no matter how much you care for his kids. Your happy faces, together, will only provoke her.

> *Second, don't compete with your husband's ex.* You may comfort yourself with the practical truth that you've already competed and won. Do not grind it in her face that "This man belongs to me." Everyone knows.

> *Third, don't try to replace her as the mom.* Form a relationship with your stepchildren that is separate and different. Be openly supportive of the importance of her role. Though you may prefer that your husband's relationship with his ex cease after divorce, remember how important a continued relationship is for the children. For the children's sake—for the sake of the whole binuclear family—allow that relationship to exist, and to be as agreeable as possible.

Ghosts of the Past

A client of mine, Beth, told me about the first time she met her ex's current wife. It was several years after his remarriage; the occasion was their daughter's graduation from high school. Beth said, "Shelly and I were uptight at first, but later we started to feel comfortable with each other. We even found ourselves joking a bit about

Richard's mother. At one point when Richard had gone out of the room, Shelly told me, 'I'm so glad to finally meet you. It's like you've been a ghost or something. No one in Richard's family talks about you and there are no pictures anywhere. There's tons of pictures of the kids with Richard when they were small, but all the ones of you have been removed from the albums. It's been a little creepy, knowing you were there but not knowing you.' "

Photo albums give life to our personal histories. My adult daughters still like to look at the pictures of their early childhood, many of which include their father and me during our marriage. Not only is it important for them to see themselves at that age, it's also important for them to see both their parents: they were too little at the time for them to remember us together in a loving way.

At a recent workshop I mentioned how my mother, in a fit of rage, carefully cut my exhusband out of all the family pictures. My children resented this, though it has since become a family joke. I was surprised when at least ten members of the audience got up and told similar stories. I learned that it's possible—although in a subtler way—to make unwanted relatives disappear from the family album. Airbrush out exspouses: Pretend they never were.

Don't do this. It's bad for the children. And it's also bad to include such dishonesty into your current relationship. The truth may hurt, but the pain is brief, compared to the long-term, nagging, subconscious hurt of knowing someone's around whom you can't mention. The ghosts of the past must be laid to rest.

The Exspouse Relationship After Remarriage

Exspouses often have a hard time coparenting after one of them remarries. Among the participants in the Binuclear Family Study, the number and frequency of child-rearing activities shared between former spouses was highest when neither partner had remarried; it was lowest when only the husband had remarried.

"Who wanted to deal with his new wife?" said Danielle, a study participant. "It was easier, and more fun, just to take the kids out by myself. For a while there Joe and I used to go to museums with the kids and we'd discuss things there—but after he married Rona, I felt like a fifth wheel."

The key word of the aftermath transition is *change*. And change brings uncertainty among family members. Who performs what roles and tasks changes at each developmental stage. Mom and Dad may parent together at one stage, and then be replaced by Mom and Charles in one household, and Rona and Dad in the other.

What's the Most Difficult Adjustment for Stepparents?

For the Binuclear Family Study, we originally interviewed 196 biological parents. By the time of the third interview, we had to include (in addition to the parents) 85 new partners of these parents. Most had been living with or married to the original participant in our study for two years or more by the time of this interview.

When we asked these new partners what was their most difficult adjustment in remarriage—when and where the problems came—the answers varied according to gender. The men felt that the very beginning of the remarriage was most difficult—the first six months. The women felt that it was only after the first six months that the problems intensified, and generally lasted through the time of the interview.

About three-fourths of the women and half the men thought that their partner's children had somehow affected the relationship between them and their partner. The men said the effect had been positive; the women, mixed. Fewer than 10 percent of men or women thought that their partner's children had brought only problems to their marriage.

The same percentage—three-fourths of the women and half the men—said that they argued about "my kids" versus "your kids." Nobody wanted to have less involvement with their partner's children: most wanted more involvement, and were satisfied that their partners were supportive. Most men described their relationship with their new wife's children as "parental," while women tended to say they were "friends" with their new husband's children, regardless of the children's age.

One-third of stepfathers interviewed said that their partner's children called them "Dad," but only 12 percent of the stepmothers were called "Mom." And in families where the stepfather was "Dad," the biological father was less involved with his own children.

Three-fourths of the new partners said they were happy with their relationships with their stepchildren; they also said that this relationship had improved since the beginning. More than twice as many women as men had sought advice on how to be a stepparent from books, articles, friends, or counselors.

So what was the most difficult adjustment? It was the sheer mass of all the changes, coming all at once. Michelle, the second wife of a study participant, summed it up this way: "It was like Mardi Gras. All that noise, all that yelling under all those masks, and everywhere you turned, something you didn't understand. All you could do was grin and hold on as hard as you could to something stable—and all try to enjoy the ride."

Acquaintances, Friends, or Relatives?

About half the participants in my study whose exspouses had recoupled had contact with their ex's new partner—their child's stepparent. Another quarter tried contact, but had later discontinued it. A minority said that they'd made substantial efforts to develop a relationship with their children's stepparents and were rebuffed.

Stepparents, to the biological parents, were acquaintances, rather than friends or relatives. The relationship was distant but polite, especially for the majority who admitted that the stepparent was a good influence on their kids. This fits with the early developmental stage of these remarriage families. At the time of our third interview, most had been married between one and two years.

The relationship between stepparents and biological parents shows what we've said so many times before: that the binuclear family begins, develops, and ends with the child. The more involved the stepparents were with their stepchildren, the better were their spousal relationships.

Steps and Halves: What's Your Remarriage Like for the Children?

Nancy and Jim, a client couple with two young children, Ellen and David, had been divorced for three years when Jim married Elaine, and for four years when Nancy married Craig. Craig and Elaine both brought children from former marriages.

When Elaine and Jim decided to get married, aside from sharing their histories with their exspouses, they invited each other's children over for extended play dates. At first their children got along fine; later—during the remarriage transition—Elaine's daughter Jamie acted out. Elaine said, "After living alone with Jamie for three years, I was really excited to have a family again and give Jamie more of a dad. But it's not working out. Jamie throws things at Jim's kids and yells at me that I never spend time with her. And when his kids are home, it seems that everyone's fighting over Jim."

Jim said in a separate interview, "Maybe we shouldn't have gotten married. When we were dating we made time for each other. . . . But after we got married Elaine felt guilty leaving Jamie with a babysitter. Jamie's very demanding, and Elaine can't seem to say no. Whenever I try to suggest to Elaine that Jamie should learn to play alone more, Elaine seems to get moody and quiet. Her resentment of the time I spend with my kids is hard for me to deal with. Sometimes I think she wishes I would stop seeing them, or see them as little as Tom [Jamie's father] sees her."

Remarriage is hard on children. They don't know whether the remarried parent sees the new stepparent as a substitute parent or as an additional parent. In the Binuclear Family Study, the children who had the hardest time were daughters of fathers who'd remarried. Children spend their babyhood hearing about wicked stepmothers: they wonder, will they get one? And why should they listen to a stepfather? He's not really their dad!

Craig—Nancy's second husband—developed a relationship with David (Nancy and Jim's son) that was a case in point. He said sadly about a year into the stormy remarriage transition, "All the kids seemed to get along pretty well at first. I wanted to be very careful not to do anything that would make Jim feel like I was taking over as father of his kids. But I was also used to being a father and liked the idea of having a couple more kids. My relationship with Ellen was pretty good—I know how to father girls. But David was difficult for me. He seemed to resent my taking over the household. I tried being his friend but he just seemed to fight with me about everything. We're not at all alike and more and more we just try to avoid each other. It upsets Nancy a lot. And when Sally and Meg live with us, things get worse. David really resents them and withdraws to his room."

David had his own ideas on the subject. "Craig's brats drive me crazy. They move into the house and just take over. Meg sneaks into my room and messes up my models and Craig just excuses her because she's a little kid. Mom bends over backward to please them and all they do is complain. For the part of the month they live with us the whole place is topsy-turvy. I'm supposed to be 'understanding'—so Mom says—but I get to a point where I feel like I'd rather just go live with Dad."

Craig added, "I find myself yelling at my own kids more now in my attempts to keep them from bothering David." In turn, Nancy complained that Craig's girls, Sally and Meg, were whiners. She'd redecorated their rooms, bent over backward to please them, and tried to be friendly, but they just ran to Craig and complained about her. "And it seems that whenever they are with us Ellen hangs all over me. The minute Craig and I go off into our bedroom we can count on a fight starting downstairs, usually between Ellen and Sally. Sometimes I think that the only thing that will save our marriage is the one weekend each month when all the kids are gone!"

In blended households, there tends to be quite a bit of friction between kids who live at the house and kids who "visit." If all the members of a new binuclear family do not perceive nonresidential children as part of the family, the children will likely not be assigned chores or given roles, nor do they have to act according to the same rules as do those who live in the household. The result is fighting. Sometimes the resident child is jealous of the visitor's special status; sometimes it's the other way around.

For Nancy and Jim's child Ellen, sharing her father with Jamie was even more difficult than sharing her mother with Craig's children, Sally and Meg. "It just doesn't seem fair. Every time I go to see Dad, Jamie is there. She always wants to hold his hand and sit on his lap and wants him to take her every place we go. I used to be able to sit in the front seat of the car with Dad ... but now Jamie and I have to share the back seat. And sometimes she even calls him 'Daddy.' I can't stand it! She gets to live with him all the time.

"It's not so bad with Sally and Meg. Meg and I get to have some fun when we're together. Sometimes we fight but we get to play together a lot. And Mom always does something special with me alone when they're in our house. I don't have to share my things with them because Craig brought a lot of their stuff. . . . Sometimes I get kind of upset when they get special privileges because they're not here all the time, but then sometimes we all get to do fun things together."

The relationship between a child and an out-of-home parent is a hard one throughout the early stages of the aftermath of divorce and the remarriage transition. But as the child adapts to the new reality, and the parent-child relationships stabilize within the binuclear family, the child can begin to look forward to those times together as very special.

What do children feel when parents remarry? This binuclear family just scratches the surface. Social scientists need to study the stresses and developmental phases of adding new members to the binuclear family. We need to know about the relationships that decline as well as the relationships that grow.

It's my belief that for many children the transition to remarriage is often more stressful than the transition to divorce. The changes children need to make when a parent inherits new children, the losses they feel, the general stress and disorganization as the household adapts to accommodate all the new needs and schedules, even the parents—who may be so wrapped up in their new mate that they're insensitive to the child's needs—all must be studied. We still know so little.

The New Family Album

For centuries, African-American families have coped with some of the same issues faced by all binuclear families of today. Through necessity and invention, many African-American families evolved complex and flexible kinship structures. There's a high incidence of children living in homes without one or both biological parents; there's also the minority relationship with the majority society—having these family structures defined as deviant by the dominant culture.

African-Americans have created what social scientists call a *pedi-focal family system*. In a pedi-focal system, children are assumed to belong to the community; they are the responsibility of any adults who are able to contribute to the child's well-being. In the African-American culture, children are prized, and being part of their rearing is a privilege, not a burden.

Given the way our dominant family structures devalue children, my suggestion is that we'd do well to learn from the pedi-focal model. If we would stop clinging so tenaciously to our nuclear family bias—that a child needs two parents and *only two* parents—we might find better ways to meet our children's needs in today's world.

According to stepfamily experts, John and Emily Visher, the lessons one can learn by living in stepfamilies are invaluable and unique: how to accept, even to grow to love, people entirely different from oneself; how to establish new but profoundly meaningful family rituals; how to calculate risk and gain in an unknown environment. Let's look at three families who have tried their best to learn those lessons.

"We're the Family": Eileen and Fred

Eileen and Fred, a housewife and engineer, had been married for nine years when they divorced in 1974. They'd known each other almost all their lives. Their three sons were five, three, and two at the time the couple divorced.

Eileen left the marriage; she moved out without the children. "I felt that since I was the one who wanted the divorce," she said at our interview, "I had to leave him with the kids. I was involved with someone else and I was terrified of a custody fight."

I met this binuclear family only once. During research for this book, a cousin of Eileen's put me in touch with this family, who she said "had a good divorce—an excellent divorce." I spent several hours one evening with Eileen and Fred, and with their remarriage partners, Joe and Bonnie.

There were no children from either of the second marriages. The seven children now in the extended family group included Eileen and Fred's three sons; Joe's two daughters (he was the noncustodial parent) from his first marriage; and Bonnie's two children (she was the custodial parent)—a boy and a girl—from her first marriage.

The divorce hadn't started well. In fact, the central couple of this

We're the Family

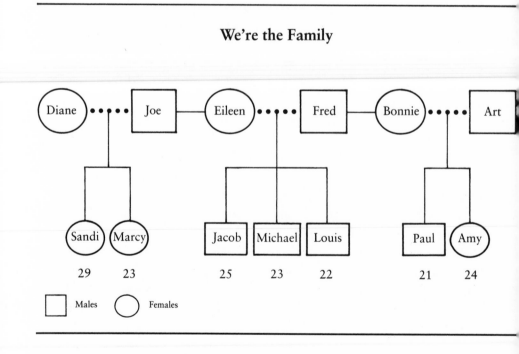

binuclear family—Eileen and Fred—had begun as Angry Associates after Eileen walked out. They rapidly developed a Cooperative Colleague relationship. Fred says, "We didn't get along, but we had a common view of what we thought was right for the kids." Also, at an early choice point, when Fred could have gotten revenge on Eileen for leaving him by keeping her away from the children, he instead chose to include her. "Our sons needed their mother." He says he was angry at Eileen, but never hated her. "Hate is something deep inside that never goes away."

In 1976, two years after her divorce from Fred, Eileen married Joe, whose marriage with her friend Diane had broken up around the same time as her original marriage. Several years later, in 1981, Fred met Bonnie at religious services, and they married a year later.

All of the adults are friendly with each other—especially Bonnie and Eileen. Bonnie had been impressed when she and Fred first got together with his exwife. "Eileen and Fred talked to each other very nicely. And Eileen embraced me. She seemed glad Fred was with a good woman." The two women soon became good friends. "It started when I'd drop the kids off," said Bonnie. "We'd have tea together, and talk."

What sparked this friendship? The women allowed themselves to like each other—and they defined their roles extremely well. Bonnie was especially generous. She never tried to replace Eileen as the three boys' mother. Pointing to Eileen in our meeting, Bonnie strongly asserted, *"This* is the momma." She turned to Eileen and repeated, *"You're* the momma. Nobody takes the place of the momma."

At important occasions and rituals, this extended family is very careful and respectful about giving everyone their rightful roles. For example, when Eileen and Fred's eldest son was bar mitzvahed, Joe and Bonnie stood back on the stage while Eileen and Fred stood proudly at the center, with their son.

They've had to make up their own rules for the family life cycle. "At school conferences," said Eileen, "the four of us just walked in together." They consciously took turns in dealing with authority figures—rabbis, doctors, teachers. No one adult was perceived by the outside world as the primary parent. Everybody worked. Everybody contributed.

All the relationships in this family did not turn out similarly rosy. Neither Joe nor Bonnie have good divorces with their exspouses. Diane and Joe had a Fiery Foe divorce that has only recently become civil; they're neither cooperative nor friendly. Bonnie, also, has little to do with her exspouse. She noted at our meeting, "Art divorced us all."

Bonnie and Joe both agree that their own children suffered from bad divorces. Said Bonnie, "Our kids aren't making the same kinds of adjustments as Fred and Eileen's kids, who got to watch their parents together as they grew up." Fred added, "I don't think the kids had to decide between the two of us. There were no loyalty conflicts."

This doesn't mean there weren't any difficult times with the kids. They went through all the transitions and choice points of the families described in this chapter. From Bonnie's point of view—the new step-parent, the outsider looking in at the cozy family—"Sometimes I wished there weren't so many people! On our honeymoon, we took a van and piled all five kids inside. My own children and I felt like we were invaded. Our family of three suddenly became a family of seven. My kids were uncomfortable with this big clan at first. Joe's kids and Eileen and Fred's kids all knew each other from before the divorces. They already felt like siblings."

Eileen and Bonnie each had the same roles: this helped them be sympathetic toward each other. They are both mothers; they are both stepmothers. They identify with each other because of this interchange of roles. For example, when Eileen and Fred's middle son got the measles while staying with Bonnie and Fred, Bonnie invited Eileen to visit so she could take care of him. "I know how bad it would feel to be the momma and not be with your sick son."

This family has defined itself as one large but close-knit group, all sharing a sizable common ground. "We are *the* family," said Eileen at our meeting. Bonnie and Fred both nodded their enthusiastic agreement. Eileen and Fred's limited partnership agreement produced one kind of good divorce.

This is a pedi-focal family: the needs of the children come first. When a child is sick, the adult caregiver who's present cares for the child, then calls in the mother.

Eileen summarized: "The four of us became family within itself. We were family because of the children at first, concerned with their problems and issues. But now, we have become friends as well."

"We're Like Sisters": Stacey and Bill

Stacey and Bill had been married for sixteen years and divorced for seven when I met with them for an afternoon while researching this book. I was doing a day-long workshop in the Northeast, and asked the sponsors for a family of divorce with which to work on stage. I was surprised when five adults and five children showed up.

There were Stacey and Bill, in their forties, and their two daughters, ages ten and sixteen; Stacey's current husband Howard; Howard's exwife Tess and their fourteen-year-old son and sixteen-year-old daughter; Tess's current husband Rick and their four-year-old son, Erik. Bill was single.

Their binuclear family is, in Stacey's words, "marginally middle class." One common denominator is the importance that the adults all place on being with the children. Stacey says, "Although I didn't want the divorce, in my gut, this was never a question. The kids needed and would have their dad."

When Stacey was first dating Howard, they double-dated with Rick and Tess, who were already married at the time. Stacey said, "It was clear to me that Tess was completely done with Howard, and only wanted him to be happy." She went on: "One of the things when Tess and I first met was, we were simpatico about wanting our kids to have dads."

This family has its problems. For example, in our meeting they spoke cautiously about "places where we have little tugs of war, when

We're Like Sisters

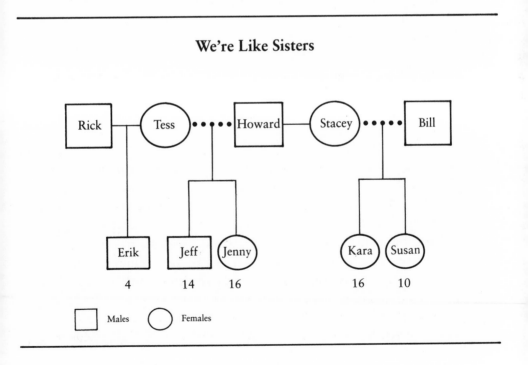

Males □   Females ○

one side of the family's interest conflicts with the other side." Upon exploration, the tugs of war proved not to be so little. In fact, there was a major tug of war over money issues. With three fathers and two mothers, and limited income, there's a lot of currency flow, and a lot of debate over who controls what.

Another tug of war was about having simultaneous coparenting relationships with exspouses and with new partners, over the same child. Stacey noted, "It's difficult to have partial partnerships with both dads." She doesn't wholly agree, either with her exhusband (the children's father) or with her current husband (the children's stepfather), about how the children should be raised. Stacey would prefer to have total control but what she's learned is to compromise, even when the end result goes against the grain. "There are things I'd like to change if I could. But, I have to be part of the 'crew.'" This "crew" decision with a bunch of teenagers has come to mean that the kids can make requests, but the parents have the final word. Sometimes those requests require a meeting of the "crew."

Tess and Stacey, however, tend to agree on child-rearing matters, which leaves them the strongest political bloc in the binuclear family system. They agree on nutrition, bedtime hours, discipline, and how the kids should dress. And together they often get their way. The two of them can argue down the men.

"We're like sisters," said Stacey proudly. "Not blood sisters—sisters in the movement."

Again, this is a pedi-focal family—centered around the children's needs. Stacey and Bill's limited partnership produced a good divorce.

"We're Good Friends": Eve and Paul

Eve and Paul, on the other hand, show how a couple can change their divorce over time, from Fiery Foes to good friends—more than Cooperative Colleagues but not quite Perfect Pals. Both are successful, high-powered, creative professionals who spent their marriage straining to balance the enormous demands of work, children, travel, and each other. Eve was and is the CEO of a major fashion empire; Paul's written many ambitious novels, and has been honored many times by the literary community. They'd been married for two years (after a ten-year relationship) when Eve discovered—through a gossip column—that Paul was having an affair with Elizabeth, a very high-profile magazine editor. Paul and Eve's only child, Adam, was two years old at the time. Eve was enraged. She immediately moved out, taking Adam with her.

Even though they were Fiery Foes—almost incendiary—when they separated, both Eve and Paul shared a strong mutual concern about Adam. This concern and care brought them into my office. At first— five years ago—they couldn't talk to each other, and I met with each individually. Both were determined to avoid a custody battle and a long, drawn-out legal divorce. How did they manage to let go of their anger and eventually end up as friends?

It didn't happen immediately. And both of them faced hard work. Paul was willing to make many concessions about support and property but one thing he wouldn't concede on was his son's living arrangements and custody. He wanted his son to be with him half of the time. In their limited partnership agreement, Eve made quite a concession. Because Adam and Paul were extremely close, she agreed to give up the idea of sole custody, and agreed to joint physical custody. Both— albeit reluctantly—made many compromises due to their shared love for their young son.

So at the start of this divorce we had noncommunicating spouses, an affair, and enormous publicity—ingredients for disaster. Another factor could have exacerbated their problems even more. Over a short span of time I watched Eve and Paul's binuclear family balloon out from a small, polarized group of three, to a crowd of four adults and

We're Good Friends

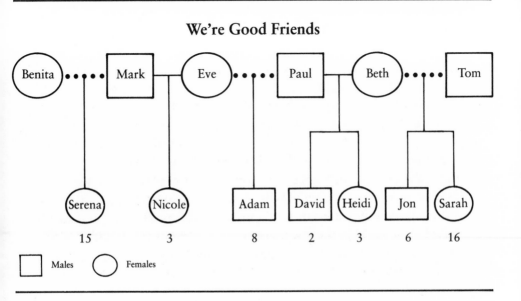

seven children. Paul and Beth married within two years after Eve and Paul's divorce, and over the next two years had two babies, which added to the two children that Beth had from her former relationships. Meanwhile, Eve also remarried, to a doctor, Mark, who was the custodial father of an eleven-year-old girl from a previous marriage. Within a year Eve and Mark had a baby of their own—Nicole. Paul and Eve's son Adam, in four incredibly eventful years, had gone from being an only child to being one of seven children.

Instead of things getting worse, surprisingly, they got better. The setup for a disastrous divorce—a unilateral split, quick remarriages, many new children, complexity, publicity, personality—became, instead, quite a good divorce. Today, Eve and Paul both say, "We're good friends." How did they accomplish this?

Eve, especially, had to make an enormous effort. She took control quickly and set her ground rules. "I want to have nothing to do with Beth. And I want it clear that she is not to take on a parent role with Adam. No taking him to the doctor. No taking him to school. No going to parent-teacher conferences." There were small crises when Beth became involved in ways that Eve would have none of. As these became resolved, more rules were developed to make sure similar incidents didn't reoccur. Eve knew herself well enough to know that she didn't want to fuel her rage with continued contact.

Even though Eve wanted no contact with Beth nor did she want her to take on a parenting role, she still wanted to stay in close communication with Paul about Adam. In the beginning they set times when they could talk about Adam, what problems he might be experiencing, who would take him to what, how they would divide holidays. Over time, as their relationship improved, they didn't need a formal time to discuss Adam but were able to do so on an ongoing basis, whenever an issue arose.

Paul and Eve diligently worked through their emotional divorce. Eventually, he apologized for the pain he'd caused. Although he felt remorseful about some of his behavior and wished their marriage had not deteriorated so badly, he didn't regret the divorce, but he did regret the way the announcement erupted. Eve contained her rage, and slowly, over time, it diminished. With professional help, they developed a limited partnership based on their strong kinship tie through Adam, with Beth on the far periphery of the common ground. The situation was helped by the fact that Paul and Mark—Eve's second husband—liked one another. Also, Beth's youngest child, Jon, from an earlier marriage, and Paul and Beth's oldest child, Heidi, come over on occasion to Eve and Mark's house to play with Adam and Nicole.

The children have sparked a partial rapprochement between the adults. Each year the two women, Eve and Beth, come one small, painful step toward making peace with one another. Eve invited Beth to Adam's last birthday party and she attended. Though the situation was socially uncomfortable and Beth left early, they'd made a huge step in the right direction.

Although Beth is not at all pleased with the ground rules set by Eve—and it sometimes creates an issue between her and Paul—she abides by them because she doesn't want to create more anger. She doesn't like the feeling of being an outsider, but she is respectful of Eve's feelings.

Honoring Family Ties

Like Eileen and Fred, like Stacey and Bill, Eve and Paul were able to structure a good divorce out of materials that at first did not seem promising. There are so many permutations for successful divorces, we would need a computer to keep track of them all. Erma Bombeck has a good idea: "The computer would not only keep pace with how many tickets are needed for graduation and seats for the wedding, but with whether the separation would allow for three mothers and three fathers to sit in peace and love, or be scattered throughout the crowd."

The binuclear family's children are that computer: they can tell us, by their anger or distant sadness, or by their healthy and happy growth, whether to scatter ourselves through the crowd in our aftermath transition—or whether to sit close together in peace and love.

8

Pathways to a Good Divorce
20-20 HINDSIGHT

ANY PROCESS AS complex as the good divorce cannot be summarized with facile "how-to's." It's easy in hindsight to say—as did many of my study parents—"I should have communicated with my ex"; "I shouldn't have badmouthed my ex in front of the kids"; or "If only I'd let go of my anger." It would be easy to quickly compile a huge list of "shoulds," "shouldn'ts," and "if only's." But as anyone in the midst of the upheaval knows, to actually follow this list would be difficult, if not impossible. In fact, such a list may even add to your pain, making you feel guilty for not being able to do something that sounds so simple.

Throughout this book, while presenting the realities of divorce, I have tried to arm you with some road maps to help you ease your losses and reintegrate your life at each stage. Along the way I hope you have also felt my hope and optimism in your courage and ability to make it through the difficult transitions.

As we are coming to the end of this journey together, I want to provide you with a list. This is not a list of "how-to's"—it's a list of pointers; each will remind you of sections of the book in which the ideas were explained in more depth. And if you've started with this last chapter—as I often do—this list will show you which parts of the book you may want to read next: the parts that challenge our basic beliefs about divorce; those that encourage you to reframe your assumptions about divorce; those that outline approaches and pathways; those that recount the experiences of other binuclear families in process.

Challenging Our Basic Beliefs

Your divorce has probably already challenged some of the beliefs you had on your wedding day. Perhaps you've lost some of your romantic notions about what marriage is like, or perhaps you wonder about your ability to choose a good partner, or perhaps you're feeling disillusioned about relationships in general.

Your old belief may have been that you'd stay married "Till death do us part." In order to work toward a good divorce, you must first challenge your fundamental beliefs about marriage, its beginnings, and endings.

Endings are an inherent part of life.
Anything that has a beginning also must have an ending.
Change is inevitable and implicitly requires endings as well as beginnings.

Although, at some level, we all accept these seeming truisms, we go on to live life denying the very real ending of marriages. In his very wise and moving book, *Soul Mates,* Thomas Moore tells a story of a man who had lived with bitterness for years after his wife left him. In conversation with the man, Moore learns how unhappy the man, too, had been in the marriage. Moore asks him why he would continue to live in a relationship that was "obviously soulless and lifeless." The man replies that he kept hoping one day it would change. To this, Moore reflects: "It takes courage to read the signals of fate asking for change, asking us to acquiesce to the bitter truths that are revealed slowly and painfully. An ending may be part of the special logic of relationship, an expression of its *logos,* its deeply inherent nature and its own laws and requirements."

That's not to say that one should leave a marriage at the first glimpse of problems, or when one first faces the inevitable disillusionment that marriage wasn't all it was cracked up to be, or when the romance wanes under the pressures of daily intimacy. Although I have said this earlier, it bears repeating. People rarely leave marriages easily; they usually struggle with their feelings for years. But one common wish of the divorced, in 20-20 hindsight, is, "If only we'd ended our marriage sooner." The data are beginning to support this belief by showing that much of the damage children suffer was caused in the last few years of their parents' troubled marriage.

If we could change our basic belief about the "shoulds" of marriage being "till death us do part" we might be in a better position to acknowledge which problems are relationship-breakers. In so doing, we could honestly confront these problems and look for healthy, constructive ways to perhaps resolve them. If, however, our fears make us unable to accept the very real possibility that our marriage may not be a lifelong contract, we are more likely to deny these early warning signs, sweep them under the rug, pretend all is well. It is only years later that most people remember these early signals of trouble, using them to substantiate their case and ease their guilt about their divorce.

Therapists note that it is the rare couple who seeks help when it is most needed and could be the most helpful; most arrive at the therapist's door years later. Now it may be too late. Serious damage has already been done. One person is more propelled to move on rather than to recommit to the present partner.

Judith Viorst, in her bestselling book *Necessary Losses*, examines the inevitability of loss. She also suggests ways that we need to integrate loss—to make losses and endings a productive part of our lives. "Losing sucks. But to look at loss is to see how inextricably our losses are linked to growth. And to start to become aware of the ways in which our responses to loss have shaped our lives can be the beginning of wisdom and hopeful change."

If we accept this very basic fact that endings and loss are woven into the fabric of our lives, we will change our beliefs about divorce. Rather than seeing divorce as the end of the family, as the failure of self and even of society, we can accept it as the end of a relationship, a traumatic and painful loss.

Reframing Our Assumptions

Societal Assumptions

Divorce ends the family.
Divorce ruins children.
Divorce is abnormal.
Divorce is mysterious and totally catastrophic.

The starting point to good divorce must be to remake the very assumptions on which the divorce is based. Since negative images of divorce are likely to inundate you just when you're feeling most vulnerable, you must change these images. This may not be easy because your reframed assumptions will contradict what society generally believes. But in fact you must internalize new assumptions and make them your own. Without this necessary change of attitude, even the most well-intentioned and the most practical of self-help suggestions will be meaningless. Your new assumptions will provide the foundation for making positive family changes and implementing a good divorce.

New Assumption #1

Divorce redefines your family. If you and your ex are parents, you are forever connected as kin. It's true that divorce ends your family as society defines it. But what it ends is your nuclear family. Handled well, divorce transforms your nuclear family into a binuclear family—which is rapidly becoming the most prevalent family form in our society.

New Assumption #2

Children in binuclear families can be as healthy as children in nuclear families. Your children will experience difficult times, but they can emerge healthy—and so can you. It's upsetting for children to change family type, from nuclear to binuclear, but it doesn't follow that you have damaged them for life. You have the opportunity to provide them with love and nurturance no matter what form your family takes.

New Assumption #3

Divorce is normal. Divorce is not deviant; therefore, you are not deviant; nor are you a failure. Like most other people in the same situation, you will love—and be loved—again. Not only are you not a failure, but your marriage isn't necessarily a failure because it ended in divorce.

New Assumption #4

The process of divorce is predictable—it can be charted. It's true that initially divorce is crazy-making. Accepting that your emotions will be volatile, powerful, and vacillating will help you manage them better. Knowing that these emotions are temporary and that others have felt the same way will help you embrace what you're feeling, and move on. Making the unknown known allows you to make reasoned choices that meet your long-term objectives.

While I was working on this chapter I shared these four basic assumptions with some friends and clients. One of my clients—recently separated after a twelve-year marriage—told me that she was going to turn these assumptions into her personal mantras. She wrote them in her journal. When she was scared and overwhelmed she repeated her mantras to herself. "They calm me. Whenever I start berating myself for being angry or vengeful or depressed I recite them—sometimes a dozen times over. They help me accept myself better and give me the courage to make it through another day."

A friend—divorced after a twenty-year marriage—told me she found these new assumptions helpful to her flagging self-esteem. She decided to start a notebook, jotting down the things people said to her that contradicted her own inner messages. She titled her notebook *Shaming and Blaming.* "When I wrote down the things that other people, TV, and the popular press were saying about divorce, I realized how often they made me feel bad about myself. When I started to write my personal answers to these comments, I found I grew stronger and more certain about my own beliefs—and I understood myself and my divorce better. It feels good to be able to stand up straight and tall and not let those others bully me into thinking of myself as an irresponsible failure."

Once you integrate these new assumptions, in your own way, whatever it is, you've cleared the road. Now you can define your goals and identify the pathways by which you can reach those goals.

Realizing Major Goals

A good divorce, mercifully, has clear, straightforward goals, and there are only three of them:

Keeping your family a family.
Minimizing the negative effects on your children.
Integrating your divorce in your life in a healthy way.

The goals are your destination. Keep them vividly in your mind. Write them on a piece of paper and post them in a prominent place, as a constant reminder. These goals are simple enough, but certainly not easy to accomplish.

Your pathways to these goals will be less clear, less simple, and more difficult to find than are the goals themselves. Don't expect yourself to be able to master all these pathways at once. Don't be discouraged. Remember, your divorce remains a permanent part of your life. You will be presented with many opportunities to correct your mistakes and improve the quality of your life.

Keeping Your Family a Family

Accept that all-out war is not inevitable and is in fact destructive.
Recognize that compromise is absolutely necessary.
Stay in charge of your divorce.
Construct a vision of your binuclear family.
Make new rules for how the two households will be linked.

Eileen and Fred, the Chapter 7 couple who'd divorced and who (after a few years) called their binuclear family of four adults and seven children *"the* family," are a case in point. Though they had all the potential for war—Eileen making the unilateral decision to leave and already being involved in a serious relationship with Joe, the man she married two years later—they very soon realized how destructive a war would be.

Eileen and Fred both made difficult compromises. Eileen's decision to have her three sons continue to live with their father in the family home was a tremendously painful compromise for her to make. She considered it long and hard before she came to the conclusion that Fred was in a better place at that point in time to provide the kind of security their sons needed. She also knew that a bitter custody battle would only make the divorce more difficult for them. Fred, in deciding not to punish Eileen for leaving him, made a critical compromise for the sake of his children. He knew his sons needed their mother. For their sake he wrote Eileen a letter confirming that informally they would have joint custody. During our meeting, Eileen turned tearfully to Fred: "I value who you are, Fred. I feel like I did you a terrible injustice. You never cut me out; you always allowed me to stay part of the family."

To be able to construct their binuclear family on their own terms meant that Fred and Eileen often had to counter expectations from their families and society in general. In 1974, for a mother to voluntarily make the decision to leave her husband, her children, and the family home was considered deviant. She often felt scorned by their families and the community. Their decision to remain a family in spite of the resistance they met in the community required them to be vigilant in their determination. They had a vision of their family that included both parents and they kept making that known to their extended families, to their children's teachers, and to their friends, thereby enabling their sons to have a two-parent family.

When each of them remarried, they included the new stepparents in the family circle. Again, the friendships they developed were viewed with curiosity and even with some disdain by those around them. Their vision of a binuclear family—of four parents and seven children, who felt like family, who celebrated important life events and developmental rituals together, who respected one another's rightful place in the family—was not an easy one to communicate to the world around them, but was indeed a healthy family environment for children and parents.

Although your actions and individual decisions and compromises will be different, you may take many of the same pathways as did this family. Personalities may determine how family members interact. With the goal in mind of keeping your family a family after divorce, you will be able to make the necessary compromises and will find creative ways to make that possible.

Minimizing the Potential for Negative Effects on Your Children

Slow down the process—children need time to adjust.
Accept that your child needs—and has a right to—both parents.
Cooperate with your ex if only for the sake of your children.
Establish a limited partnership agreement with clear rules.
Accept that your child's family will expand to include nonbiological kin.

Stacey and Bill, the Chapter 7 family in which the women said, "We're like sisters," beautifully demonstrate an exspouse pair who have done all they can to minimize negative effects on their children. All the adults placed enormous importance on being with the children. Stacey said, and this bears repeating, that one of the first pathways she decided to take was, "The kids needed and would have their dad." This led to cooperation with Bill, for the sake of the children—even though Bill had initially wanted the divorce and Stacey hadn't.

Stacey and Bill are quite different in their parenting styles as well as in many other aspects of their lives. When I met with them I was impressed by their ability to put their children's needs before their own. I watched them pass up many opportunities to engage in battle by silently making the compromises to cooperate for the sake of the children.

That Stacey and Bill established a limited partnership with consistent rules is shown when Stacey says that her bottom line is, "If the kids are doing okay, even when I don't like it [the father's decision], I have to accept it." She turned to a family therapist and gradually learned to live more comfortably with the knowledge that she could not always control her children's daily lives. When, as a young teenager, her older daughter Kara chose to move in with Bill—who tended to allow the children more independence at an earlier age than Stacey felt comfortable with—it was a difficult time for her. Carefully, she had to look at each situation, and if her daughter was not in danger in some way, she had to accept that for her daughter living with her dad was going to be different than living with her mom.

When I was discussing with the family how they managed to have these compatible relationships, the men in the family agreed on one important pathway they each chose. Bill, who was still single but currently in a serious relationship, noted: "After having a couple of bad experiences I learned to date only women who would warmly welcome my children." Howard noted that he, too, made that his priority. Thus they'd accepted that their children's family would expand to include nonbiological kin, but they'd also maximized the possibility of success and of ultimately establishing more peaceful households.

This binuclear family expanded to include not only Stacey's new spouse Howard and his exwife Tess and their two children, but also Tess's spouse Rick and their son Erik. When I began the interview with this family, I asked each person to tell me who they were and how they were related to everyone else. Stacey introduced herself, her current spouse and her ex, her children, her stepchildren, and when she came to Erik, she just said, "This is Erik. He's my family too." Although Erik is only related to her through the divorce chain of her current husband's exwife and her new husband, she clearly felt like he was kin.

Integrating all these nonbiological kin as family has produced a binuclear clan that is often greeted with surprise and disbelief from those around them, but which functions as a supportive kinship network. When acquaintances hear that the three men in the family have on occasion gone camping together with all the children, they are both confused and surprised. On the occasion of anyone's birthday, and on Thanksgiving and Christmas, the whole clan assembles, including a couple of grandmothers and other assorted extended kin.

Again, your pathways to maximizing the children's health may well be different. Which choice points are most difficult for you is an individual matter. What's important is your commitment to meeting this goal.

Integrating Your Divorce in Your Life in a Healthy Way

Remember the good—as well as the bad—parts of your relation-ship.
Accept the inevitable ambiguities.
Face your losses without drowning in the pain.
Forgive yourself—and your ex.
Let go of the anger.

Eve and Paul, the Chapter 7 couple who were Fiery Foes and now are friends, show that even in the toughest divorces, it's possible to remember the good parts of your relationship; to forgive yourself as well as your ex. When Paul's affair was painfully revealed to Eve, and again when Paul remarried, Eve's anger (which initially exploded) could have built and built and ultimately destroyed Paul and Eve's son, Adam. Instead, the concerns about Adam, which she shared with Paul, allowed Eve to start to forgive him. That she's had to take small steps, and that each step has been extremely painful, is a fact of life; her willingness to take these steps is a sign of courage, maturity, and commitment. Angry feelings still well up in her sometimes, and she occasionally still vents her anger at Paul, but both she and Paul are able to let the incident pass without allowing it to define the relation-ship.

Paul's concessions about support and property, his ability to apol-ogize for the pain he caused Eve, his staying put on custody issues, and Eve's ultimately agreeing that Paul equally share custody demon-strates that both exspouses faced loss and did not allow themselves to wallow in it. They accepted the ambiguities as issues that would never be resolved fully: for Eve, balancing her vision of Paul as a good dad with her resentment of him as an unfaithful spouse; for Paul, balancing his vision of Eve as a dedicated mother with the unpleasantness of taking her anger.

In this binuclear family, the letting go of anger has allowed them all to move on with their lives, integrating their divorce as best as they can. Although Eve and Beth don't talk with one another, they both accept the other's role in this complex family. Eve accepts that Beth is Adam's stepmother, although she has carefully drawn the boundaries of how Beth may or may not participate. Beth, on the other hand, struggles with not crossing these boundaries, and also has had to accept the continuing friendship that Paul has with Eve.

To integrate your divorce as part of your life means you have to accept that there may be some feelings that remain ambiguous and unresolved. There are also losses that you may have to grieve even years later. Remembering that the marriage contained good times as well as bad times, that your ex has good characteristics as well as bad ones, that not staying married for life doesn't mean you, your ex, or even your marriage have failed, allows you to fully accept your life and integrate the past with the present.

Five years ago I had just begun to write this book—I began my sabbatical year with a brief holiday in Big Sur. In a split second, while walking down a hill, lost in my thoughts and in the beauty of the day, I slipped and broke my leg. When I woke up after surgery to find myself in a full leg cast, I was terrified.

I was 300 miles from home, a home I lived in alone, with a big dog to care for, a private practice to attend to, and a book to write. My well-planned life had totally collapsed.

Intellectually I knew that I would survive. But emotionally, I was flooded with anxiety. How would I even go to the bathroom with a totally immobilized and casted leg, let alone prepare my meals, take care of my dog, go to work? I was overwhelmed with new and unwelcome problems.

But in the middle of the night, when I woke scared and alone, I read and reread one very special book, a book that brought me great comfort: *A Leg to Stand On,* by Oliver Sacks, the eminent neuropsychologist. The author spoke not only as a physician but as a patient who had a similar injury to mine: "I was astonished at the profundity of the effects [my injury] had on me . . . an abyss of bizarre and often terrifying, effects. . . . I found the abyss a horror, and recovery a wonder; and I have since had a deeper sense of the horror and wonder which lurk behind life and which are concealed, as it were, behind the usual surface of health."

As corny as it sounds, with 20-20 hindsight, years later, I now see the breaking and mending of my leg as teaching me invaluable lessons. With Oliver Sacks as my understanding guide, I learned about patience, aloneness, loneliness, friendship, dependency, and coping. His empathic understanding of the transitions along the path to healing gave me both the courage and the knowledge to weather difficult passages and emerge healthy and whole. It is my fervent hope that *The Good Divorce* will help you navigate a similar road.

Epilogue

I HAD JUST written the final chapter of this book when a surprise letter arrived in the mail. It was from my younger daughter, who was in the process of applying to graduate programs in business administration. She enclosed an essay she had written for the personal section of her application to Stanford University. She'd spontaneously chosen to write about how my divorce from her father shaped the person she is today.

As I read my daughter's essay, I began to cry. You see, no matter how expert one is or how hard one tries to achieve a good divorce, even if one is confident that one has, finally, achieved one, there remains some fear—fear that one's choices, no matter how reasoned and correct, have adversely affected the children. As you have seen throughout this book, my exhusband and I started off very badly, as Fiery Foes. For most of our children's growing-up years, we did parallel parenting rather than cooperative coparenting. Although as the children grew up we were able to achieve a more amicable (though still distant) relationship, although today my exhusband and I do indeed feel like family, I had wished—and my wish grew stronger over the years—that we could have had a divorce all along that epitomized the principles from which this book grew.

My daughter's letter put my fears to rest.

Here is the question my daughter was asked to respond to: **Each of us has been influenced by people, events, and situations of our lives. How have these influences shaped who you are today? (Our goal is to get a sense of who you are, rather than what you have done.)**

Here is my daughter's essay, in its entirety:

When I was four years old, my family moved from suburban New Jersey to Madison, Wisconsin. My clearest memory of this move was, during our drive to the Midwest, the stop we made at Niagara Falls. My mom has a photo of my sister and me with big, black slickers on, taking a boat ride under the falls. My mom or dad must have taken the picture. They were still married at the time. They stayed married for one year after our move, then divorced. My father, who was enrolled in law school, moved back to the East Coast and completed his degree there.

In 1965, divorce was not as common as it is today. And, in particular, a father who wanted custody was unheard-of. But my father was not one to be influenced by the norm. He was determined to keep his children with him. He was so determined, in fact, that one day he came to my sister's and my summer camp, picked us up without my mother's knowledge, and drove us from Madison to his mother's house on the Jersey shore. I cannot imagine what my mother must have felt that afternoon when she arrived at the bus stop and no daughters got off the bus. From conversations we have had only recently, I now know that only with the help of her brother, and after hiring a detective, was she able to find us.

At the time, I had just assumed my dad was taking us on vacation. My mom came to the beach in New Jersey looking for us. I vaguely remember there being some type of confrontation between my parents and my uncles. I have to honestly say, I think most of my memories are from discussions that ensued many years later.

Thirty years have passed. This event still brings up many unanswered questions and raw emotions. Although much of the research in this area highlights the negative impact divorce has on children, and indeed, I still have some pain, there have been numerous positive results for me and also influences that have positively shaped who I am today.

First, I was forced to be independent at a young age. With my mother being a single parent and working on her graduate degree, my sister and I took on many of the responsibilities of the household. Also, as we lived in Wisconsin and my father lived on the East Coast, this did not facilitate easy visitation. Fortunately, my parents did not play out their hostilities for one another, and I was able to develop a relationship with each of them. Visiting my father regularly throughout the year meant travelling from one destination to another; this created situations which continually tested my independence.

Second, I have had the opportunity to be exposed to two lifestyles and a myriad of cultural environments. My parents are extremely different in how they live and approach life. Living in Madison during the sixties and seventies, with my mother and stepfather, who are professors, allowed me to experience a less conventional, more liberal upbringing. To counter that, my time with my father, who is an attorney, exposed me to a more conservative, conventional lifestyle. In addition, each family loved to travel, but in vastly different ways. I feel extremely fortunate to have travelled Europe when I was nine years old and Scandinavia when I was thirteen. My mother and stepfather chose to buy a car and travel for over a month each time, staying at little pensions, picnicking along the roadside and visiting historical sights. In contrast, with my father and stepmother (and later my younger brother and sister from my father's second marriage), I experienced Caribbean resorts, New York theater, and a family trip to Israel.

The divorce of my parents, and subsequently each of their remarriages, gave me four parents as potential role models. Each parent has influenced me greatly. My mother is always striving for new goals. While I was growing up, she worked on getting her masters degree, her Ph.D., and then tenure. Now she is working on her second book and deciding the next step in her career. She has helped me understand how to set goals and achieve them. She has given me a great deal of confidence that I can complete anything I put my mind to. My stepfather, having already secured tenure, was the one who kept the household going. I spent time with him making family dinners, learning how to use a hand drill and other tools to fix things around the house, and enjoying old Sherlock Holmes movies. He made sure that I would be able to take care of myself once I went out on my own, and that I would know how to take time out for fun.

My father started his own law firm and went through many ups and downs of partnership. He has shown me how to persevere and come out on top. Family is the most important thing to my father. The close ties he maintains with his large extended family have given me a sense of belonging, and shown me the importance of generosity, dependability and integrity. My stepmother managed my father's office while raising two children and having two step-daughters come and go as though through a revolving door. She always remains easy-going, good-humored, and open-hearted, despite the chaos. She has shown me how to make someone feel welcomed and part of the group, as well as how to let certain things roll off your shoulder.

My older sister and I have the same parents. It is hard to imagine not having someone like her with whom to share this experience. She is always there when I need her. She knows when to let me cry on her shoulders and when to push me to seek the next challenge. My younger sister and brother are from my father's second marriage. They have brought a new meaning, for me, to the word "family." In one family, I was the baby, and in the other, the older sister. Having younger siblings has allowed me to be a role model and to understand what type of influence that can be, developmentally.

My parents' divorce and the evolution of my family since then have had an amazing impact on my life. There have been difficult times, but overall, I have gained from the divorce. Though I would not wish it on anyone, and I hope never to experience it personally, my parents' divorce has afforded me many wonderful opportunities which I could not otherwise have experienced. My close family ties form the foundation that has allowed me to become who, and what, I am.

I include my daughter's essay not only because of its content, not only because it meant a lot to me, but because it is the heartfelt reaction of a child of divorce, thirty years after the initial shock. My daughter's letter can give hope to other parents that even when the divorce is not as good as one might wish, even when the relationships start off with great hostility, we can still gain from setting up and living in a binuclear family. The process will bring gifts of amazing value, when we least expect them. Some of the gifts will be immediate. Some, like my daughter's gift to me, will land on our doorstep thirty years later, and give us cause to appreciate all the good things that even the worst of shocks may bring us—with work, with time, with luck, and with our own goodwill.

Appendix

THE BINUCLEAR FAMILY STUDY
METHOD AND SAMPLE

Research Sample

With funds provided by the National Institutes of Mental Health and the University of Wisconsin Graduate School, this intensive study of ninety-eight divorced families began in 1979.

The population for this study was identified through 1977–79 public divorce records in Dane County, Wisconsin. Dane County consists of the city of Madison and its surrounding suburban communities, small towns, and rural areas. The population of Dane County is quite homogeneous along ethnic and racial lines. In 1978, the city of Madison had a population of about 170,000, and the whole county had 319,000 inhabitants.

Since the major purpose of this study was to explore how families changed after divorce, we selected a sample that had been legally divorced for one year. All cases in Dane County in which the divorce was finalized in 1977 were investigated. Due to the small number of joint and father custody cases in 1977, we also reviewed divorces finalized in 1978 and 1979 to identify additional nonmother custody cases.

Criteria for inclusion in the study were: (1) that the divorced spouses have at least one child under eighteen residing with one or both of them at the time of the study; (2) that both former spouses reside in Dane County; (3) that the couple has not reconciled; (4) that the nonresidential parent visits the child at least once every two months; and (5) that both former spouses agree to participate.

Of the 1,288 divorced in 1977, 675 (52.4 percent) did not have a minor child. Of the 613 remaining cases with minor children, 232 cases (37.8 percent) were identified from court records as not meeting the county residence criterion. This left 381 cases (762 individuals) identified from the 1977 divorce records that appeared to meet the first two study criteria (a child under eighteen and residence within Dane County). These eligible cases represented approximately 30 percent of all couples divorced in 1977 in Dane County. The overwhelming majority (349 or 92 percent) of the eligible cases were mother custody cases. Based on refusal rates of earlier studies and the stringent criteria of this study, a 60-percent sample of eligible mother custody cases was randomly selected. This yielded a mother custody sample of 195 cases. An additional five mother custody cases were incorrectly identified in court records as nonmother custody cases and were later counted in the mother custody sample; thus, the mother custody sample included 200 cases. Because of the low number of nonmother custody cases available in 1977, 1978 cases and six months of 1979 cases were used to provide the nonmother custody sample.

Since only 32 father, split, and joint custody cases were identified as eligible from the 1977 records, it was necessary to review 1978 and 1979 records to obtain an adequate sample. All 1978 father, split, and joint custody cases meeting the child and residence criteria were included in the sample as were 82 percent of the eligible nonmother custody cases granted in the first six months of 1979. This sampling procedure yielded a final pool of 379 potentially eligible couples (758 individuals).

Selection Procedures

Letters explaining the study and requesting participation were sent to all eligible individuals (379 couples). When possible, addresses were updated through the support court records prior to sending out the letters. Each letter was individually typed and included the respondent's phone number when that number was available from the records, phone books, or operator-assisted information. A precoded postcard was enclosed requesting that the respondent supply us with a phone number if the number was not publicly available, or provide us with a corrected or preferred phone number. The letters were sent out in eight waves to prevent long lapses of time between the receipt of letters and actual interviewing. Approximately ten days after the letters were mailed, follow-up phone calls were made to assess whether the respondent met the criteria of the study, to request the eligibles' participation, and to conduct a brief telephone interview when possible with those who refused. The interviewers then recontacted the respondents who agreed to participate and set up appointments for in-person interviews.

The initial telephone calls to the 379 couples who apparently met the first two criteria (minor child and residence within the county) resulted in identifying 92 (24.3 percent) who were determined ineligible for reasons other than refusal of the former spouse. Either there was no child under eighteen in the parental home, at least one spouse had moved from the county, the couple had reconciled, or one parent had not seen the child at least once in the past two months. Seven couples were found ineligible for other reasons (death of a child, institutionalization of one parent, or mother custody status ascertained after completion of mother custody interviews). In two cases the reason for ineligibility was not reported. In 65 cases neither person could be contacted. In an additional 30 cases, one party was unreachable (in most of the cases, the contacted spouse refused to cooperate in locating the other party). Thus, a total of 95 couples (25.1 percent) were not reachable. This left an eligible and locatable sample of 192 couples (51 percent of those identified as potentially eligible). Of the eligible sample, 98 couples or 51 percent agreed to participate.

Of the 98 couples who participated in the first wave of the study, 54 were cases of maternal custody, 28 were joint custody, and 16 were either split custody (with some children living with the father and some with the mother) or paternal custody. Two years later (three years following their divorce), 176 of the original 196 divorced persons (90 percent) participated in the second wave of the study (Time 2). This represented 80 couples as well as one member from an additional 16 couples. After another two years (Time 3, five years postdivorce), a total of 178 parents participated, including several who were not interviewed in Time 2. This 90 percent response rate is unusually high for longitudinal studies, with a loss of only two families from the original sample who were unavailable for any follow-up over the five years.

In the second and third wave of interviews (Times 2 and 3) the participants identified new partners, either married or cohabiting. Of the 122 new partners at Time 2, 91 (75 percent) were interviewed. At Time 3, 115 new partners were identified and 85 (74 percent) were interviewed. A partner was defined as cohabiting if he or she lived with our study participant for twelve or more nights a month. Combining the biological and new partner sample, the total of people interviewed at Time 2 was 267, and at Time 3, 263 people were interviewed.

Characteristics of the Sample

The sample is predominantly white and middle class, due to the composition of Dane County. The biological parents were, on the average, in their mid-thirties with an age range of nineteen to sixty-four. The length of marriage ranged from one to twenty-five years, with the average couple married for about eleven years prior to their divorce. Two-thirds of the couples had been separated before filing for divorce; these separations were about one to two years in length. A little over half of the fathers and 38 percent of the mothers were college graduates. About 75 percent of the women were employed full-time. The annual average household income prior to divorce was approximately $21,000 for both men and women. After divorce, it had dropped to about $15,000 for women while remaining the same for men.

At the time of the original data collection, the number of children per family ranged from one to six, with an age range of two to eighteen years. Seventy percent of the sample had more than one minor child, with an average of two children per family. Twenty percent of the children were preschool age, 50 percent were elementary-school age, and 30 percent were adolescents.

At Time 1, all the former spouses lived in Dane County. By Time 3, 11 percent of them lived more than 300 miles from each other. At that time, 45 percent of the mothers had remarried, compared with 72 percent of the fathers.

During the course of the study, nine families changed their custody disposition. Six cases of maternal custody at Time 1 changed during the two-year interval prior to Time 2, two to paternal custody and four to split custody. Between Time 2 and Time 3, two cases of maternal custody changed disposition, one to split and the other to joint custody. During that same time, a joint custody case switched to paternal custody.

By one year after divorce, approximately 14 percent of the women and 22 percent of the men had remarried, and another 13 percent of each were planning remarriage in the near future. By the second interview, three years postdivorce, 35 percent of the women and 55 percent of the men had remarried. Another 23 percent of the women and 21 percent of the men had cohabitors. The new partners were similar in education and employment to the biological parents. Two-thirds of the respondents' new partners had themselves been married before, and somewhat over half had children from the previous relationships. Seventy percent of the new wives and 30 percent of the new husbands with children had the children residing with them in the new remarried household. About 10 percent of the married or cohabiting couples had a new child born to this relationship.

Methodology

Data were collected through in-depth interviews conducted by the research staff in the participants' homes. All the interviewers had clinical training and they were matched by sex with the participants. Different interviewers were used for each member of a family. In Time 2, blank binuclear diagrams were used to collect identifying data on the family system. The diagrams were used to establish rapport with the respondent while familiarizing the interviewer with names and relationships in these complex family systems. The diagrams were used throughout the interview so that the interviewer could refer back to them and address family members by first name during the interview process.

The interview was semistructured: most of the questions could be analyzed quantitatively—that is, questions had specific response categories, such as from always to never; other questions were qualitative—that is, the participants were asked questions that they answered in their own words.

The interviews averaged one and a half hours in Time 1, and ranged from one to four hours in Time 2 (depending on the binuclear family structure, e.g., whether they were remarried, whether their new partner had children from a prior marriage, etc.) and from two to six hours in Time 3.

Variables

The two major dependent or outcome variables were: (1) the quality of coparental communication and (2) the nonresidential parents' involvement with the children. The quality of coparental communication scale (eleven items) was comprised of two major dimensions, interparental conflict and mutual support. These two constructs of support and conflict were identified in the literature as major factors of the coparental relationship affecting the child's adjustment to the divorce. Each dimension was composed of several items that tapped slightly different dimensions of the variable. The variable, the nonresidential parent's involvement with the child, included the frequency and duration of time spent with the child as well as the extent of involvement. Ten major parental responsibility areas (i.e., disciplining, attending school functions) comprised the nonresidential parent involvement scale.

A major independent variable was custody, and was measured by the legal custody determination. The second cluster of independent variables included background information on parents and children, marital and divorce history. Included in this cluster were items such as length of marriage, mutuality of divorce decision, length and duration of separations, occupation and education of parents, etc.

The third cluster of psychological variables consisted of eight major variables: (1) anger toward former spouse; (2) guilt about the divorce; (3) positive feelings toward former spouse; (4) attachment for former spouse; (5) psychological distance from former spouse; (6) generalized attitudes about divorce; (7) feelings toward former spouse as a parent; and (8) psychiatric symptomatology. In six of the eight variables, measures were developed for this research and were tested and refined in pilot work. All were measured by multi-item scales. The attachment variable was assessed using the Attachment Index developed by Kitson and Sussman; psychiatric symptomatology was assessed with the Hopkins Symptom Checklist (HSCL), a ninety-item paper-and-pencil test consisting of five dimensions or symptom clusters.

A fourth cluster of independent variables, coparental interaction, were family process variables. Conceptually, coparental interaction was comprised of two dimensions, parental and nonparental. The parental component of the relationships included interactions between divorced spouses related to child-rearing issues; the nonparental component included those interactions not concerned with child rearing. The contents of both dimensions were measured by multi-item scales.

In Times 2 and 3, three and five years postdivorce, the sample was extended to include the new partners of the original sample parents. The event and quality of remarriage, the relationships between new and former spouses, and stepparent-child relationships were new independent variables for these later phases of the research. Additional variables were included in these two phases to assess qualitatively the process of binuclear family reorganization and stepfamily development.

Extensive pilot work and pretesting was conducted prior to Time 1 interviews. The first pilot was conducted primarily to test a preliminary interview schedule and to assess the feasibility of obtaining a sample selected from court records that would include both parents. Using a semistructured interview procedure, 22 individuals were interviewed at three months after separation. The results of that pilot study indicated that it was possible to select a sample from court records in which both parents could be interviewed but that three months post-separation was not a suitable time frame in which to study postdivorce family reorganization. The interview schedule was refined based on this pilot and a second more extensive pilot study was conducted in San Diego, California, with 41 joint-custody parents. The data from this pilot study were used to conduct preliminary analyses on the scales and to further refine and develop the instrument. In Time 2 and Time 3, new items were pretested by project staff on a sample provided by the Dane County Family Court.

Data Analysis

Reliability estimates were calculated on all the major scales. Factor analyses of the eleven items comprising the "quality of coparental communication" scale confirmed that there are two factors, one measuring interparental conflict and one measuring mutual support.

Preliminary analyses of the data included paired T tests to examine sex differences and differences between custody groups by sex. Multiple regression techniques were used to assess the effects of some of the independent variables on the dependent variable of father involvement. Analysis of variance was used to identify differences in coparental relating.

The typologies were formed by combining the scores of the divorced couples on thirteen questions. These questions assessed the amount of conflict, and how often and about what issues couples continued to interact. Cluster analyses were used to form the typologies. Once the typologies were formed, multivariate analyses of variance (MANOVAs) were used to see how the groups differed on important variables.

Acknowledgments

I am enormously grateful to many people who have contributed in many different ways to this book.

I especially want to thank my family: My father, who never lived to see most of my accomplishments but who never failed to let me know that I was accomplished; my mother, who never quite understood my choices in life but who believed in me anyway; my brother, who has always been a loyal cheerleader; and especially my daughters, who never doubted for one minute that I would write this book. They and the newest member of my family, my son-in-law, were a constant source of support and encouragement.

I have been blessed to have four remarkable people who, each in their own special ways, brought this book to life. Thank you—

To Sandra Dijkstra, my agent, who waved her magical wand and made possible this remarkable opportunity in my life. I am very grateful for her enthusiastic and steadfast belief in me and her continuing interest and support.

To Janet Goldstein, my editor at HarperCollins, who believed in this book way before she even read the proposal. Her vision guided this book, her wisdom of the writing process and her unwavering support gave me the courage to break though difficult transitions, and her incisive suggestions kept my writing focused.

To Betsy Amster, whose enthusiasm, guidance, and editorial assistance in the early stages of the book helped me formulate the proposal and structure my unwieldy first drafts. Her persistant reminders of "show, not tell" are stamped indelibly in my mind.

To Jaqueline Austin, who took time out from her own writing to answer a rescue call in the last stages of the book. She became my energetic writing coach, providing encouragement, structure, guidance—and friendship. Her extraordinary gift for words has greatly enhanced this book.

I am especially grateful to three dear friends who gave generously of their time, energy, and wisdom, who provided gentle criticism and insightful suggestions on the manuscript at many stages:

To Marilyn Mason, who never wavered in her enthusiasm and who is the best and most generous friend anyone could ever ask for.

To Myrna Silton-Goldstein, who protected my time by taking over the day-to-day responsibilities of our therapy office and whose humor kept me sane.

To Yossi Guttmann, who kept my spirits up with his early-morning faxes and helped me gain a healthy perspective.

For their conversations, support, understanding, encouragement, and wisdom during the long gestation of this book, my utmost appreciation and thanks to: Howard Craig, Susan Evans, Barbara Fromm, Laura Geller, Abby Hellwarth, Richard Lapkin, Diana Meehan, Woody Mosten, Isolina Ricci, Fern Topas Salka, and Barrie Thorne. And to Barbara Lipscomb, my assistant, who kept my life together and who makes incredibly nourishing chicken soup. A special thanks to Judith Kay and Judy Perkins of Age Concerns, who were loving caregivers for my mother when my own energies were absorbed elsewhere.

My research never could have been done without the financial support of several institutions. I am very grateful and indebted to the University of Wisconsin, for its belief in my ideas before they were very well defined and for its faith in my ability to carry them out. They generously provided the seed money and research assistance that got the Binculear Family Research Project off the ground. I am also grateful to the National Institutes of Mental Health (NIMH) for providing funds for the longitudinal follow-up studies and for supporting my participation in the Cross National Project, and to the University of Southern California for providing the funds for the Young Adult Study and for the gift of time by granting me a sabbatical to begin writing this book. In the research phases of my work, literally hundreds of graduate students and research assistants have been involved.

Thank you one and all for your commitment, enthusiasm, hard work, and stimulating ideas.

Last but not least, I am especially grateful to Roy H. Rodgers, my co-author of *Divorced Families,* for the many years of our collaborative work; his ideas, now so intertwined with my own, are very much a part of this book.

Notes

Introduction

xi their subjects were not randomly selected: In the Wallerstein and Kelly study, "The sixty families who participated in the study came initially for a six-week divorce counseling service. The service was conceptualized and advertised as a preventive program and was offered free of charge to all families in the midst of divorce. Parents learned of the service through attorneys, school teachers, counselors, social agencies, ministers, friends, and newspaper articles describing divorce as an expectable period of high stress." Judith S. Wallerstein and Joan Berlin Kelly, *Surviving the Break-up* (New York: Basic Books, 1980), p. 319. The five-year findings are presented in the above-cited book, and the ten-year follow-up findings appear in Judith S. Wallerstein and Sandra Blakeslee, *Second Chances* (New York: Ticknor and Fields, 1989). For further discussion of the implications of this sampling procedure see Chapter 1 notes.

The subjects in the Hetherington study (E. Mavis Hetherington, Martha Cox, and Roger Cox, "Effects of Divorce on Parents and Children," in Michael E. Lamb [ed.], *Nontraditional Families* [New Jersey: Lawrence Erlbaum Associates, 1982], pp. 233–288) were recruited in Virginia through the schools and attorneys.

xiii who joined these families as stepparents: some of these "stepparents" were not legally married to the biological parent but considered themselves to be stepparents.

xiii cross-national study: The cross-national comparative project, "Divorce and Its Consequences for Families with Dependent Children," was organized by the European Coordination Centre for Research and Documentation in Social Sciences (Vienna Centre) in 1978 in Budapest, Hungary. The need for the research was documented because it was clear that research on families of divorce was lagging behind the rapidly growing phenomenon in Europe.

At that first meeting four problem areas were identified, namely, the economic, the emotional, the legal, and the social, and it was decided that although in each of the countries the study would be conducted independently, all four areas were to be covered by every participant.

The findings are reported in L. Cseh-Szombathy, I. Koch-Nielsen, J. Trost, and I. Weda (eds.), *The Aftermath of Divorce—Coping with Family Change: An Investigation in Eight Countries* (Budapest, Hungary: Akademiai Kiado, 1985).

Chapter 1

2 divorce rate in the United States doubled: In Norway—Scandinavian countries are second only to the United States—the number of divorces tripled in the period from World War II until today. In fact, most industrialized nations have experienced a rapid increase in divorce rates in the past twenty-five years. England's rates doubled between 1960 and 1970, then more than doubled between 1970 and the early 1980s. In France, the explosion held off throughout the 1960s, but rates more than doubled between 1970 and the early 1980s. In Sweden and Germany, the rates doubled between 1960 and 1988.

2 binuclear family: The term *binuclear family* first appeared in print in 1979 in an article I wrote that reported findings from my study of joint custody families in San Diego. The title was "Binuclear Families: Two Households, One Family," and it was published in the journal *Alternative Lifestyles,* 2 (1979): 499–515. Not yet part of the mainstream culture then, it has gradually over the past fifteen years become integrated into the social science vocabulary. Most new editions of marriage and family textbooks now identify binuclear families as a common family form. Although it is not yet a household word, it has gained acceptance in the popular culture, as evidenced by an article in *Cosmopolitan* (August 1991) titled: "His, Hers and Theirs: Binuclear Family Ties."

4 "The vulgar 'my ex'": See Margaret Mead's chapter, "Anomalies in American Postdivorce Relationships," in Paul Bohannan (ed.), *Divorce and After: An Analysis of the Emotional and Social Problems of Divorce* (New York: Anchor Books, 1971), p. 125. Although this book was written nearly twenty-five years ago, it remains a classic in the field of divorce. Anthropologist Paul Bohannan presents in this volume a way of analyzing divorce across cultures that is still highly relevant today.

6 descriptive, alliterative, and easy-sounding names: Articles citing the findings I presented with the newly coined types appeared within the next few days in the *New York Times* (October 21, 1985) and *Los Angeles Times*

(November 11, 1985). They had been officially launched and accepted: new language to expand role models for exspouse relationships.

7 Letty Cottin Pogrebin likens it to a hydra: Letty Cottin Pogrebin, *Family Politics: Love and Power on an Intimate Frontier* (New York: McGraw-Hill, 1983), p. 36.

8 the difference between household and family: See Paul Bohannan's *All the Happy Families: Exploring the Varieties of Family Life* (New York: McGraw-Hill, 1985) for an excellent discussion of kinship and family.

14 less than 10 percent of the total number of divorces: Although we tend to think that most divorces are adversarial, less than 10 percent of divorces in the United States end up being litigated in court. A 1993 study released by the American Bar Association's Committee on Delivery of Services found that in 1991, in Maricopa County (Phoenix, Arizona), 52 percent of the divorces had no attorney and in over 80 percent at least one of the parties was unrepresented. The study found that persons with incomes under $50,000, no children, without real estate, and married less than ten years were less likely to use lawyers.

15 divorce does leave women poorer: Although studies differ somewhat in their exact numbers, most show that, on average, women end up about 30 percent poorer than they were when married.

15 Wallerstein notes: See Judith S. Wallerstein, "Children After Divorce: Wounds That Don't Heal," *New York Times Magazine* (January 22, 1989), pp. 19–44; and Judith S. Wallerstein and Sandra Blakeslee, *Second Chances: Men, Women, and Children a Decade After Divorce* (New York: Ticknor and Fields, 1989).

For an excellent critique of this work see E. Mavis Hetherington and Frank F. Furstenberg, Jr., "Sounding the Alarm," *Readings: A Journal of Reviews and Commentary in Mental Health* (June 1989), pp. 4–8. The well-respected social scientists Hetherington and Furstenberg offer this summary: "The authors venture beyond, and often without, data to deliver a sweeping and dire message not only to mental health professionals but to the public and to the members of divorce and divorcing families. . . . The claim that some children experience severe long-lasting problems following divorce is not controversial: the prevalence, duration, and severity of the disordered behavior suggested by the case histories is controversial, indeed" (p. 6).

They further conclude: "Without more convincing evidence that links the prevalence of problem behavior in early adulthood to marital dissolution, their effort to sound the alarm ends up producing too shrill a note" (p. 8).

It has been unfortunate that Wallerstein and Blakeslee's report of the findings of a small clinical study have all too often been accepted by the media and the general public as if the study reported on a large national sample. The frequent citations of only the highly popularized negative findings have led them to be labeled as facts. A conclusion that may have been based, for example, on less than a dozen children of one gender in one developmental stage gets restated in sweeping generalizations by those reporting it. Sociologist Richard J. Gelles ("Violence in the Family: A Review of Research in the Seventies" in the *Journal of Marriage and the Family*, 1980, 42[4]: 873–885) calls this the "whoozle effect." Without considering the limitations of the sample or the methodology, only the conclusions are remembered and more credibility is attributed to them than even the authors of the original study intended.

16   solicited for a counseling program: See the first book published on the study findings by Judith S. Wallerstein and Joan Berlin Kelly, *Surviving the Break-up: How Children and Parents Cope with Divorce* (New York: Basic Books, 1980), Appendix A, p. 319.

On page 328 of the Appendix the authors describe their sample: "Fifty percent of the men and close to half of the women . . . were chronically depressed, sometimes suicidal individuals, the men and women with severe neurotic difficulties or with handicaps in relating to another person, or those with long-standing problems in controlling their rage or sexual impulses . . . 15 percent of the men and 20 percent of the women were found by us to be severely troubled during their marriages, perhaps throughout their lives."

This left just a third of the sample with normal or above normal functioning. These psychological characteristics were judged to be present prior to the separation.

16   Are children from nuclear families faring any better: Hetherington and Furstenberg, *op. cit.* (p. 7), note the problems with generalizing from the Wallerstein data: "The absence of any control group leaves Wallerstein free to speculate about how her subjects might have fared had they received the parental attention and support provided to children in a 'normal' family. It almost appears that Wallerstein and Blakeslee share the fantasy of many of their subjects that they would have enjoyed a happy, harmonious life if only their parents had not divorced. But it is highly doubtful that many children would have realized such ideal outcomes had their parents remained together. It seems far more likely that many would have had to contend with a life of conflict, deprivation, and uneven parenting even if their families remained intact. Existing studies of the effects of conflict-ridden marriages on children are not very reassuring."

19 new study from England shows: For a discussion of the British study of over 17,000 families, see Andrew J. Cherlin, Frank F. Furstenberg, Jr., P. Lindsay Chase-Lansdale, Kathleen E. Kiernan, Philip K. Robins, Donna Ruane Morrison, and Julien O. Teitler, "Longitudinal Studies of Effects of Divorce on Children in Great Britain and the United States," *Science,* 1991, 252(5011): 1386–1389.

For an excellent analysis of the research on the effects of divorce on children, see Paul Amato and Brian Keith, "Parental Divorce and the Well-Being of Children: A Meta-analysis," *Psychological Bulletin,* 1991, 110(1): 26–46. The researchers concluded that overall, studies showed only a slight negative effect, and that was only on a small number of outcome variables.

Joan B. Kelly in her review of the current research ("Current Research on Children's Postdivorce Adjustment: No Simple Answers," *Family and Conciliation Courts Review,* 1993, 31[1]: 45) concludes: "Overall, the evidence suggests that when children begin the divorce experience in good psychological shape, with close or loving relationships with both parents, their adjustment will be maintained by continuing their relationships with both parents on a meaningful basis."

Chapter 2

23 prevalent reasons for divorce: In a recent study, 64 percent of women and 65 percent of men checked sexual intimacy problems as an important factor in their divorce, compared with 11 percent in 1967 and 4 percent in 1956. See Lynn Gigy and Joan B. Kelly, "Reasons for Divorce: Perspectives of Divorcing Women and Men," *Journal of Divorce and Remarriage,* 1992, 18(1/2): 169–187.

Using data from a large midwestern study, Gay C. Kitson with William H. Holmes (*Portrait of Divorce: Adjustment to Marital Breakdown,* New York: Guilford Press, 1992, pp. 143–146) found that some reasons increased or decreased in importance over time and some remained consistent throughout their longitudinal study. The ones that did not change over time were alcohol, lack of communication or understanding, too young at time of marriage, problems with in-laws and relatives, and extramarital sex. Reasons that were stated at the first interview but not stated subsequently were arguing all the time, inflexible, stubborn, overcommitment to work, not enough time together, and joint conflict over roles.

23 "four-year itch": See Helen E. Fisher, *Anatomy of Love: The Natural History of Monogamy, Adultery, and Divorce* (New York: W. W. Norton and Co., 1992).

23   median duration of recent marriages: Duration is calculated from all divorces in a given year. Therefore, some of the marriages used in the calculations began decades ago, under very different social conditions, and are not indicative of the likelihood of the duration for a couple marrying now. See William J. Goode, *World Changes in Divorce Patterns* (New Haven, CT: Yale University Press, 1993), p. 146.

23   "women's subordination": Carl Degler, *At Odds: Women and the Family in America from the Revolution to the Present* (New York: Oxford University Press, 1980).

24   cohabitation: Data from the National Survey of Families and Households show that women who cohabit have a 50 percent higher divorce rate than those who do not cohabit prior to marriage. See Larry L. Bumpass, Teresa Castro Martin, and James A. Sweet, "The Impact of Family Background and Early Marital Factors on Marital Disruption," *Journal of Family Issues,* 1991, 12(1): 22–42.

24   rise in the divorce rates: See Dennis A. Ahlburg and Carol J. DeVita, "New Realities of the American Family," *Population Bulletin,* 1992, 47(2): 15.

25   marriage remains as popular today: Although marriage rates are still high, especially in the United States, which has one of the highest rates in the world, the percentage of thirty-year-olds who have never married almost doubled between 1970 and 1990. Because the probability of getting married declines with age, this pattern of delayed age at first marriage could eventually lead to fewer people ever getting married. See Dennis Ahlburg and Carol J. DeVita, "New Realities of the American Family."

25   postponing marriage: In 1950, the average age at marriage for women was 20.3 and 22.8 for men; by 1970, it was 20.8 for women, 23.2 for men; by 1980, it was 22.0 for women, 24.7 for men; by 1991, it had increased to 24.1 for women, 26.3 for men. These U.S. patterns are similar to those of other industrialized countries.

For blacks, the age at first marriage now exceeds that of whites by two years, and a smaller proportion of black women marry.

See Dennis A. Ahlburg and Carol J. DeVita, "New Realities of the American Family," for further information.

26   first self-help book: Glenda Riley, *Divorce: An American Tradition* (New York: Oxford University Press, 1991), p. 128.

27 early American divorce laws: For an excellent and very readable history of divorce laws, see Roderick Phillips, *Untying the Knot: A Short History of Divorce* (Cambridge: Cambridge University Press, 1991).

28 the debate flourished: See Glenda Riley, *Divorce: An American Tradition,* p. 73.

28 Horace Greeley: For an interesting discussion of the progression of the divorce reform movements, see Lynne Carol Halem, *Divorce Reform: Changing Legal and Social Perspectives* (New York: The Free Press, 1980), p. 25.

29 divorce rates have risen: From the time of the first census figures, divorce rates have been rising. There was a slight downward trend during the depression of the early 1930s and an increase in the prosperous 1970s. Rates increased after the Civil War, World War I, and World War II. For more discussion of economic trends and fluctuations in rates, see Maxine Baca Zinn and D. Stanley Eitzen, *Diversity in Families* (New York: Harper-Collins College Publishers, 1993), pp. 362–367

Increasing Rate of Divorce, 1860–1990

Year	Divorce rate per thousand people	Percentage of marriages begun in each year ending in divorce
1860	.3	—
1879	.3	7%
1880	.4	8%
1890	.5	10%
1900	.7	12%
1910	.9	14%
1920	1.6	18%
1930	1.6	24%
1940	2.0	25%
1950	2.5	30%*
1960	2.2	39%*
1970	3.5	48%*
1980	5.2	49%*
1990	4.7	—

* Projections.
Source: Leonard Beeghley and Jeffrey W. Dwyer, "Social Structure and the Divorce Rates," *Population Today* 19(July/August 1991), p. 9.

30   increase in divorces in every country: The following table shows the divorce rates for major industrial countries:

U.S.	4.70	1991
Russian Federation	3.96	1989
Canada	3.15	1989
Former German Dem. Republic	1.9	1990
United Kingdom	2.98	1990
Denmark	3.0	1989
Democratic Germany	3.0	1989
Sweden	2.2	1991
France	1.9	1990
Netherlands	1.9	1991
Switzerland	2.0	1990
Japan	1.3	1990
Italy	0.5	1990

The data are from *1991 Demographic Yearbook* (New York: United Nations), pp. 752–757.

31   racial differences: The explanations for racial differences are very complex and far from conclusive. Good discussions can be found in Joseph Guttmann, *Divorce in Psychosocial Perspective: Theory and Research* (New Jersey: Lawrence Erlbaum Associates, Publishers, 1993); Dennis Ahlburg and Carol J. DeVita, "New Realities of the American Family"; and Maxine Zinn and Stanley Eitzen, *Diversity in Families*.

31   demographic trends: Demographer Paul Glick ("American Families: As They Are, and Were," *Sociology and Social Research,* 1990, 74[April]: 139–145) predicts the lower rate while demographer Larry Bumpass ("What's Happening to the Family? Interactions Between Demographic and Institutional Change," *Demography,* 1990, 27[November]: 483–498) predicts a higher rate.

32   the golden age of families: Because these problems were viewed as family problems and not reported, we have no accurate figures of how prevalent they were. However, there is no reason to assume that the incidence was any less than it is today. The current societal norms strongly support—and in the case of abuse, laws even require—bringing these family problems out in the open. Twelve-step groups for alcohol, drug, and other addictions are very common and even quite mainstream today. In fact, in Los Angeles, twelve-step groups have become one of the most popular places for singles to meet.

34   Entering the workplace: See Dennis Ahlburg and Carol J. DeVita, "New Realities of the American Family," note 58.

35   Gary Becker: Interview by John Ydstie, "Dollars and Sense," *Modern Maturity,* August–September 1993, p. 66.

35   "daddy track": See Amy Saltzman, *Downshifting: Reinventing Success on a Slower Track* (New York: HarperCollins Publishers, 1991). Although there is some beginning discussion of a slowing down of the work track for workers in the parenting years, there is little evidence of that change in the industrial complex yet.

35   Women still carry the major responsibilities: See Arlie Hochschild with Anne Machung, *Second Shift* (New York: Viking Books, 1989).

36   poor will be elderly women: Heather Joshi, a British economist, reported that the problem could be particularly severe for British women because pension rights are rarely divided at divorce. She has estimated that the "lifetime earnings of a married mother of two may be little over a quarter of those of a similarly qualified man." ("The Bargain Breaks," *The Economist,* December 26, 1992–January 8, 1993, p. 39.)

36   family values: Constance R. Ahrons, "21st-Century Families: Meeting the Challenges of Change," *Family Therapy News,* 23(5), October 1992.

36   "solutions to our family's problems": Stephen Lai, Ph.D., "Letter to the Editor," *Family Therapy News,* February 1993.

37   other nations have better child-care policies: Marian Wright Edelman in her book *The Measure of Our Success* (Boston: Beacon Press, 1992, pp. 43–45) notes: "Our leaders mouth family values they do not practice. As a result, our children lag behind the children of other nations on key child indicators like infant mortality, poverty, and family supports. Seventy nations provide medical care and financial assistance to all pregnant women; we aren't one of them. Seventeen industrialized nations have paid maternity leave programs; we are not one of them. . . . Sixty-three nations worldwide provide a family allowance to workers and their children; America does not."

British pediatrician Dr. Penelope Leach (*Children First,* New York: Knopf, 1994) reminds us that Sweden, unlike most other countries, prioritizes the interests of children by having an eighteen-month child-care leave policy and a six-hour workday until a child's eighth birthday.

37   twin deficit in terms of our children: Sylvia Ann Hewlitt, *When the Bough Breaks: The Cost of Neglecting Our Children* (New York: Basic Books, 1992), p. 18.

39   self-reliance is practically impossible: For interesting discussions of why the nuclear family appears to be in crisis, see Jan E. Dizard and Howard Gadlin, *The Minimal Family* (Amherst: University of Massachusetts, 1990); Stephanie Coontz, *The Way We Never Were: American Families and the Nostalgia Trap* (New York: Basic Books, 1992); Arlene Skolnick, *Embattled Paradise: The American Family in an Age of Uncertainty* (New York: Basic Books, 1991).

41   "single-parent family": Traditionally, sociologists, psychologists, and policymakers have defined families of divorce as "single-parent families," and lumped them together in their analyses with families in which the parent never married, or in which one parent has died. It assumes that divorced families contain only one parent, usually the mother. Calling all families of divorce "single parent" is a misnomer with serious consequences. For years, therapists also went along with that view and left fathers out of their therapy room; sociologists also went along with this view and in their research left fathers out of their studies. What has resulted has been studies examining father absence instead of studying father presence.

See Constance Ahrons, "Redefining the Divorced Family: A Conceptual Framework," *Social Work,* 1981, 25(6): 437–442; Constance Ahrons and Roy H. Rodgers, *Divorced Families: Meeting the Challenge of Divorce and Remarriage* (New York: W. W. Norton and Co., 1989).

41   nuclear family bias: See, for example, David Popenoe, "American Family Decline, 1960–1990: A Review and Appraisal," *Journal of Marriage and the Family,* 1993, 55(3): 727–741; David Blankenhorn, Steven Bayne, and Jean Bethke Elshtain, *Rebuilding the Nest: A New Commitment to the American Family* (Wisconsin: Family Service of America, 1990).

42   "President who was reared": See Judith Stacey, "Good Riddance to 'The Family,' A Response to David Popenoe," *Journal of Marriage and the Family,* 1993, 55(3): 545–547.

43   average length of a marriage: See Ken Dychtwald, Ph.D., and Joe Flower, *Age Wave: The Challenges and Opportunities of an Aging America* (Los Angeles: Jeremy P. Tarcher, Inc., 1989).

44   Neither intellect nor vigor: Research in the new field of adult development has shown that intellect does not decline with age. The issue of leisure

time has become a major topic of interest as more and more retired people are healthy and active. Even the mandatory retirement age has risen, with people now often working well into their seventies, and some into their eighties. Not only do we live longer, but we are healthier and more active. The average person of seventy today is much more active than he or she was a century ago.

Chapter 3

50 exspouse relationship: Anne-Marie Ambert ("Relationship Between Ex-spouses: Individual and Dyadic Perspectives," *Journal of Social and Personal Relationships,* 1988, 5: 327–346) conducted an exploratory study of 85 exspouse pairs in the metropolitan Toronto area; Carol Masheter ("Postdivorce Relationships Between Ex-spouses: The Roles of Attachment and Interpersonal Conflict," *Journal of Marriage and the Family,* 1991, 53[1]: 102–110) analyzed questionnaires from 265 people, but she did not get responses from both partners in most cases. Only in 39 of the cases did both partners respond. David Wright and Sharon Price ("Court-ordered Child Payment: The Effect of the Former-Spouse Relationship on Compliance," *Journal of Marriage and the Family* 48[November 1986]: 869–874) interviewed 58 divorced parents in the South and Midwest but none of their sample were couples. Jean Goldsmith ("Relationships Between Former Spouses: Descriptive Findings," *Journal of Divorce,* 1980, 4: 1–20) interviewed 100 divorced couples in the Chicago area.

50 "smacks of incest": Margaret Mead, "Anomalies in American Postdivorce Relationships," p. 121.

51 Forming typologies: The questions for the typologies were derived from scales specifically designed and constructed for this research. For more complete details on the construction and analyses, see Constance Ahrons and Lynn Wallisch, "The Relationship Between Former Spouses," in Daniel Perlman and Steve Duck (eds.), *Intimate Relationships: Development, Dynamics and Deterioration* (Newbury Park: Sage Publications, 1987), pp. 269–296.

52 Perfect Pals: It is important throughout this book when percentages are presented to keep in mind that the sample size of biological parents (I'll present information on the new partners in Chapter 7) in the Binuclear Family Study was 98 couples (196 individuals). So, for example, the 12 percent who are Perfect Pals are 12 couples.

61 Prince Charles and Princess Diana: "Charles, Diana Reportedly Plan Separate Lives," *Los Angeles Times,* November 16, 1992.

61   Kati Marton and Peter Jennings: *Los Angeles Times,* August 13, 1993.

61   Joyce Brothers: "After Split, Try Joint Custody of Mutual Friends," *Los Angeles Times.*

61–62 Audrey Hepburn: *People* magazine, February 8, 1993.

62   Farentino and Lee: "James Farentino and Michele Lee Draw on Their Past for Dramatic Movie," *Los Angeles Times TV,* November 15–21, 1992, p. 7.

62 Joyce Maynard: "My Turn," *Newsweek,* December 21, 1992, p. 12.

70   reversal of the marriage ritual: Pat Lewis, "Innovative Divorce Rituals: Their Psycho-Social Functions," *Journal of Divorce,* 1983, 6(3): 71–81.

70   wedding ring ritual: Michael Haederle, "With This Ring . . . ," *Los Angeles Times,* July 7, 1993, pp. E1–2.

71   family rituals: For an excellent discussion of the meaning of rituals in relationships, see Evan Imber-Black and Janine Roberts, *Rituals for Our Times: Celebrating, Healing, and Changing Our Lives and Our Relationships* (New York: HarperCollins, 1992).

Chapter 4

77 transitional processes were already named: For a more in-depth discussion of the transitions of divorce, see Ahrons, "Divorce: A Crisis of Family Transition and Change," *Family Relations,* 1980, 29: 533–540; "Redefining the Divorced Family: A Conceptual Framework," *Social Work,* 1980, 25(November): 437–441.

78 stabilize their feelings: See, for example, Robert Weiss, *Marital Separation* (New York: Basic Books, 1975); Mavis Hetherington; Judith Wallerstein and Joan Kelly, *Surviving the Break-up;* Gay Kitson, *Portrait of Divorce.*

79 stressful life events: T. Holmes and R. Rahe, "The Social Readjustment Rating Scale," *Journal of Psychosomatic Research,* 1967, 11: 213–218.

82 expressing anger: For a discussion of the research on anger, see Carol Tavris, *Anger: The Misunderstood Emotion* (New York: Simon & Schuster, 1982).

83   unresolved anger: Harriet Goldhor Lerner, in her book *The Dance of Anger* (New York: HarperCollins, 1985), clearly demonstrates how our family-of-origin patterns of dealing with anger are revisited in our later intimate relationships. She also provides some excellent advice on understanding, coping, and developing more productive ways of dealing with anger.

83   "To forgive": Beverly Flanagan, *Forgiving the Unforgivable: Overcoming the Bitter Legacy of Intimate Wounds* (New York: Macmillan Publishing Company, 1992). The first part of this quote can be found on page 5, and the last part on page 234.

84   terminal illness: When parents are divorced, how parents and hospital staff handle a child's illness has important implications for the child's recovery. For a discussion of an exploratory study about these situations, see Constance Ahrons and Sandra Arnn, "When Children from Divorced Families are Hospitalized: Issues for Staff," *Health and Social Work,* 1981, 6(August): 21–28.

85   Being peaceful . . . more possible than people think: A recent study of over 1,100 families in California supports this conclusion. The authors note:". . . many divorced people, even though they harbor strong resentment toward the former spouse and try to avoid contact, nevertheless are capable of civilized and even considerate behavior when they do need to interact" (Eleanor Maccoby and Robert Mnookin, with Charlene Depner and H. Elizabeth Peters, *Dividing the Child: Social and Legal Dilemmas of Custody*, Harvard University Press, 1992, p. 294).

87   first step toward divorce: For an excellent description of this stage of the process, see Robert Weiss, *Marital Separation.*

89   The leaver and the left: Some writers use the terms *initiator* and *partner, seeker* and *opposer, dumper* and *dumped partner.* I chose to use the terms *leaver* and *left* because this is the language most people used in my research.

89   leavers and lefts switch roles: For an interesting discussion of how divorced people change their accounts of the split after the fact, see two articles by Joseph Hopper, "Oppositional Identities and Rhetoric in Divorce," *Qualitative Sociology,* 1993, 16: 133–156; and "The Rhetoric of Motives in Divorce," *Journal of Marriage and the Family,* 1993, 55(November): 801–813.

Therapists and authors Patricia O'Hanlon Hudson and William Hudson O'Hanlon note: "When people get into difficulties, they usually develop stories that don't enhance their relationships. . . . People often become convinced that their stories are the truth, that their map is the territory." "Rewriting Love Stories," *Family Therapy News* (October 1993): 9.

91   an account of the breakup: For a more in-depth discussion of the psychological importance of developing an account, see Robert Weiss, *Marital Separation*.

94   all-too-familiar pattern: See, for example, Lillian Rubin, *Intimate Strangers* (New York: Harper & Row, 1982); and Deborah Tannen, *You Just Don't Understand* (New York: William Morrow and Co., 1990).

100   Extramarital affairs: Although we still hang on to the stereotype that men's sexual desires are more powerful than women's, current research informs us that the increased incidence of affairs is less gender-related than the stereotype reflects. Affairs seem to depend on an individual's power and access to external opportunities. As more women are employed outside the home, their behaviors have begun to parallel those of men.

Chapter 5

123   "asparagus syndrome": Letty Cottin Pogrebin, "Asparagus Syndrome," *Family Politics*, p. 2.

124   Shaming families: For a discussion of how shame and family dysfunction are related, see Merle Folsum and Marilyn Mason, *Facing Shame* (New York: W. W. Norton and Co., 1986).

126   no long-term disturbances: Sociologist Andrew Cherlin (*Marriage, Divorce and Remarriage*, p. 78), in his review of the research findings, concludes: (1) almost all children experience an initial period of great emotional upset following a parental separation; (2) most return to a normal developmental course within one or two years following the separation; and (3) a minority of children experience some long-term psychological problems as a result of the breakup that may persist into adulthood.

129   parenting across two households: For a wealth of practical information and sample parenting plans, see Isolina Ricci, *Mom's House, Dad's House* (New York: Macmillan, 1980).

130   "binuclear house": Personal communication, Samuel Hurst, Professor Emeritus and Former Dean, School of Architecture, University of Southern California.

139   The judge made the unusual decision: "Divorced Parents Can Visit, But the Kids Get the House," *Minneapolis Tribune,* January 20, 1982 (Associated Press).

142   clarifying boundaries: My discussion of the importance of boundaries is based on the work of family therapist Salvador Minuchin, *Families and Family Therapy* (Cambridge, MA: Harvard University Press, 1974).

146   variation of this traditional arrangement: The patterns among the parents in the traditional families varied considerably in terms of how often the noncustodial father "visited" the children. For more information on these patterns, see Constance Ahrons and Annamette Sorensen, "Father-Child Involvement," in L. Cseh-Szombathy, I. Koch-Nielsen, J. Trost, and I. Weda (eds.), *The Aftermath of Divorce—Coping with Change* (Budapest: Akademiai Kiado, 1985); Madonna Bowman and Constance Ahrons, "Impact of Legal Custody Status on Fathers' Parenting Postdivorce," *Journal of Marriage and the Family,* 1985, 47: 481–488; Constance Ahrons and Richard Miller, "The Effect of the Postdivorce Relationship on Paternal Involvement: A Longitudinal Analysis," *American Journal of Orthopsychiatry,* 1993, 6(3): 441–450.

149–50   "Hi, Daddy, it's Josh": In her collection of short pieces, Delia Ephron in *Funny Sauce: Us, the Ex, the Ex's New Mate, the New Mate's Ex, and the Kids* (New York: Viking Press, 1986, p. 38) writes from the personal perspective of being a stepmother. Her essays and poems about "the new extended family" are insightful, poignant, and humorous.

152   father's involvement . . . stabilizes: For a more detailed analysis of this finding, see C. Ahrons and R. Miller, "The Effect of the Postdivorce Relationship on Paternal Involvement: A Longitudinal Analysis."

153   the "most involved father": For further information about the involvement of fathers in the cross-national comparisons, see C. Ahrons and Annemette Sorensen, "Father-Child Involvement," in L. Cseh-Szombathy et al. (eds.), *The Aftermath of Divorce—Coping with Family Change: An Investigation in Eight Countries* (Budapest: Akademiai Kiado, 1985).

155   "parallel" parenting: In the Maccoby and Mnookin study (*Dividing the Child*), they found that the most common pattern by three and a half years after separation was what they called "spousal disengagement," which they describe essentially as parallel parenting with little communication. They note that this pattern became more common as children became

older and could manage more of the arrangements themselves. They conclude that although this is not the "first best" alternative, it is far better for children than open conflict (p. 292).

155   crossings: This term was coined by Myrna Silton-Goldstein in her doctoral dissertation, "The Relationship Between Coparenting and Psychological Crossings: An Exploratory Study," The Los Angeles Psychoanalytic Institute, 1986.

Chapter 6

167   divorce is big business: For an excellent discussion of how divorce has become such a big business in the United States, see Paul Bohannan, "The Divorce Industry," in his book *All the Happy Families*.

177   they have partitioned: See Forrest S. Mosten's paper "Unbundling of Legal Services in Family Law," presented at the Advanced Family Law Conference (Queensland, Australia, September 17, 1993). He notes: "The concept of unbundling these various services means that the client is in charge of selecting a portion of the full package and may contract with the lawyer accordingly." He identifies seven different services: gather facts from client, advise client, discover facts of opposing party, research law, draft correspondence and documents, negotiate, represent clients in court.

179   the specialty of family law: For an interesting discussion and suggestions for improving the profession of family law, see Fern Topas Salka, "A Not So Modest Proposal to Humanize the Legal Profession," *Family and Conciliation Courts Review*, 1992, 30: 26–31.

180   the more the litigants will have to pay: Elliott H. Diamond, "Children as Victims of Divorce," in David Levy (ed.), *The Best Parent Is Both Parents: A Guide to Shared Parenting in the 21st Century* (Norfolk, VA: Hampton Roads Publishing Co., 1993), pp. 15–28, notes that about one and a half billion dollars are spent annually nationwide. He calls this a "conservative lower limit" and calculates that the average cost per divorcing couple is $1,260.

182   mandatory mediation: As of 1992, thirteen states had mediation statutes: California, Colorado, Connecticut, Florida, Louisiana, Maine, Michigan, New Hampshire, North Dakota, Oregon, Rhode Island, Texas, and Washington. The majority of these states grant the courts broad discretion in ordering mediation. In Michigan, New Hampshire, and Oregon, mediation is purely voluntary.

183 choosing a mediator: At present, there is no licensing for mediators, so it is difficult to monitor the profession. The best way to select a mediator is to ask professionals who have knowledge of the divorce practices in your community. The family court in most jurisdictions will have a list of private mediators in your community.

192 in the shadow of the law: This concept was introduced by Stanford Law Professor Robert Mnookin in his article co-authored with L. Kornhauser, "Bargaining in the Shadow of the Law: The Case of Divorce," *Yale Law Review,* 1979, 88: 950–997.

196 joint custody statutes: For a state-by-state description of the laws addressing child custody, see David Levy's *The Best Parent Is Both Parents* (Appendix B).

200 first study of joint custody: Constance Ahrons, "Joint Custody Arrangements in the Postdivorce Family," *Journal of Divorce,* 1980, 3: 189–205.

Chapter 7

210–11 "we are in the same family": Ellen Goodman, "The Family That Stretches Together," *Keeping in Touch* (New York: Summit Books, 1985), p. 264.

215–16 stepfamily photos: Dear Abby, *Los Angeles Times,* November 17, 1992.

219 maternal grandmothers continue to see their grandchildren: Constance Ahrons and Madonna Bowman, "Changes in Family Relationships Following Divorce of Adult Child: Grandmothers' Perceptions," *Journal of Divorce,* 1982, 5: 49–68.

224 "expectation of 'instant love'": Emily Visher and John Visher, *How to Win as a Stepfamily* (New York: Dembner Books, 1982), p. 80.

233 stepfather called "Dad": Constance Ahrons and Lynn Wallisch, "Parenting in the Binuclear Family: Relationships Between Biological and Stepparents," in Kay Pasley and Mariyn Ihinger-Tallman (eds.), *Remarriage and Stepfamilies* (New York: Guilford Press, 1987), pp. 225–256.

237 pedi-focal family system: For an interesting discussion of the strengths of the African-American Family and an application to stepfamilies, see Edith Lewis and Margaret Crosbie-Burnett, "Use of African-American

Family Structure and Functioning to Address the Challenges of European-American Postdivorce Families," *Family Relations*, 1993, 42: 243–248.

245 "three mothers and three fathers": Erma Bombeck, "Here Come the Stepfamilies," *Wisconsin State Journal*, March 25, 1984.

Chapter 8

247 endings of relationships: Thomas Moore, *Soul Mates: Honoring the Mysteries of Love and Relationship* (New York: HarperCollins, 1994), p. 192.

248 integrating loss: Judith Viorst, *Necessary Losses: The Loves, Illusions, Dependencies and Impossible Expectations That All of Us Have to Give Up in Order to Grow* (New York: Ballantine Books, 1987), p. 5.

Index